Kosher for Everybody

The Complete Guide to Understanding, Shopping, Cooking, and Eating the Kosher Way

Trudy Garfunkel

An Arthur Kurzweil Book

JOSSEY-BASS
A Wiley Imprint
www.josseybass.com

Published by Jossey-Bass
A Wiley Imprint
989 Market Street, San Francisco, CA 94103-1741   www.josseybass.com

Readers should be aware that Internet Web sites and businesses listed within may have changed or disappeared between when the book was written and when it is read.

Jossey-Bass books and products are available through most bookstores. To contact Jossey-Bass directly call our Customer Care Department within the U.S. at 800-956-7739, outside the U.S. at 317-572-3986 or fax 317-572-4002.

Jossey-Bass also publishes its books in a variety of electronic formats. Some content that appears in print may not be available in electronic books.

Library of Congress Cataloging-in-Publication Data

Garfunkel, Trudy.
  Kosher for everybody: the complete guide to understanding, shopping, cooking, and eating the kosher way / Trudy Garfunkel.—1st ed.
    p. cm.
  "An Arthur Kurzweil book."
  Includes bibliographical references.
  ISBN 0-7879-7587-7 (alk. paper)
  1. Kosher food. 2. Jews—Dietary laws. I. Title.
  BM710.G36 2004
  296.7'3—dc22

                                                          2004006419

Printed in the United States of America
FIRST EDITION
PB Printing   10 9 8 7 6 5 4 3 2 1

Contents

For Aunt Chip—with love and appreciation

Author to Reader

> **kosher** *adj*. Honest; authentic; valid; ethical;
> fulfilling the minimum requirements of honesty or
> ethics. From *kosher* = clean and acceptable,
> according to Jewish dietary laws. (Word taken from
> Hebrew to Yiddish to English.)
> —The Dictionary of American Slang

You don't have to be Jewish to buy and eat kosher food. In fact, only 8 percent of the consumers who purchase kosher food in the United States do so for religious reasons. In the past decade, kosher has become one of the fastest-growing and hottest trends in the food industry. Eighty thousand products in the United States are already certified kosher, and a thousand new products are added to the list each year.

Kosher is big business: the U.S. market for kosher food is approximately $7.5 billion annually. Over 9,200 companies—including such giants as Procter & Gamble, Pillsbury, Kraft, Coca-Cola, General Mills, Hershey, Nabisco, Heinz, and Dannon—have spent time, effort, and money to earn the coveted kosher certification.

Why has kosher become so popular? There are a number of reasons. In recent years, there has been a resurgence of people going back to their Jewish roots and becoming more observant of kosher laws. American Jews today may observe the laws of kashrut in varying degrees. Strictly kosher observant Jews follow all the dietary laws to the letter. Others may practice "biblical kashrut," abstaining only from foods forbidden in the Bible. Still others buy only kosher meats and poultry and do not eat meat and milk products at the same meal. And then there are Jews who become vegetarians, following the commandments to revere all animal life. (There are several branches of Judaism, with differing interpretations and views on keeping kosher. Orthodox and Conservative branches, practicing so-called rabbinic kashrut, expect their adherents to follow all the dietary laws as set down in the Bible and in the later rabbinic commentaries. Both Reform Judaism, a movement that began in nineteenth-century Germany as a way to reconcile tradition with modernity, and Reconstructionism, a twentieth-century American movement that sees Judaism as an evolving religion, affirm the importance of a kosher lifestyle but allow for a more lenient interpretation. Reform Judaism allows its members to decide which laws to follow, although in 1999, it began encouraging a more encompassing reconsideration of this traditional observance; Reconstructionists believe that the dietary laws are to be followed only if the individual wishes to follow them.)

Other groups also purchase kosher foods to remain true to their religious beliefs. These include six million American Muslims, who follow dietary laws similar to those of observant Jews, and eight hundred thousand American Seventh-day Adventists, who are encouraged to follow the dietary guidelines given in the Bible—the basis of kosher.

Another reason for the burgeoning kosher market is the growing number of health-conscious consumers who believe that because kosher certification is given by independent, nongovernmental agencies (and certification has its own strict labeling laws and stringent meat and poultry inspection), it represents a kind of extra "Good Housekeeping seal of approval." For them, buying and eating kosher means healthier, safer food. Then there are the millions of Americans who are vegetarians. And the 2 to 3 percent of the American population who suffer from a variety of allergies or food intolerances: people who are allergic to shellfish or milk, for example, and who, like vegetarians, must know exactly what ingredients are in the processed foods they buy.

Kosher for Everybody is a consumer's guide to the ever-growing world of kosher food and kosher products. It explains the meaning of kosher and how to interpret the variety of symbols used to designate kosher products. There are chapters on buying kosher meats and poultry and on identifying kosher products for vegetarians and those who are lactose-intolerant or allergic to milk. There are tips on how to buy foods that are both healthy and kosher, including a selection of easy-to-prepare kosher recipes from the kitchens of my family and friends, as well as information on kosher wines, buying kosher products by mail, kosher summer camps, kosher travel, eating kosher while at college, and where to find kosher hotels, restaurants, supermarkets, and caterers.

Glossary

bodek The trained inspector who looks for abnormalities in a slaughtered animal's lungs and other organs.

fleishig (sometimes *fleishedik*) Yiddish for kosher meat, including poultry. Also used to refer to meat dishes and utensils. In Ladino, the language of the Sephardim, *dela carne*; in Hebrew, *basar*.

halakha (sometimes *halacha*) The body of Jewish law, including the laws of kashrut. Literally, "the path that one walks." Consists of 613 *mitzvot* or commandments, good deeds, and meritorious acts from the Torah, laws enacted by rabbis, and established customs and traditions.

hechsher (sometimes *heksher*) The symbol that indicates kosher certification. Literally, "authorization" or "fitness."

kashering, koshering The act of making something kosher; the process by which utensils and equipment are made fit for kosher use.

kashrut (*kashrus, kashruth*) The complete written code of religious dietary laws governing every single act of eating. Also, the state of being kosher. Literally, "validity," "propriety," "fitness."

kosher Meeting the requirements of the Jewish dietary laws. Literally, "valid."

Ladino Language of Sephardic Jews from Spain, Portugal, North Africa, and the Middle East; a mix of Spanish, Arabic,

Hebrew, and other languages. (*Sepharad* is the Hebrew name for Spain.)

mashgiah (sometimes *mashgiach*) A kosher investigator or supervisor; someone sufficiently familiar with laws of kashrut and qualified to supervise the production of food in accordance with the dietary laws. This person need not be a rabbi.

milchig (sometimes *milchedik*) Yiddish for dairy products. Also refers to dairy dishes, utensils, and equipment. In Ladino, *dela mantika*; in Hebrew, *halav*.

pareve Neutral, applied to foods containing neither dairy nor meat ingredients (for example, eggs, fish, and vegetables). From a Czech word meaning "pair."

shehitah (sometimes *shechita*) The conditions that meat and poultry must satisfy in order to be considered kosher; the process of ritual slaughter of meat and poultry.

shohet (sometimes *shochet*) A ritual slaughterer.

Talmud The massive encyclopedia of Jewish thought and commentary, a compilation of oral tradition that interprets the Torah, compiled in the first few centuries of the Common Era. Literally, "learning."

Torah The first five books of the Bible; the Five Books of Moses and the oral law given to the Israelites on Mount Sinai. Sometimes used to refer to all Jewish books and wisdom. Literally, "law" or "teaching."

trayf (sometimes *trayfe* or *treif*) Food that is unfit or improper to eat according to Jewish dietary laws. Yiddish variant of the Hebrew *trefah*, "torn."

vaad A community board of rabbis who give kosher certification.

Yiddish The language spoken by the Ashkenazic Jews of central and eastern Europe, a mix of German, Hebrew, and Slavic tongues. (*Ashkenaz* is the Hebrew name for Germany.)

Chapter 1

What Is Kosher?

Kosher is the anglicized version of the Hebrew word *kasher*, meaning "fit" or "proper." Food is kosher when its ingredients and the means of its manufacture or preparation have adhered to a certain set of stringent and demanding laws and restrictions. You can't make foods kosher just by saying prayers over them. Nor does it have the same meaning as "kosher-style," a phrase used to describe certain ethnic dishes or food preparations (such as "kosher" dill pickles or "kosher-style" delicatessen) or foods derived from eastern European Jewish cuisines.

Kosher means adhering to the Jewish dietary laws—some nearly 3,500 years old—that have their origins in passages of the Torah (the first five books of the Bible: Genesis, Exodus, Leviticus, Numbers, Deuteronomy). These were later elaborated on by rabbis who, in the Talmud, added further requirements and restrictions. (The *Talmud*—Hebrew for "learning"—is the massive encyclopedia of Jewish thought, commentary, and civil and religious law compiled in the first few centuries of the Common Era.) The word *kosher* itself does not appear in the five books of Moses, although it can be found a few times in later books of the Bible. But even here it does not refer to food specifically but to the "fitness" of items used in religious rituals.

The kosher dietary laws and rules, known as *kashrut* (also spelled *kashrus* or *kashruth*), govern many aspects of food preparation, cooking, and consumption for observant Jews. They include instructions for the ritual slaughter of animals, which foods are permitted, and which are prohibited. Although the purpose of these laws may have had a positive effect on health (see Chapter Seven), their original purpose was religious, an act of devotion and affirmation of faith that expressed spiritual and moral values. They provided a diet for the soul as well as for the body. The dietary laws imposed a type of self-discipline on one of the most basic elements of life—eating.

In Jewish teaching, eating is regarded as a hallowed act. The twentieth-century religious philosopher Martin Buber (1878–1965) wrote that kashrut hallowed the everyday by turning a natural function, eating, into something holy. Kashrut also teaches a reverence for all life. There are many admonitions in the Torah forbidding cruelty to animals, including the mandate not to "cause pain to any living creature." The Torah preaches compassion and respect for all living things, going so far as to prohibit eating animals killed by hunters, adding that animals should not be killed for anything other than food or self-preservation.

Some of the dietary laws are stated clearly in the Bible; others took on interpreted meanings through the writings and commentaries of generations of Talmudic rabbis who refined and commented on the biblical injunctions. No explicit reasons are given in the Bible for many of the prohibitions and mandates in the dietary laws. The observant accept this apparent arbitrariness because they are commanded by God to do so. The dietary laws are considered divine directives that need no rationale or explanation other than that following them leads to holiness. (The Hebrew word for holiness is *kedushah*, which is derived from the word *kodesh*, meaning "separateness.") As *The Jewish Book of Why* by Alfred J. Kolatch explains, "Whatever was holy was something apart, to be set aside. To be a holy people, Israel had to be apart, separated from their idol-worshipping neighbors. The dietary laws were instituted as one means of making the Jewish lifestyle different from that of their neighbors." Through the ages, the dietary laws have helped define Jewish life, giving the Jewish people a cohesive yet distinct identity.

The basic dietary laws include the following:

- A *prohibition against mixing meat and milk:* "You shall not seethe a kid in its mother's milk" (Exod. 23:19; also Exod. 34:26 and Deut. 14:21). This commandment, which is mentioned three times, led to the rule against cooking or consuming both meat and milk or dairy products together at one meal. As with other dietary laws, the Bible offers no reason for this prohibition, although some scholars think it may have derived from an abhorrence of pagan practices or rituals (offering meat boiled in milk was both a pagan form of hospitality and a pagan form of worship) or as an extension of the commandment against cruelty to animals. For what could be more indifferent or cruel than first to kill an animal and then mix its flesh with the liquid that gave it life?

- A *prohibition against the consumption of blood:* "You shall eat the blood of no manner of flesh; for the life of all flesh is the blood thereof" (Lev. 17:14). There are numerous mentions in the Bible of blood as the symbol of the essence of humankind. In Judaism, eating or drinking of blood is considered a desecration of life itself. This belief led to a key element of kosher food preparation—the removal of blood from meat. The early rabbis concluded that when animals are killed for food, care should be taken to remove or drain as much blood as possible before the meat is cooked.

- A *list of permitted animals:* "Of the animals you may eat any that hath both true cloven hooves and that brings up its cud" (Lev. 11:3); "Among the mammals that you may eat are the ox, the goat, the gazelle, the deer, the antelope, the ibex, the chamois, the bison, and the giraffe" (Deut. 14:4); "You may eat any creature that lives in salt water or fresh water, as long as it has fins and scales" (Lev. 11:9); "Of all the pure birds you may eat"; twenty-four forbidden species of fowl are then listed (Deut. 14:11).

- A *prohibition against eating certain animals:* "All creatures in seas and rivers that have no fins and scales, whether invertebrates or mammals or other creatures, are an abomination to you" (Lev. 11:10); "These are the smaller animals that breed on land which are unclean to you" (a list of rodents, reptiles, and mollusks follows; Lev. 1:29); "All the winged swarming things are unclean to you;

they shall not be eaten" (Deut. 14:19). Again, no reasons are given in the Bible as to why some fish and animals are proper to eat and others are forbidden. However, the identifying characteristics that make a creature fit for consumption are provided: mammals must both chew their cud and have a split or cloven hoof; fish must have both fins and scales that are removable without damaging or tearing the skin. The characteristics of permitted birds are not listed; later traditions, however, allowed that domestic fowl and birds that have a projecting claw, a crop, and a gizzard or stomach whose inner lining can readily be peeled were kosher.

• *The ritual slaughtering of animals for food:* "Then shall you slaughter of your herd and of your flock" (Deut. 12:21). Although not described in the Bible, ritual slaughter is one of the central elements of kashrut. Ethical considerations stressing the importance of compassion and respect for all living things led to creating humane methods of animal slaughter, methods that were designed for the quickest and most painless death for the animal. Exactly what is involved in ritual slaughter and what else is done to meat to make it kosher will be discussed in detail in Chapter Five.

Kosher and Nonkosher Animals

Permitted mammals: Animals that both chew their cud (ruminants) and have a split or cloven hoof, including antelope, bison, buffalo, cattle, deer, eland, gazelle, goat, hart, moose, ox, sheep, and yak

Forbidden mammals: Camel, dog, dolphin, donkey, horse, pig, porpoise, rabbit, rodents, whale

Permitted fowl: Birds that have a projecting claw, a crop, and a gizzard or stomach whose inner lining can readily be peeled; most domestic fowl, including capon, chicken, Cornish hen, duck, dove, goose, pigeon, songbirds, squab, and turkey

Forbidden fowl: Wild birds or birds of prey, including eagle, heron, ostrich, owl, pelican, stork, swan, falcon, raven, hawk, and vulture

Permitted fish: Must have both fins and scales that are removable without damaging or tearing the fish's skin; seventy-five species including anchovy, bass, blackfish, bluefish, butterfish, carp, chub, cod, flounder, fluke, haddock, halibut, herring, mackerel, mahimahi, mullet, perch, pickerel, pike, pompano, porgy, red snapper, sablefish, salmon, sardine, shad, smelt, snapper, sole, tilefish, trout, tuna, weakfish, whitefish, and whiting. The eggs (caviar) of permitted fish are kosher.

Forbidden fish and seafood (partial list): Catfish, eel, lamprey, marlin, rays, puffer, sailfish, shark, sturgeon, swordfish, and turbot. The eggs (caviar) of nonkosher fish are not kosher. No shellfish or mollusks are kosher; this includes clam, lobster, octopus, oyster, scallop, shrimp, snail, and squid.

Also forbidden: Reptiles, invertebrates, and amphibians, including crocodile, frog, lizard, snake, toad, turtle, and worms; all insects are also forbidden.

Did You Know?

There is no such fish as the gefilte fish. *Gefilte* (Yiddish for "stuffed") is an eastern European Jewish dish, a dumpling made of chopped whitefish, pike, and carp that is poached in a vegetable broth. It is most often eaten cold, as an appetizer, especially at Sabbath or Passover meals. The copyeditor of this book told me the following story, a gefilte fish tale that makes the origin of both the dish's name and its traditional shape much clearer. In Europe, he was served gefilte fish prepared with the chopped fish mixture stuffed into the cavity of a whole carp before the entire fish was poached. After the fish was cooked, the hostess removed the stuffing in a single lump that looked very much like the tubular-shaped "loaves" of gefilte fish we are familiar with in this country.

The dietary laws of kashrut divide all foods into two categories: kosher (Hebrew, *kasher*), or permitted, foods and *trayf* (sometimes spelled *trayfe* or *treif*), food that is unfit or improper to eat. (Derived from the Hebrew word for "torn" or "damaged," *trayf* originally meant "torn from a wild beast" and therefore unfit to be eaten.)

Kosher or permitted foods are then divided into three categories:

1. *Dairy (milchig)*: Milk and all its derivatives, excluding milk from nonkosher animals. (Labels on dairy products are marked "D" after the symbol of kosher certification.)

2. *Meat, including poultry (fleishig)*: From permitted animals (ones that chew their cud, generally cows and sheep, and have split hooves), that have been ritually slaughtered, and have undergone the koshering process of soaking and salting to remove any residual blood (see Chapter Five). This procedure, which is also referred to as kashering, must be done under the supervision of a *mashgiah*, or rabbinic supervisor. (Labels on meat and poultry products are marked "M" after the symbol of kosher certification. An "M" may also mean that the product was processed on equipment that was used to process meat products.)

3. *Neutral (pareve)*: Foods that are neither dairy nor meat. Based on the verses in Genesis (1:29–30) in which God gives Adam and Eve permission to eat "every seed-bearing grass" and "every fruit-bearing tree," everything that grows in the ground is considered both intrinsically kosher and pareve. This includes, in their natural state, all plants, herbs, grains, fungi, fresh fruits and vegetables, flowers, roots, seeds, and nuts, as well as food products made from them, such as sugar, tea, flour, coffee, spices, pasta, salt, oils, and most condiments.

However, once a fruit or vegetable has undergone any form of processing, it may no longer be either pareve or kosher, since a nonkosher ingredient or a meat or dairy ingredient may have been added or it may have been processed by machines that are also used to process nonkosher foods. For example, coffee beans and ground coffee are pareve, but flavored coffees may not be, since they may include nonkosher or dairy ingredients. Similarly, canned tuna fish[1] processed in water or oil would be pareve, but some tuna fish is processed with milk byproducts and therefore would be considered dairy. Also pareve are eggs (from kosher birds), as long as there is no blood in the yolk, and fish with fins and scales. Unlike kosher meat and poultry, kosher fish need not be killed by a ritual slaughterer, nor is it soaked and salted. (Labels on pareve foods have neither "D" nor "M" after the symbol of their kosher certification.)

For observant Jews, pareve foods may be eaten with both meat and dairy foods. Because of the biblical injunction against "seething [cooking] a kid in its mother's milk," observant Jews do not cook or eat meat and milk together at the same time. Depending on local traditions, they wait between three and six hours (about the time it takes to digest meat) after a meat meal before eating any milk or milk products. (If the dairy is eaten first, there is no need for this waiting period.)

Because they may be made of porous materials that allow particles of meat or dairy to be absorbed, cooking utensils and dishes have also come under this dietary law. Observant Jews have at least two sets of pots, pans, plates, bowls, knives, forks, and so on—one for milk dishes and one for meat. For the same reason, they have two sets of dish towels and two separate bars of soap for washing dishes. In this way, they can be sure that there is no inadvertent mixing, however small, of meat and milk. Pareve foods can be cooked and eaten on either meat or dairy plates and utensils.

Although observant Jews consider fish to be pareve, it is not mixed with meat or poultry. This is another example of how sometimes enigmatic biblical injunctions were elaborated by later rabbis. The admonition to "verily guard your souls" was interpreted by Talmudic scholars to mean that you should closely guard your health, and therefore fish and meat should not be consumed together because you might not be scrupulous in looking for fish bones when eating the latter and therefore might choke on one.

Foods that are prohibited by the laws of kashrut are called trayf and will never be found in food products that have been certified as kosher. Trayf foods include the following:

- Meat from pigs, dogs, rabbits, horses, camels (four-footed animals that do not chew their cud)
- All insects[2]
- Rodents, reptiles, and creeping animals such as worms, snakes, and lizards
- Invertebrates and amphibians, such as frogs and toads
- Shellfish and mollusks
- Animal blood
- Certain sinews and fat, even if from kosher animals (probably because the fat from oxen, sheep, and goats were used as part of pagan sacrificial rites; rabbis later extended this prohibition to the fat of cows as well)
- Products such as gelatin and bone meal that are derived from prohibited animals
- Any limb that has been cut or torn from a living animal (a graphic example of the biblical admonition against "causing pain to any living creature")
- Meat from any animal that has been killed by another animal or that died a natural death (one more extension of the prohibition against eating the flesh of an injured animal; also, such animals could not have been ritually slaughtered)
- Any food or food product that mixes milk, or milk products or derivatives, with meat or products derived from meat (of special importance for lactose-intolerant individuals and vegetarians)

What Makes a Product Kosher?

1. Even though kosher foods already meet safety standards set by the U.S. Department of Agriculture (USDA) and the Food and Drug Administration (FDA), they must also meet certain additional requirements of Jewish law pertaining to raw materials and processing. Although there are several branches of Judaism—including Orthodox, Conservative,

Reform, and Reconstructionist—it is Orthodox rulings that usually determine what is kosher. The major certifying agencies follow Orthodox rulings.

2. Rabbinic inspectors and other members of kosher certifying agencies are trained specialists; they include food and flavoring chemists and processing experts, as well as authorities on kosher law.

3. All the ingredients in a processed food or product must be certified as kosher. This includes all of the raw materials as well as flavorings, colorings, stabilizers, and other ingredients that are added to processed foods. Certain additives, such as those derived from civet cats (civet), beavers (castoreum), and whales (ambergris), are intrinsically nonkosher. Others, such as glycerin, gelatin, enzymes, emulsifiers, and fatty acids, may be derived from kosher or nonkosher sources.

4. Before a kosher endorsement is given to a product, the plant in which it is manufactured—the equipment it is processed on, as well as the container or packaging it comes in—must be inspected by a representative of the endorsing agency. Traces of nonkosher substances can remain on machinery and processing equipment and can be absorbed into the food, affecting its aroma and taste. If the equipment was previously used for nonkosher items, it must be washed with caustic soap and sterilized with boiling water before kosher products can be processed on it.

5. Even after a product is deemed kosher and receives certification, regular unannounced on-site inspections are made. Kosher inspectors have access to a company's records and storerooms, as well as plant machinery. In some instances, such as in meat and poultry slaughterhouses and processing plants, there may be one or more kosher supervisors on duty at all times, around the clock.

6. Kosher meat and poultry must be ritually slaughtered and butchered and prepared for the consumer by the prescribed method of salting and soaking.

Why Be Kosher?

There are a number of reasons to follow the rules of kashrut. For observant Jews, the dietary laws are God's commandments, to be obeyed without question. Keeping kosher can be a means of connecting with coreligionists, a way of exhibiting Jewish identity. There are also other spiritual, ethical, and moral considerations and dimensions involved in keeping kosher that can appeal to and be appreciated by Jews and Gentiles alike.

Kashrut elevates a simple and necessary act, that of eating, into a sanctified ritual, an observance that is good for your spiritual health. Perhaps it is a good thing to not eat wild animals or birds and beasts of prey—an ongoing reminder of the qualities of character we should avoid. Keeping kosher forces you to think about where the food you consume ultimately came from and to be very careful about the foods we allow into our bodies. The dietary laws also impose a self-discipline that can be transferred to all aspects of life. As the noted Jewish philosopher and physician Maimonides (1135–1204 C.E.) wrote, the dietary laws "train us in our mastery of the appetites. They accustom us to restrain both the growth of desire and the disposition to consider the pleasure of eating as the event of man's existence." Or as Benjamin Franklin succinctly put it some six hundred years later, "One should eat to live, not live to eat." By eliminating certain foods from your diet, you can gain self-control over your passions. By following the dietary laws, what we consume does not consume us and become the end-all of our existence. We learn to say no.

There is also a moral and ethical component to keeping kosher. It promotes a respect and reverence for all life, including compassion toward the animals with which we share the earth. In Jewish tradition, animals are not to be abused and should be treated with respect. If you must eat meat, you must slaughter that animal in the most humane way possible—by a single stroke that brings almost instant unconsciousness—and you cannot eat meat that has been hunted for food, for to kill by hunting is not humane.

In the 1970s, Rabbi Zalman Schacter-Shalomi coined the term *eco-kosher* to describe a growing response to global ecological crises. Individuals who wish to keep eco-kosher—many of whom are vegetarians—consider the impact of what they eat and how it is raised on both the environment and society. Was the food raised organically, without use of pesticides and chemicals? Were the workers who produced the food treated fairly and paid a living wage? Were natural resources wasted or destroyed in the production of the food? Were the animals that were ultimately consumed for food treated well before their slaughter? These are just a few of the questions that the eco-kosher ask.

Finally, there is the idea of eating kosher for physical health. It is impossible to be sure if the Jews of biblical times knew that certain animals—such as pigs or shellfish—or blood could carry disease and therefore were forbidden to be consumed, but today, a cogent argument can be made that in some ways, kosher beef and poultry is a healthier choice (see Chapters Five and Seven) because of the way animals for kosher slaughter are raised and processed. As Rabbi Wayne Dosick says in *Living Judaism*, "Today there is medical evidence of the effects that eating, or avoiding, certain foods have on health. A kosher diet—with its unlimited portions of fruit and vegetables, its limits on certain cuts of red meat, its requirement to eliminate as much fat as possible, and its focus on chicken and fish—may very well contribute to good health."

And as the sages say, "It couldn't hurt."

❧ Kosher Voices ❧

"I started keeping kosher as a young adult to create a sense of Jewishness and tradition I did not have in my parent's home. Keeping kosher connects me with other Jews and gives me a sense of identity. I'm surprised at the number of non-Jews here who keep kosher or buy kosher food. When I've asked some of my Gentile friends for an explanation, I've gotten responses that range from their belief that kosher food (especially beef) is healthier or tastes better to the ongoing debate among Bible-oriented Christians about whether the dietary laws as set down in the Torah are laws for Jews only or are also for Christians. This connects with the idea [held by a number of] Christians [here] that they too are part of the household of Israel."

—Peter, a rabbi and the director of a Hillel program at a major Texas university in an area often referred to as part of the Bible Belt

It should be noted that two of the dietary laws cited in the first books of the Bible were indeed given to all humanity, not just the Jews. These are the prohibitions against consuming blood and eating the limb of a living animal. One could also include the vegetarian ideal set down for Adam and Eve, the ancestors of all people (see Chapter Eight).

❦

Chapter 2

A Brief History of
Kosher Foods in America

In the fall of 1654, sixteen vessels carrying Spanish and Portuguese Jews—Sephardic families and Maranos (so-called Crypto-Jews, who publicly converted to Christianity but continued to practice Judaism in secret) fleeing the Inquisition—set sail from Recife, Brazil, seeking a haven on the more tolerant shores of Holland. One of the ships, blown off course, was set upon by pirates, who confiscated the passengers' goods and scuttled their boat. Rescued by a passing French ship, the passengers were eventually deposited at the nearest port, the Dutch colony of Nieuw Amsterdam, a community of 750 souls speaking eighteen languages. The twenty-three Jews were allowed to remain in the colony, "provided the poor among them shall not become a burden to the company or to the community, but be supported by their own Nation," according to a Dutch West India Company document.

Most of the men in the Jewish group—among the first of their religion to settle in North America—were merchants, but several were also butchers, versed in the laws of kosher slaughter. In 1660, one of their number, Asser Levy, applied to the town council for a license to sell both kosher and nonkosher meat, although the license he received explicitly exempted him from having to slaughter pigs. The Jews of Nieuw Amsterdam could trade and own real estate but could not hold public office or establish a synagogue. In 1664, the English captured Nieuw Amsterdam, renaming it New York. It was the British who allowed the Sephardim to found what would be the first official synagogue in North America, Congregation Shearith Israel, which still exists today. By 1752, this congregation had a monopoly on supervising the kosher slaughtering in the New York colony. New York kosher beef, perhaps because the koshering process of washing and salting made it safer for transport, began to be exported to Jamaica and Curaçao, as part of the burgeoning West Indies trade.

In the years before the Revolutionary War, other Jewish congregations in the colonies arose—in Savannah, Georgia (1734), in Charleston, South Carolina (1740), in Philadelphia, Pennsylvania (1740), and in Newport, Rhode Island (1763)—and quickly became involved in providing kosher food for their communities. Philadelphia's Congregation Mikvah Israel was not only the source for matzo, the unleavened bread of the Passover holiday, but also made sure that Jewish citizens could celebrate national occasions in a kosher way. In 1788, the congregation prepared a kosher table—laden with "soused salmon and crackers"—for the city's outdoor festivities honoring the ratification of the Constitution.

After the War for Independence, Jewish peddlers, following the new country's westward migration, introduced kosher meat to the frontier, although keeping kosher was for them, and for Jewish pioneers, a most difficult task. Perhaps it simply meant eating a vegetarian diet or abstaining from eating pork and horsemeat and slaughtering your own beef and poultry as humanely as possible. As travel across the Ohio and Mississippi Rivers became easier, *shohets* (ritual slaughterers) from the east began to visit frontier towns and newly established Jewish communities in Cincinnati, New Orleans, Louisville, Chicago, and Cleveland. There are records that *shohets* visited the Pacific gold fields during the California Gold Rush.

In the Jewish communities along the Atlantic Coast, the production of kosher meat remained in the control of the synagogues. In 1813, however, the first independent *shohet* set up shop in New York City, signaling the end of congregational control of the ritual slaughterers. This led to a decline in the standards of what constituted kosher meat, a situation not remedied until 1897, when the *shohets* themselves formed a union called the Meleches Hakodesh ("Holy Work") to improve standards as well as the wages of ritual slaughterers.

There were approximately two thousand Jews in America at the end of the Revolutionary War. Over the next 150 years, two great waves of Jewish immigration helped expand the kosher food market in the United States. Between 1820 and 1880, half a million German Jews migrated to America; between 1880 and 1920, more than two million Russian and eastern European Jews followed. By the end of the nineteenth century, there were more than five thousand kosher butchers and one thousand ritual slaughterers in New York City.

The demand for kosher foods continued to grow in the United States. The first American kosher cookbook, *Jewish Cookery Book*, a collection of mostly German recipes collected by Esther Jacobs Levy, was published in 1871. By 1911, besides kosher meats and poultry, consumers could purchase such kosher products as Dr. Brown's Cel-Ray Tonic (1869), Fleischmann's yeast (1870), Manischewitz matzo (1887), Breakstone butter (1888), Hebrew National frankfurters (1905), and Crisco (1911), an all-vegetal shortening that Procter & Gamble advertised as a product for which the "Hebrew race has been waiting four thousand years." (American icon Coca-Cola became kosher in 1937; in 1997, yet another American institution, Oreo cookies, received kosher certification.)

In 1924, the Union of Orthodox Jewish Congregations of America, which had been founded twenty-six years earlier to act as a single voice of Orthodoxy in America, decided to enter the field of kosher certification. The organization's OU symbol, indicating that a product is kosher, was originally devised for the H.J. Heinz Company for its vegetarian baked beans; Heinz had not wanted the label to include the word *kosher* or any other symbol that might imply that the food was for Jews only.

As more and more manufacturers sought kosher supervision for their products, additional certifying agencies arose: the Organized Kashrus Laboratories, founded in 1935; the Jewish Council of Baltimore's Star-K, established in 1947; and the Kof-K, dating from 1969, are among the largest. Today, there are more than four hundred certifying agencies and individual certifying rabbis.

In the mid-1960s, two mass market advertising slogans did much to spread the word about the "benefits" of kosher food: Hebrew National's campaign for hot dogs, claiming, "We answer to a higher authority," and Levy's rye bread's "You don't have to be Jewish to like Levy's" brought kosher foods to the attention of an even wider audience, perhaps lending support to the notion that kosher meant better, purer, and more carefully prepared.

Today, kosher foods are part of the American mainstream, a multibillion-dollar-a-year industry with potential customers numbering in the tens of millions.

From Colonial Times to Today

Revolutionary War Problems

"The Jews in particular were suffering [in Newport, Rhode Island] due to a scarcity of kosher food. They had not tasted any meat, but once in two months. Fish was not to be had, and they were forced to subsist on chocolate and coffee."
    —Letter, written by Aaron Lopez, a Jewish merchant, 1779

What Every Good Housewife Should Know

"Few persons are aware of the injury they sustain by eating the flesh of diseased animals. None but the Jewish butchers, who are paid exclusively for it, attend to this important circumstance."
    —The Virginia Housewife, 1824

"From having been forbidden to use butter with meat, oil enters more largely into their cookery of both meat and vegetables. Their fish fried in oil, and so cooked that it can be eaten cold or hot, enjoys a deservedly high reputation. As the Mo-

saic law forbids the use of any flesh as food which is not free from 'spot or blemish,' the meat supplied by the Jewish butchers is of the best quality."
—*Smiley's Cook Book and Universal Household Guide*, 1901

Kosher Dining Away from Home

"An offshoot of the kosher restaurant is the kosher delicatessen and lunchroom, of which there must be many hundreds in Greater New York. If you take a glance into the plate-glass window you will see such a display of food, tastefully decorated with strips of varicolored paper, as Rabelais might have catalogued for one of Gargantua's heartier meals."
—*Saturday Evening Post*, 1929

Kosher Today

"[There was] a head-spinning array of kosher products, such as gnocchi in tomato and basil sauce, margarita mix–flavored nuts, ginger teriyaki marinade, $400 bottles of French wine, and Poppy Chocky Wocky Doodah Gourmet Popcorn Sensations."
—*New York Times, reporting on the 2003 Kosherfest, a yearly trade show of kosher foods and products*

🌿 Kosher Voices 🌿

"I started keeping kosher a few years ago as part of my conversion to Judaism. I wanted to show my commitment to the traditional observances of my (then) future husband, Oliver. When we first met, he didn't keep kosher, but as I studied for my conversion, he became more and more interested in his Jewish identity." Adds Oliver, "Keeping kosher helped bring me back to Judaism. It makes our home a sanctuary and turns eating into a holy experience, something that resonates for both of us now."
—*Jeana, originally from the Midwest, and her husband, Oliver, now residents of a suburb of New York City*

Chapter 3

Understanding the Kosher Symbols

Once you have decided to look for kosher products, you need to become familiar with the different symbols, called *hechshers*, used to designate kosher. More than four hundred organizations and individuals in the United States and Canada issue kosher certifications, and each has its own kosher symbol. A number of these certifying agencies, however, are regional groups or local rabbis.

Generally, when shopping for processed and packaged foods, the average consumer will need to recognize the symbols of the four major national certifying organizations. These four groups tend to share the same high standards for certification and are likely to accept each other's certification for ingredients and suppliers. They all employ experts in food chemistry, flavor processing, factory engineering, and food transport technology, as well as experts in religious law. Their supervision system extends worldwide, since they provide certification for companies that produce key raw materials and ingredients. The following symbols, used by the major certifying organizations, are registered trademarks:

 A circle with a U in its center, called the "OU," is the symbol of the Union of Orthodox Jewish Congregations, often referred to simply as the Orthodox Union, 11 Broadway, New York, NY 10004, (212) 563-4000. Founded in 1898, this is the largest kosher certifying

agency in the world, a not-for-profit public service
program for kosher certification that supervises approximately 60 percent of U.S. kosher products, produced
by more than six thousand companies in the United
States and sixty-eight countries overseas, and certifies
over a quarter of a million products, brand names,
hotels, restaurants, companies, and services, and
nearly five thousand manufacturing plants. Its Web
site, http://www.ou.org, contains listings of kosher
products and manufacturers.

A circle with a K in its center, known as the "OK,"
indicates certification by the Organized Kashrus Laboratories (OK Kosher Certification), 391 Troy Avenue,
Brooklyn, NY 11213, (718) 756-7500. Founded in the
1930s, the OK has 150 rabbis who certify the products
of over six hundred companies on six continents. Its
state-of-the-art computer system keeps track of all the
ingredients in all the products it certifies. The OK publishes a bimonthly magazine, *The Jewish Homemaker*,
which includes a "Kosher Food Guide of Products." A
list of the products the OK certifies can also be found
on the company's Web site, http://www.ok.org.

A letter K within the Hebrew letter *kof*, the first letter
of the word *kasher*, indicates certification by Kosher
Supervision Services, 201 The Plaza, Teaneck, NJ
07666, (201) 837-0500. The so-called Kof-K is an
international organization of Orthodox rabbis and
experts in kosher food production. It was the first
kashrut organization to introduce computer technology to kosher supervision and management. A
list of the products it certifies is available online at
http://www.Kof-K.org.

A five-pointed star with a K in its center (STAR-K) indicates certification by STAR-K Kosher Certification, 122 Slade Avenue, Suite 300, Baltimore, MD 21208, (410) 484-4110. This not-for-profit service issues a quarterly, *Kashrus Kurrents*. Information on the products it certifies can be found at the Web site http://www.star-k.org. STAR-K also administers the certification of STAR-D, the (dairy) kashrut symbol of the National Council of Young Israel.

In addition to the symbol of the certifying agency, the labels of kosher products also indicate their dairy, meat, or pareve status. Products marked "D" either contain dairy ingredients or have been processed on equipment that is also used to process dairy products. Products marked "M" either contain meat ingredients or have been processed on meat-processing equipment. If neither a "D" nor an "M" appears by the product name, the product is considered pareve.

The Generic K

Some products on supermarket shelves are marked with a simple K symbol, but this tells you nothing about their true kosher status. A letter of the alphabet cannot be trademarked or copyrighted in the United States. Although the Food and Drug Administration permits use of the K for kosher whether or not there has been rabbinic or kashrut supervision of the product, the simple letter K only means that the *manufacturer* claims that the product is kosher. The generic K is not as reliable as other symbols since it offers no clue as to who actually certified the product or according to what standards. If consumers have a question about a generic K, they should ask the manufacturer for more specific information about actual rabbinic supervision. More than fifty individual rabbis and local rabbinic authorities also use the K as their certifying symbol. (Their names and credentials are usually available from the product's manufacturer.)

A Kosher Joke

A rabbi, out on a walk, is horrified to see one of his observant congregants walk into a nonkosher Chinese restaurant. Looking in the window, the rabbi sees this man talk to the waiter, who soon appears with dishes filled with shrimp in lobster sauce and pork spare ribs. As the man picks up chopsticks and begins to eat, the rabbi rushes into the restaurant to confront him.

"What are you doing! I saw you come into this nonkosher restaurant, order, and now eat trayf food in violation of everything we're taught in the dietary laws."

Putting down his chopsticks, the congregant replies: "Did you see me come into this restaurant?" The rabbi nods yes. "Did you see me give my order to the waiter?" Another nod yes. "Did you see the waiter bring me the food?" Another nod. "Did you see me eat the food?" Another nod. "Then, rabbi, I don't see what the problem is. This entire meal has been under rabbinic supervision!"

Some twenty states, however, do have consumer protection laws regarding kosher labeling.[1] In New York State, for example, the law requires that any kashrut symbol, including the K, must have a rabbi or supervising agency backing it, and *that* individual or organization must be registered with the state's department of agriculture. This information must be posted in a visible place. (In 2000, a federal judge, citing separation of church and state, struck down New York statutes that set standards for kosher foods but left in place the sections of the law that require kosher food sellers to disclose what rabbinic authority certified a product or restaurant as kosher.) New Jersey has one of the most comprehensive kosher food laws in the nation. The law provides that a K or kosher claim must be backed up by posting the name of the certifying organization in each establishment, or else the food producers must file a thorough disclosure form and prominently post a sign describing just what kosher standards were adhered to. Failure to keep the standards is considered fraud and is subject to fine by the state. For further information on New York and New Jersey state laws, contact:

In New York State: Kosher Law Enforcement Advisory Board, New York State Department of Agriculture and Markets, 55 Hanson Place, Brooklyn, NY 11217, (718) 722-2852, fax (718) 722-2836.

In New Jersey: Kosher Enforcement Division, Office of Consumer Affairs, P.O. Box 45023, Newark, NJ 07101, (973) 504-6100. (The full text of the regulations governing the sale of foods represented as kosher is available on written request.)

Other Certifying Organizations

The following is a selection of the more than four hundred certifying agencies in the United States and Canada. These and other city, state, and regional organizations and individual rabbis are often the ones that certify local restaurants, markets, butchers, and catering facilities. Some of these groups issue their own publications and lists of kosher products.

United States

Association for Reliable Kashrus, 104 Cumberland Place, Lawrence, NY 11559, (516) 239-5306

Atlanta Kashruth Commission, 1855 Vista Road, Atlanta, GA 30329, (404) 634-4063

Central Rabbinical Congress of the USA and Canada, 85 Division Street, Brooklyn, NY 11211, (718) 384-6767

Certified Kosher Underwriters, 1310 Forty-Eighth Street, Brooklyn, NY 11219, (718) 436-7373

Chicago Rabbinical Council, 2701 West Howard Street, Chicago, IL 60645, (773) 465-3900

Community Kashrus of Greater Philadelphia, 7505 Brookhaven Road, Philadelphia, PA 19151, (215) 745-2968

Houston Kashruth Association, 9001 Greenwillow Street, Houston, TX 77096, (713) 723-3850

Igud Hakashrus of Los Angeles, 186 North Citrus Avenue, Los Angeles, CA 90036, (323) 935-8383

Kashruth Inspection Services of the Vaad Hoeir of Saint Louis, 4 Millstone Campus, Saint Louis, MO 63146, (314) 569-2770

KOA Kosher Supervisors, 72 Ascension Street, Passaic, NJ 07055, (973) 777-0649

Kosher Certification Service, 401 North Laurel Avenue, Los Angeles, CA 90048, (323) 782-1433

Kosher Overseers Association of America, P.O. Box 1321, Beverly Hills, CA 90213, (323) 870-0011

Kosher Supervision of America, P.O. Box 35721, Los Angeles, CA 90035, (310) 282-0444

Mid-Atlantic Orthodox Rabbis, 1401 Arcola Avenue, Silver Spring, MD 20902, (301) 649-2799

Organization of Orthodox Kashrus Supervisors, 3301 West Ardmore, Chicago, IL 60659, (773) 539-8049

Orthodox Rabbinical Board of Broward and Palm Beach Counties, 5840 Sterling Road, Suite 256, Hollywood, FL 33021, (945) 797-7888

Orthodox Rabbinical Council of San Francisco, 1851 Noriega Street, San Francisco, CA 94122, (415) 564-5665

Rabbinical Council of Bergen County, P.O. Box 1233, Teaneck, NJ 07666, (201) 287-9292

Rabbinical Council of California, 617 South Olive Street, Los Angeles, CA 90014, (213) 489-8080

Rabbinical Council of Greater Washington, 7826 Eastern Avenue N.W., Washington, DC 20012, (202) 291-6052

Sephardic Kashrus Lemehadrin Laboratory, 30 Lancaster Avenue, Brooklyn, NY 11223, (718) 743-3141

Twin Cities Rabbinical Kashruth Council, 4330 West Twenty-Eighth Street, Minneapolis, MN 55416, (612) 920-2183

Vaad Hakashrus of Dallas, 7800 Northaven Road, Dallas, TX 75230, (214) 739-6535

Vaad Hakashrus of Denver, 1350 Vrain Street, Denver, CO 80204, (303) 595-9349

Vaad Hakashrus of the Five Towns and Far Rockaway, 597A Willow Avenue, Cedarhurst, NY 11516, (516) 569-4536

Vaad HaKashrus of Miami, P.O. Box 403225, Miami, FL 33140, (786) 390-6620

Vaad Hakashrus of Raritan Valley, P.O. Box 4119, Highland Park, NJ 08904

Vaad Hakashruth of Northern California, 2520 Warring Street, Berkeley, CA 94704, (510) 843-8223

Vaad Harabbanim of Flatbush, 1575 Coney Island Avenue, Brooklyn, NY 11230, (718) 951-8585

Vaad Harabonim of Massachusetts, 177 Tremont Street, Boston, MA 02111, (617) 426-2139

Vaad Harabonim of Queens, 90-45 Myrtle Avenue, Glendale, NY 11385, (718) 847-9206

Canada

Calgary Kosher, 1607 Ninetieth Avenue S.W., Calgary, Alberta T2V 4V7, (403) 253-8600

Chief Rabbinate of Quebec-Kashruth Commission, 5850 Victoria Avenue, Montreal, Quebec H3W 2R5, (514) 738-1004

Jewish Community Council of Montreal, 6825 Decarie
  Boulevard, Montreal, Quebec H3W 3E4, (514) 739-6363

Kashruth Council of Canada, 4600 Bathurst Street, Suite 240,
  Toronto, Ontario M2R 3V2, (416) 635-9550

Orthodox Rabbinical Council of British Columbia, 8080
  Francis Road, Richmond, British Columbia V6Y 1A4,
  (604) 275-0042

Ottawa Vaad HaKashrut, 1780 Kerr Avenue, Ottawa,
  Ontario K2A 1R9, (613) 798-4696

Vaad Ha'ir of Winnipeg, C306-124 Doncaster Street,
  Winnipeg, Manitoba R3N 2B2, (204) 487-9571

Listings of certifying agencies in the United States and Canada
can be found at http://www.kashrusmagazine.com (including both
Orthodox and Conservative agencies), http://www.kashrut.com,
and http://www.kosherquest.com.

🌿 Kosher Voices 🌿

"I'm observant and have kept kosher my entire life as a way to perfect Creation and bring more holiness into my daily life. It's a way
of making me more connected to *Hashem* [God] through fulfilling
his commandments."
  —*Yitzchak, a Hassidic attorney from New Jersey*

Chapter 4

The Growth of Kosher Certification

The market for kosher food has grown dramatically in the past ten years, expanding, it is estimated, at a rate of 15 percent annually. Today's consumers are much more health-conscious than those of a generation ago. The public is increasingly aware of potential food contaminants: news stories about such events as the deadly outbreaks of "mad cow disease" and *E. coli* infections make headlines around the world. For many people, a kosher certification is perceived as an extra level of quality assurance and good manufacturing procedures for the products they buy. For them, "kosher" has come to stand for wholesomeness and purity.

Virtually every major food and beverage company has therefore turned to kosher certification—for at least some of their products—as a means of improving their market share in this highly competitive industry. Kosher food and products—nationally known brands and supermarket private labels—can now be found on store shelves all across America. A number of supermarket chains have specific kosher food sections in their stores.

For large manufacturers, the cost of kosher supervision—about $3,000 to $6,000 per plant per year—does not show up in the retail prices they charge for dairy or pareve items. They often absorb the certification cost into their advertising and marketing budgets. This saving to the consumer does not occur with kosher meat and poultry, which can be much more expensive than their nonkosher counterparts, due to the labor-intensive methods of slaughter and preparation (to be discussed more fully in Chapter Five).

How Certification Is Obtained

When companies seek kosher certification, they agree to keep their manufacturing plants and products open to sometimes constant supervision. A kosher investigator or supervisor, called a *mashgiah*,[1] may have a personal set of keys and can make unannounced on-site inspections, visiting plants more frequently than federal investigators do.[2]

The *mashgiah* is particularly concerned about the ingredients that go into a product and the machinery on which it is manufactured. Machinery that has been used to produce nonkosher products or that once processed meat products and is now to process dairy products (or vice versa) must undergo a special kosher cleansing that may go beyond the cleaning procedures companies generally use.

Every single ingredient that is used in the food or comes in contact with the food—no matter where it is produced—must undergo the same thorough investigation.[3] This means that there are kosher inspectors in almost every country in the world. This attention to ingredients extends to processing aids such as pan liners and release agents (used in baking) and to the containers and wrappings, which must also be certified, because minute amounts of chemicals in them can leach into the food.

Since many companies that manufacture kosher products also produce nonkosher ones, the same machinery may be used for different products or lines. If the supervisor finds that a piece of equipment was used for a nonkosher product, it must undergo a specific and stringent cleaning process overseen by the *mashgiah*. This includes a thorough washing with a caustic soap and sterilizing the equipment with boiling water. Equipment may also be disinfected with heat from blowtorches or steam guns.

Although kosher inspectors are not primarily looking for cleanliness, if they find that food has come in contact with a nonkosher ingredient such as bugs, rodent hairs, or droppings, they will deny it certification.

Major food manufacturers that have obtained kosher certification for their products include Amway, Beatrice Foods, Ben & Jerry's, Best Foods, Borden, Carvel, Chock Full O'Nuts, Coca-Cola, Dannon, Del Monte, DowBrands, General Foods, General Mills, Great Atlantic & Pacific Tea Company, Hain Celestial Group, Heinz, Hershey, Horowitz-Margareten, Hunt-Wesson, Keebler, Kellogg's, Kraft, La Choy, Nabisco, Pillsbury, Procter & Gamble, Quaker Oats, Rokeach, Stella D'oro, Stuckey's, Thomas J. Lipton, Tropicana, and U.S. Mills.

National Brands with Kosher Certification

The following is by no means an all-inclusive list of kosher products. Consumers should also be aware that the kosher status of products can and does change, so they should carefully check labels for current certification. The same caution applies to the dairy or pareve status of products. If you have any question about the kosher designation of a specific item, contact the manufacturer or the certifying agency or consult with your rabbi.

Baby Care Products

Adwe Laboratories/Dr Fisher's Nursery Line (shampoos, soapless soap, creams, sunscreen)

Baby Foods

Alsoy, Beech-Nut, Gerber, Heinz, Similac

Baking Mixes and Baking Products

Arm & Hammer baking soda, Arrowhead Mills bread mixes, Atkins Quick Cuisine Low Carb muffins and bread mixes, Betty Crocker, Bisquick, Duncan Hines, Goodman, Keebler Française dough for puff pastry, Old Fashioned Kitchen Crepe Shells, Ostreicher's Cookie Dough, Pepperidge Farm pastry shells and pastry sheets, Pillsbury, Presto

Beverages and Drink Mixes

A&W Cola, Canada Dry, C&C Cola, Ceres Fruit Juices, Coca-Cola, Coors beer, Dr. Brown's beverages, Droste cocoa, Dr Pepper, Fruitopia, Hawaiian Punch, Holland House mixes, RC Cola, Sea-gram's club soda, ginger ale, seltzer, and tonic water, Shasta soda, Snapple natural tea, soda, and seltzer, Tab, Tropicana citrus juices

Breads, Muffins, and Rolls

Arnold, Damascus Bakeries lahvash wraps and pitas, Bellacicco Italian bread, Devonsheer, Entenmann's baked goods, Kemach breadsticks, Kineret frozen challah, Lender's bagels, Levy's, Mrs. Butterworth, Pepperidge Farm, San Luis sourdough breads and bagels, Sara Lee, Stella D'oro, Stroehmann's, Thomas's, Weight Watchers

Cakes, Pies, and Donuts

Drakes, Entenmann's, Heisler's, Krispy Kreme, Pepperidge Farm, Pillsbury

Cereals and Grains

Arrowhead Mills organic flours, Atkins Morning Start Low Carb cereals and breakfast bars, Back to Nature flakes and granola, Casbah flavored rices, Eden Foods whole wheat and quinoa flours, Energy Food Factory Uncle Roy's Cereals, Familia, General Mills cereals (Cheerios, Cocoa Puffs, Total, Wheaties), Kellogg's cereals (Corn Flakes, Froot Loops, Nutri-Grain, Rice Krispies), Kemach cereals and flours, Manischewitz cake meal, Maypo, Nabisco cereals (Shredded Wheat, Cream of Wheat), Near East rice mixes,

Quaker Oats cereals (Cap'n Crunch, Instant Oatmeal, Puffed Wheat), Post cereals, Sahara Natural Foods couscous mixes, Sovex Natural Foods Good Shepherd cereals, Streit's cake meal, U.S. Mills Cereals (Skinner's Bran, Erewhon brand cereals, Wheatena), Wolff's kasha

Cheese Substitutes

Formagg cheeses, Soyco Parmesan cheese, Soymage cheeses, ToTuFu soy cheeses

Chinese Food Products

Bokek vegetable egg rolls, Canton chow mein noodles and egg roll skins, China Pack's duck sauces and hot mustards, Kemach chow mein noodles, La Choy Chinese vegetables (bamboo shoots, bean sprouts, chow mein, noodles, water chestnuts), Mrs. Adler's hoisin and soy sauces, Nasoya egg roll wrappers and wontons, Seasons Oriental vegetables (including baby corn, bamboo shoots, broken-star mushrooms, stir fry vegetable mix, and water chestnuts), Soy Vay marinades, Wonton Foods egg roll skin dough, fortune cookies, and wonton skin dough

Chocolates and Candies

Baby Ruth, Barricini chocolates, Barton's, Cadbury bars, Chuckles, Ghirardelli chocolates, Glenny's 100 percent natural candies, Godiva chocolates, Hershey's Kisses, M&M's, Nestlé bars, Peter Paul Almond Joy and Mounds, Reese's Peanut Butter cups and pieces, Schrafft's, Sorbee hard candies, Starbucks, Stuckey's log rolls, Toblerone milk chocolates

Cleansers, Detergents, and Soaps

Ajax, Amway products, Arm & Hammer bleaches and detergents, Cascade, Cheer, Cinch, Clorox, Dow Oven Cleaner, Electrasol automatic dishwashing detergent, Fab, Fantastik, 409 cleaners,

Hagarty silver cleaners, Ivory Snow, Kleen Bright, Lysol, Mr. Clean, Palmolive, Rokeach kitchen soap, Spic and Span, Sunbright

Coffee

Chock Full O'Nuts, Folgers, General Foods international coffees, Gillies certified organic coffees and natural decaf coffees, International coffees, Maxwell House, Medaglia d'Oro, Sanka instant coffee, Starbucks coffees, Taster's Choice instant coffees, Y&S coffee and instant cappuccino mixes, Yuban

Condiments

B&G Relishes, Blanchard & Blanchard mustards, French's mustards, Gold's horseradish, Grey Poupon mustard, Heinz relishes, Ortega salsas, Westbrae mustards

Cookies and Crackers

Devonsheer melba toast, Drakes, Duncan Hines, Entenmann's, Girl Scout cookies, HeavenScent Reduced Carb cookies, Kedem tea biscuits, Keebler cookies, Nabisco's Oreos, Nonni's biscotti, Ostreicher's cookies, Parco cookies, Pepperidge Farm cookies, Stauffer's, Stella D'oro, Steve's Mom rugelach, Walker's shortbread, Westbrae natural cookies

Cosmetics and Beauty Products

Adwe hand cream, Cinema Beauté lipsticks, Maxx bath oil beads, Nehedar cosmetics, Reflections cosmetics, Shain Dee lipsticks, blush, foundation, and eye shadow

Creamers

Carnation Coffee-mate, Hershey's Non Dairy Creamer, Rich's Creamer

Dairy Products

Boursin spiced gourmet cheeses, Breakstone's butter, cream cheese, and sour cream, Breyer's yogurt, Carnation milk, Dannon yogurt, Farmland Dairies, Friendship Dairies, Horizon Organic Milk, J & J butter, cheeses, sour cream, and yogurts, Kinor cheeses, Maggio ricotta cheeses, Mehardrin butter, cheeses, and sour cream, Miller's cheeses, Parmalat, Philadelphia Brand cream cheese, Polly-O ricotta, Sealtest cottage cheese and sour cream, Sorrento mozzarella and ricotta, Taam Tov cheeses (American, cheddar, Gouda, mozzarella, Muenster, Swiss), Tuscan Dairies

Egg Products and Substitutes

Better 'n Eggs, Egg Beaters, Egg Watchers, Ener-G Egg Replacer, Wonderslim fat and egg substitutes

Fish Products

Brunswick herring, kipper snacks, and sardines, Bumble Bee tuna fish and salmon, Chicken of the Sea tuna, Empress anchovies, Nathan's herring, Progresso tuna in oil, Season salmon, sardines, anchovies, and tuna, Starkist tuna, Vita herring

Frozen Foods

Hain's meatloaf, Macabee Foods bagels and pizza, Mon Cuisine entrees, S'Better Farms chicken entrees (wheat- and gluten-free)

Greek Food Products

Athens frozen spinach and cheese filos, baklava, spanakopita, filo, and strudel leaves, Aunt Trudy's Frozen Filo Pocket Sandwiches, Krinos feta cheese and Greek olives, Oasis frozen moussaka, stuffed grape leaves, and nondairy spinach pie

Ice Cream, Sorbets, Ices, Frozen Yogurt

Ben & Jerry's, Borden ice cream, frozen yogurt, and sherbet, Breyer's ice cream and ice milk, Ciao Bella Gelato sorbet, Cyrk gourmet desserts and sorbets, Dannon frozen yogurt, Dolly Madison ice cream, Edy's ice cream and frozen yogurt, Friuli sorbet, Frozfruit, Good Humor, Häagen-Dazs ice cream and frozen yogurt, House of Flavors ice cream and frozen yogurt, Howard Johnson, I Can't Believe It's Yogurt, Klondike, Mama Tish's Italian ices, Mehadrin frozen deserts, ice cream, Italian ices, sorbet, and yogurt, Nestlé's Turkey Hill ice cream, Rosati Italian ices, Schrafft's ice cream, Sealtest ice cream, Sedutto ice cream and sherbert, Sharon's sorbet, Starbuck's ice cream, Stoneyfield organic frozen yogurt and ice cream, Uncle Louie G's ice cream and ices

Jams, Jellies, and Preserves

Hero preserves, Knott's Berry Farms, Kraft Foods jellies and preserves, Polaner, Roadside Farms, Tiptree preserves

Japanese Food Products

Eden Foods brown rice, miso, sea vegetables, soba and other traditional noodles, rice crackers, teas, wheat-free tamari, and shoyu sauces, and pickled Japanese vegetables, Erewhon miso, ramen, soba, nori, tamari, rice vinegar, tea, candies, and seaweed, Gold's wasabi sauce, Great Eastern Sun wheat-free tamari, umeboshi plums and paste, and seaweed, Kikkoman sauces, Mitoku sea vegetables, umeboshi products, dried shiitake mushrooms, brown rice mochi, soba, udon, and ramen noodles, sesame oil, rice crackers, wheat-free tamari and shoyu sauces, and tea, Mrs. Adler's tamari and teriyaki sauces, San-J International teriyaki sauce and organic wheat-free and reduced-sodium tamari, Sobaya organic soba, udon, and sumen noodles, Soy Vay teriyaki sauce, Westbrae Natural Foods miso, rice wafers, rice cakes, wheat-free tamari, and instant miso soup

Margarine

Blue Bonnet, Fleischmann's, Imperial, Parkay, Promise, Super-brand, Weight Watchers

Marinades

Gold's Dip n Joy sauces, Hunt's barbecue sauces, Jack Daniel's grilling sauces, KC Masterpiece sauces and marinades, Mikee sauces and marinades, San-J barbecue sauces, marinades, and stir-fry and dipping sauces, World Harbors sauces and marinades

Mayonnaise

Best Foods, Chadalee Farms, Hellmann's, Kraft, Weight Watchers

Meat Substitutes

Garden Gourmet frozen vegetable patties, Green Giant Harvest Burgers, Hain frozen drumsticks and burgers, Lightlife Foods meatless protein fat-free "turkey," "ham," "bologna," "bacon strips," and "links," Morningstar Farms frozen Better N Burgers, vegetarian patties, Chik patties, and sausage links, White Wave meatless meat products, Worthington Foods meat substitutes, Zaglo's frozen meatless burgers, nuggets, and patties

Mexican Food Products

Azteca corn and flour tortillas, La Mexicana tortillas and burritos, Ortega tostada and taco shells

Mideastern Food Products

Sabra spreads (babaganosh, hummus, eggplant, tehina), Two Taam spreads

Oils and Shortenings

Bertolli olive oil, Colavita olive oil, Crisco, Kraft oils, Liberty oils, Mazola oils, Pastorelli oils, Riboizi olive oil, Wesson oils

Pancake and Waffle Mixes and Syrups

Aunt Jemima pancake mixes, Hungry Jack pancake mixes, Manischewitz potato pancake mix, Pillsbury pancake mixes, Upcountry Organics of Vermont maple syrup

Pan Coatings and Cooking Sprays

Butter Buds, Mazola NoStick, Pam nonstick cooking spray

Pasta and Noodles

Azzurro organic whole wheat pastas, Barilla pastas, Bartenura gnocchi, Cemac Foods organic wheat-free dry pasta, Contadina, Creamette, De Boles pastas, Don Peppe pastas, Eden Foods organic pasta, Goodman's noodles, Hodgson Mill organic pastas, Italpasta, Kemach noodles, Manischewitz noodles, Mueller's, Prince, Ronzoni pastas, San Giorgio, Sapore di Napoli pasta, Vitelli pasta

Peanut Butter

Jif, Peter Pan, Planters, Reese's, Skippy

Pharmaceuticals and Over-the-Counter Drugs

Adwe Laboratories nonaspirin pain reliever, antacid tablets, heartburn tablets, and Adwe-Tussin, Celestial Seasonings throat lozenges, Fruttasan laxative, Luden's throat drops

Pickles and Pickled Products

B&G, BaTampte, Claussen, Heinz, Vlasic

Poultry and Poultry Products

David Elliott organic chicken, Empire kosher poultry, Galil kosher poultry, Hebrew National, Royal kosher poultry, Wise Kosher natural organic poultry

Private Labels

Many supermarkets chains have their own private or store labels for processed foods and food wrappings. Among the chains that have received kosher certification for a number of their private label products are Finast, Food Emporium, Foodtown, Grand Union, King Kullen, Pathmark, ShopRite, and Waldbaum's.

Processed Meats

Ballpark Premium Beef Franks, Hebrew National Frankfurters, Solomon's Buffalo Frankfurters

Salad Dressings

Blanchard & Blanchard dressings, Cains, Chadalee Farms dressings, Heinz dressings, Henri's, Hidden Valley Ranch dressings, Kraft Miracle Whip dressings, Nasoya Vegi dressings, Pfeiffer, Weight Watchers dressings

Sauces

Buitoni marinara sauce, Contadina marinara sauce, Heinz sauces, Hunt-Wesson barbeque sauces, Kemach pasta sauces, Kraft barbecue sauces, Lea & Perrins steak sauces, Manischewitz tomato and marinara sauces, Ortega Taco sauces, Red Wing sauces

Snack Foods

Cape Cod potato chips, Charles' Chips, Flavor Tree, Frito-Lay corn chips, Tostitos, and Ruffles, Gabilla & Sons knishes, Garden of Eatin' organic corn chips, Keebler pretzels, Konricko rice and wheat cakes, Mrs. Maltz knishes, Newman's Own popcorn, Nutri-Grain bars, Orville Redenbacher's popcorn, Osem snack foods, Pringles, Quaker rice cakes, Quinlan pretzels, Ruffle's classic potato chips, Snyder's of Hanover chips and pretzels, Terra Chips, Uncle Roy's granola bars, Westbrae Natural Foods rice cakes, Wise chips

Soups and Soup Mixes

Campbell's condensed vegetarian vegetable soup, Goodman, Lipton soup mixes, Manischewitz, Rokeach, Tabatchnick's

Spices and Seasonings

Chef Paul Proudhomme's Magic Seasoning Blends, Corona spices, Durkee spices and blends, La Flor spices, McCormick spices, Mrs. Dash, Tones spices

Substitutes for Nonkosher Foods

Bac'n Pieces (artificial bacon-flavored bits), Bac*os bits, Bacon Bits (imitation), Finlay Foods' Cavi*art (vegetarian caviar made from seaweed)

Sweeteners

Draper's honey, Dutch Gold honey, Equal, Karo syrup, NutraSweet, Sweet 'n Low

Tea

Bigelow, Celestial Seasonings, Lipton, Nestea, Remeteas herbal tea, Tetley, Uncle Lee's

Tomato Products

Furmano's, Heinz tomato ketchup, paste, puree, sauce, and crushed tomatoes, Hunt-Wesson tomato products, Pomodora, Redpack, Red Wing, San Benito catsup, puree, crushed, and stewed tomatoes, Westbrae ketchup

Toothpastes and Mouthwashes

Airway Anti-Plaque Fluoride toothpaste, Kosher Dent toothpaste, Lander mouthwash, Melaleuca tooth polish and mouth and throat sprays and washes, Shaklee New Concept dentifrice, Tom's of Maine additive-free toothpastes

Toppings

Betty Crocker, Hershey's, Pillsbury, RediWip, Rich's nondairy topping

Vegetable and Fruit Products

Bodek kosher produce, Del Monte dried fruits, Eden Foods organic beans and tomatoes, Green Giant canned vegetables, Heinz vegetarian baked beans, Hero canned fruit, Le Sueur canned vegetables, Libby canned vegetables, Mariani dried fruits, National Produce fresh packaged vegetables, Paesana sun-dried tomatoes, Seasons canned vegetables, Seneca canned fruits and vegetables, Spratés vegetable spreads, Sun Giant raisins and nuts

Vitamins, Nutritional Supplements, Diet Aids

Boost, Ensure, Freeda Vitamins (no wheat, yeast, gelatin, salt starch, sulfites, or preservatives), General Nutrition Products/Diet Center vitamins and mineral tablets, Kyolic garlic tablets and liquid, Landau children's and adults' vitamins (no sugar, starch, salt, milk, dyes, or additives), MaxiHealth Research vitamins, mineral and herbal supplements, and vegetarian capsules, Naturemax energy boosters, Shaklee vitamins and nutritional supplements, Slimfast and Ultra Slimfast, Solgar vitamins, Sunrider International vitamins and nutritional supplements, Sustacal, Twin Labs vitamins, minerals, food supplements, and sports supplements

Wrappings and Paper Goods

Alcan foil products, Chinet molded dishes and trays, Glad wraps and storage bags, Hefty freezer and storage bags, James River Dixie cups and plates, Reynolds Cut-Rite wax paper, aluminum foil pans and foil, and plastic film, Sweetheart paper plates and cups, White Star paper cups and plates

❧ Kosher Voices ❧

"A Jewish friend told me about the different way in which kosher chickens are raised and processed, and it seemed more organic and cleaner and more humane than nonkosher brands. So I decided to give it a try, and I liked what I tried. Most supermarkets here in New York City carry kosher chicken, so finding it in my neighborhood is not a problem and I don't mind the slightly higher price."

—*Sue, a non-Jewish researcher who buys kosher poultry*

Chapter 5

Meats and Poultry

Because of the costly and time-consuming steps involved in their breeding, slaughter, and processing, kosher meats and poultry are notoriously more expensive than their nonkosher counterparts. But many people are willing to pay higher prices for the extra assurances that a kosher certification brings to these products.

To be considered kosher, meat and poultry have to satisfy a number of conditions (called *shehitah*) that go beyond what is mandated by the U.S. Department of Agriculture for meat on sale in the United States. These conditions are as follows:

1. The meat must come from an animal considered kosher; that is, the animal for slaughter must be a permitted one. Animals for slaughter must be in apparent good health. Diseased animals are automatically considered nonkosher.[1]

2. Kosher poultry must be raised without hormones or growth stimulants.

3. Animals cannot be artificially stunned before slaughter.[2] Nor can they be slaughtered mechanically. They must be dispatched by a *shohet*, a specially trained ritual slaughterer, by the most painless and humane way possible. Because of the strength needed, *shohets* are generally men. Although the *shohet* need not be a rabbi, he is considered a religious official, knowledgeable about Jewish law and skilled in the theory and practice of slaughter, and a person whose piety has been attested to by a rabbi. The knife used by the *shohet* is

razor-sharp and extremely smooth; it must not have any visible notches so that it will cut cleanly and quickly. The knife, which is twice as long as the width of an animal's throat, is checked for nicks or dents before and after each animal is slaughtered. If the blade shows any imperfection or if a hair or a feather clings to it, the animal can be declared ritually unfit for consumption and therefore will not get a kosher certification. If the imperfections are found before slaughter takes place, the knife must be resharpened before the *shohet* can continue.

4. Before the slaughter, the *shohet* recites a blessing. Then, because the animal must be killed instantaneously, he slits the animal's throat, severing the jugular vein, trachea, and esophagus in a single uninterrupted stroke. No stabbing motions or any pressure can be used. Even a momentary delay or the least bit of hesitation will make the killing invalid. This method of slaughter cuts off the blood supply to the animal's brain almost at once. Pain is thought to be minimized, and the animal loses a huge amount of blood immediately.

5. To ensure the wholesomeness of the meat, immediately after slaughter, the animal's lungs and other internal organs are checked by a trained inspector, called a *bodek*, for any physiological abnormalities, discolorations, or symptoms of disease. Meat with certain types of adhesions, cuts, or bruises is rejected. There are over seventy defects that render an animal unsuitable. These include perforated or punctured organs, underdeveloped organs, organs of abnormal size, absence of an organ, internal cuts and bruises, hernias, fractured bones, dislocated limbs, infections, and tumors.[3] If the animal or bird is found to suffer from an illness or defects that would lead to its natural death within a year, its carcass is rejected. Some kosher meat and other kosher products carry the designation "glatt kosher." *Glatt* refers to the perfect smoothness of an animal's lungs. The term has also come to mean "extremely kosher."

6. Certain blood vessels, nerves, and lobes of fat in beef, veal, and lamb are forbidden by Jewish dietary law and are removed from the carcass.

7. After slaughter, all the remaining blood must be extracted to fulfill the biblical injunction against consuming blood. The carcass is first hung, neck down, so that the blood drains freely. Then it is butchered into the permitted cuts and all the internal organs and parts are removed. Next comes the koshering or kashering process, which is generally done for consumers by a kosher butcher before cutting and packaging the meat, although it can be done at home by the consumer. For poultry, the kashering process is completed at the slaughterhouse or packaging plant. First, the meat or poultry is washed and soaked, totally covered, in clean cool water for half an hour. (The internal organs have already been removed and are koshered separately.) It is then placed on a perforated surface or on a flat grooved board set on an incline to drain before being salted on all sides with coarse kosher salt.[4] For poultry, both the inside and outside of the bird are salted. Coarse-grained salt is a very effective method for drawing off blood; regular table salt is too fine and would dissolve before it could have any effect on the meat. Finally, after an hour, the meat is rinsed off twice, again in cool water. Liver, because it is so rich in blood, cannot be koshered in this manner. It must be broiled over a grate or an open flame. Hearts must be sliced open before being salted, to facilitate draining. For observant Jews, the rule about not consuming blood extends to eggs as well. If an egg has even a minute spot of blood in the yolk, it is discarded.

8. All meat and poultry must be koshered within three days of slaughter, because after seventy-two hours, blood becomes so coagulated that it cannot be properly removed. Freezing meat after slaughter also prevents the blood from draining. Ground meat cannot be koshered, so meat used for hamburgers and the like is koshered before grinding.

9. Supervision of the koshered meat and poultry continues until the product reaches the consumer. Meat and poultry must be properly tagged and labeled. For fowl, a metal tag, called a *plumba,* bearing the kosher certification, serves as an identifying seal. Kosher butcher shops and markets must also be under kosher supervision.

Did You Know?

Kosher salt is so named because its large grains are used in the koshering process of meat and poultry. Although chemically identical to other salts that come from the sea or from dried salt beds (sodium chloride), kosher salt differs from regular table salt in several ways. Not only is it large-grained, light, and flaky, but it also contains less salt per teaspoonful and adheres better to food. (Although there are table and sea salts that are certified as kosher, the term *kosher salt* refers specifically to the large-grained variety.)

Table salt is made by driving water into a salt deposit and evaporating the brine that is formed, leaving dried cubelike crystals that resemble granulated sugar. Kosher salt is made in the same way, but during the evaporation, it is continuously raked, giving it a lighter, flakier texture. Kosher salt also differs from its counterparts in that it has no additives such as iodine, often added to table salt to prevent goiter and as an anticaking agent, or dextrose, added to iodized salt as a stabilizer.

Kosher salt can be used as a general kitchen salt, but because it is "less salty," you will have to use almost twice as much as table salt to achieve the same degree of saltiness. But many professional chefs prefer it for cooking and seasoning, believing that the additives in regular table salt can give food an "off" taste.

Two nationally available brands of kosher salt are Morton's Coarse Kosher Salt and Diamond Crystal Kosher Salt.

A Guide to Kosher Meats

Jewish dietary laws mandate the removal of certain arteries, veins, nerves, and sinews from animals before they can be eaten. These include the sciatic nerve and its accompanying blood vessels, which run through the hip joint and hindquarters of cattle and sheep. Genesis 32:33 prohibits eating this nerve in remembrance that Jacob was touched on the thigh's sciatic nerve when he wrestled with the angel. From this biblical story, Talmudic scholars and rabbinic interpreters drew various conclusions, including proof that God would not allow the annihilation of the Jewish people.

Removal of the sciatic nerve is an extremely time-consuming and therefore expensive process, so in the United States, the hindquarters of kosher animals are usually sold to nonkosher butchers. However, some kosher butchers will undertake the tedious job of removing the sciatic nerve, and some specialty shops do sell kosher filet mignon, kosher leg of lamb, and so forth.

The kosher and nonkosher cuts of beef, veal, lamb, and poultry are as follows.

Beef

Kosher Cuts (from the forequarters)	Nonkosher Cuts (from the hindquarters)
Brisket	Loin
Chuck (ground, filet steak, pot roast)	Rump
Flanken (breast, rib), minute steak, cubed steak	Flank
	Shank
Rib top	Filet mignon
Delmonico cut	Sirloin
Short rib	Tenderloin
Standing rib roast	T-bone
Shoulder roast, shoulder steak, hanger steak	Porterhouse
Rib eye, rib steak	
Skirt steak	
Round (ground, steak, pot roast)	
Tongue	

Veal

Kosher Cuts (from the forequarters)	Nonkosher Cuts (from the hindquarters)
Breast	Loin
Cutlets	Flank
Shoulder, shoulder steak	Leg
Rib (chops, roast)	Hind shank
Brisket	
Tongue	

Lamb

Kosher Cuts (from the forequarters)	Nonkosher Cuts (from the hindquarters)
Neck	Loin
Shoulder chops	Leg
Shank	
Rib (chops, roast)	
Breast (roast, brisket)	

Poultry

All parts of a capon, chicken, Cornish hen, duck, goose, pigeon, and turkey are kosher.

Did You Know?

Approximately 10 percent of the animals slaughtered in the United States for food each year are killed by Jewish ritual law and therefore are considered kosher.

A Note on Islamic Dietary Laws

Islam, the Muslim religion, also divides foods into those that are permitted, referred to as *halal*, and those that are *haram*, or forbidden. As in Judaism, forbidden foods include blood and pig and pork products. Also forbidden are animals that have not been slaughtered in the proper manner, which is by cutting the jugular vein with a very sharp knife while reciting a prayer pronouncing the name of Allah (God). Sura 2:172 in the Koran, the Muslim holy book, forbids eating "an animal that dies of itself, and blood and the flesh of pigs, and that on which any other name has been evoked beside that of God."

Like the Torah, the Koran forbids the eating of birds of prey, rodents, reptiles, and insects (except locusts). However, unlike Jews, Muslims are permitted to eat camel meat. Meat from kosher butchers is considered *halal*, or proper for consumption.

These dietary restrictions are an important obligation for Muslims. In a study of Islamic values in the United States, 90 percent of American Muslims responding said they never ate pork or pork products, and two-thirds believed that it was important to buy and eat *halal* meat whenever possible.

Chicken the Kosher Way

Chicken is America's number one meat. Since 1975, the annual per capita consumption of poultry has doubled to more than 70 pounds per adult. According to the National Broiler Council, Americans eat 500 million pounds of chicken and turkey each week, and approximately 4 million pounds of that total is kosher.

In a number of blind taste tests sponsored by food and cooking magazines, kosher chickens invariably beat the leading supermarket poultry brands and came out at or near the top when compared to other specialty premium brands. Many experts say that kosher chickens do have a different taste, a result, perhaps of the extra steps kosher poultry processors take in the breeding, feeding, raising, and processing of their chickens, turkeys, and ducklings.

For example, the chickens bred by Empire Kosher Poultry of Mifflintown, Pennsylvania, the world's largest producer of kosher chickens, are free-roaming, rather than caged for their entire lifetimes. In bad weather, they are housed in brightly lit, environmentally controlled sheds. Galil Poultry of Livingston Manor, New York, raises its chickens on a special scientifically devised high-protein, all-natural diet of grain, soybeans, corn, wheat germ, and naturally occurring minerals. Empire also has its own rabbinically supervised feed mills and hatcheries. Indeed, all aspects of kosher poultry's growth and processing—from egg-laying conditions to transportation and slaughter, to the dressing, wrapping, and shipping of the product to market—are overseen by rabbinic supervisors. Wise Natural Poultry is certified as both kosher and organic. Antibiotic-free, the birds are fed an all-organic grain diet grown in soil free of herbicides and pesticides and are allowed to roam freely outdoors.[5]

Feed and water for kosher fowl contain no growth stimulants, antibiotics, hormones, or preservatives. In contrast, many of the chickens destined for processing by the industry giants are fed a "least-cost formulated diet," which changes as the market price for the various ingredients fluctuate. This feed may also contain additives, preservatives, by-products, or fillers forbidden by kosher laws.

Most chickens in the United States are slaughtered at six or seven weeks. Kosher chickens are allowed to "grow out," that is, they are permitted to grow to full maturity, slowly and naturally, and are not shipped to the processing plant until they are at least nine weeks old.

Once kosher chickens arrive at the processing plant, each one is checked for signs of illness and to see if it sustained any injuries during transport. If so, it is immediately rejected. All kosher poultry is handheld for slaughter; the birds cannot be stunned electronically beforehand, nor can they be slaughtered by machine. The salting process is also done by hand; other aspects of processing are done using high-tech conveyers and soaking vats. The finely honed knives used by the *shohets*, the ritual slaughterers, are constantly being checked to see that they are razor-sharp because any irregularity or minor imperfection in the blade is thought to cause the animal additional suffering, forbidden by Jewish law. Because their job requires such intense concentration, the *shohets* work for only an hour at a time.

In addition to the standard inspections done by USDA workers (who only began inspecting poultry processors in 1958), kosher supervisors are stationed all along the production line, continually checking for external and internal defects and diseases that would make a bird unfit for the kosher market. Kosher inspectors are much stricter than those who work for the USDA and reject more poultry as inedible than the government does. Birds are rejected for such things as punctured organs, abnormal growths, and certain broken bones that would pass USDA inspection.

U.S. Department of Health regulations call for the removal of all feathers from processed poultry to prevent the spread of bacteria-borne disease. Nonkosher processors make this difficult job easier by soaking their birds in hot water. Kosher chickens cannot be processed in hot water because technically that would begin to "cook" the bird before it was properly koshered. So kosher processors use cold, fresh running water for all washing and rinsing—a process, incidentally, that has been shown to help retard the growth of bacteria and to prevent cross-contamination.

It takes approximately three hours from slaughter to packaging of a kosher chicken. The U.S. industry average for all poultry is forty-five minutes.

🍃 Kosher Voices 🍃

"I've just started buying kosher meat and poultry exclusively. The impetus was the recent 'mad cow' disease scare. I read an article that talked about the way beef for kosher slaughter is treated, and it sounded healthier, so I decided 'better safe than sorry.' A number of my non-Jewish friends have also switched to kosher meat for the same reason."

—*Sylvie, a woman who lives in Los Angeles and describes herself as ethnically Jewish but nonobservant*

Chapter 6

Wine and Spirits

Wine is sure proof that God loves us and wants us to
be happy.

—*Benjamin Franklin*

Mention kosher wine, and for many people, the adjectives that
come to mind include *sweet* and *heavy*. But kosher wine is no longer
limited to the traditional "sacramental" red wines made from New
York's Concord grapes.[1] In the past fifteen years, kosher wine has
taken on a whole new look and taste. More than a dozen wineries
in California, New York, France, Italy, and Israel have begun pro-
ducing kosher varietals, including some award-winning, top-ranked
chardonnays, cabernet sauvignons, and white zinfandels.

Wine, often thought of as a symbol of joy, redemption, and hospitality, plays an important role in Jewish celebrations and holidays
such as Passover. Special prayers are said over wine before Sabbath
meals. Genesis 9:20–21 tells us that the first thing Noah did after
the Flood was to plant a vineyard. The Psalms (104:15) speak of
"wine that maketh glad the heart of man."

How Wine Becomes Kosher

Although other kosher foods and beverages may be prepared or manufactured by non-Jews as long as there is proper supervision and certification, special rules apply to kosher wines. Since biblical times,

wine has been an important part of religious rites and ceremonies, and therefore special procedures need to be taken in order for it to be considered kosher. For example, from the time the grapes are crushed to the moment the product is bottled and corked, the wine and the winemaking equipment may be handled only by Jews who observe the Sabbath (sundown Friday to sundown Saturday).[2] Other rules must also be followed:

1. Although the grapes used for making kosher wine are no different from those used to make nonkosher wines, they cannot be picked on the Sabbath or on Jewish holidays such as Rosh Hashanah, Yom Kippur, or Sukkot (which, unfortunately, usually fall right in the middle of the prime grape harvesting season).

2. Juices are fermented using kosher yeast and enzymes that do not contain *any* animal-derived ingredients. No animal-derived products can be used in any part of the winemaking process. This includes the soaps used to clean the tanks and barrels as well as the fining (purifying) and filtering agents. Since there are no commercial kosher bacteria, vintners have to make their own cultures from natural yeasts found in the air and on the grapes themselves—an expensive and time-consuming project.

3. Cleanliness is of the utmost importance: the fermenting tanks, barrels, hoppers, pumps, and presses are sterilized with purifying chemicals or steam jets and rinsed with 190-degree water before the grapes are crushed. The barrels have to be cleaned three times.

4. The entire process has to be overseen by a *mashgiah* or religious supervisor.

Other alcoholic beverages that contain grape wine, such as certain liquors, arak, brandy, champagne, cognac, sherry, vermouth, and sangria, must comply with these rules in order to be certified kosher. Alcoholic beverages and spirits such as beer, unflavored grain vodkas, rye, bourbon, and Scotch (straight and blended), which are grain- or potato-based, are considered inherently kosher and pareve, as are true fruit liquors, unless they contain flavorings and additives or grape products or derivatives. If so, their production must be under kosher supervision. Grape products or products that contain wine, grape derivatives, or grape flavoring, such as jams, jellies, grape juices, candies, and wine vinegar, must also receive kosher supervision.

A Selection of Kosher Wines and Spirits

A number of companies and wineries produce or import kosher wines and spirits. The following is a sampling of what is available in the United States.

Abarbanel Wine (Cedarhurst, New York)
http://www.kosher-wine.com; (888) MYIWINE
Wines from around the world: Beaujolais, Cabernet
　　Sauvignon, Chardonnay, Merlot
Layla Dirty Blonde Lager (from Israel)

Canandaigua Wine Company (Canandaigua, New York)
www.cwine.com; (888) 659-7900
Manischewitz: Blackberry, Cream Almonetta, Cream Peach,
　　Elderberry, Loganberry, Malaga, Medium Dry Concord

Carmel Wine Company (Israel)
http://www.carmelwine.com
Founded in 1882, today Carmel, Israel's oldest winery, is a
　　cooperative of two hundred winegrowers.
Carmel sparkling wines: Blanc de Blancs, Brut Reserve Cuvée,
　　Sparkling Chardonnay
Carmel Valley wines: Cabernet Sauvignon, Colombard,
　　Grenache Rosé, Sauvignon Blanc, Sémillon
Carmel Vineyards wines: Cabernet Sauvignon, Chenin,
　　Dry Muscat, Emerald Riesling, Sauvignon Blanc, Shiraz,
　　White Zinfandel
Rothschild wines: Cabernet Sauvignon, Chardonnay, Emer-
　　ald Riesling, Merlot, Sauvignon Blanc, White Muscat

Carmel also produces a number of brandies and dessert wines, vodkas, and cream liqueurs.

Gan Eden (Sebastopol, California)

http://www.GanEden.com; (800) 829-5686

Sauvignon Blanc, Chenin Blanc, Black Muscat, Chardonnay Cabernet, Gewürztraminer Sémillon, Syrah

Hagafen Cellars (Napa, California)

http://www.hagafen.com; (707) 252-0781

Cabernet Sauvignon, Chardonnay, Chardonnay Reserve, Harmonia red and white table wine, Johannesburg Riesling, Merlot, Pinot Noir, Pinot Noir Blanc, Syrah

Royal Wine Corporation (Bayonne, New Jersey)

http://www.royalwines.com; (718) 384-2400

Baron Herzog (California): Black Muscat, Blush Muscat, Cabernet, Cabernet Sauvignon, Champagne Brut, Chardonnay, Chenin Blanc, Red Zinfandel, Sauvignon Blanc, Special Reserve Chardonnay, Syrah, White Zinfandel

Bartenura (Italy): Amaretto, Asti Spumante, Bartenura liqueurs, Chianti Classico, Lambrusco, Merlot, Pinot Grigio, Sambuca, Soave, Valpolicella

Herzog (France): Barons Rothschild Haut Médoc, Beaujolais Villages, Cabernet Sauvignon, Chardonnay, Château de la Grave Bordeaux, Château Grande Noyer Pomerol, Château la Rèze Minervois, Chateneuf semidry white, Chinon, Muscadet

J. Furst (California): Cabernet Sauvignon, Chardonnay, Fumé Blanc, Pinot Noir, White Zinfandel

Kedem (New York State): Burgundy, Chablis, Concord, Malaga, Vermouth (dry and sweet), Sauternes, Sherry, Tokay

Teal Lake (Australia): Cabernet, Chardonnay, Merlot, Shiraz

Weinstock (Sonoma, California): Cabernet Sauvignon, Chardonnay, Gamay, Merlot, Sauvignon Blanc, White Riesling, White Zinfandel

Royal Wine publishes a kosher wine newsletter, *From the Grapevine*. See details at the company's Web site

Yarden (Golan Heights, Israel)

http://www.golanwines.com

Blanc de Blancs, Cabernet Sauvignon, Chardonnay, Merlot, Mt. Hermon red and white, Sauvignon Blanc, Syrah, White Riesling

Other kosher wines are produced by Barkan, Israel (Cabernet Sauvignon, Chardonnay, Merlot, Pinot Noir, Syrah); Dalton, Israel (Cabernet, Cabernet Sauvignon, Chardonnay, Merlot, Muscat, Sauvignon Blanc); Galil Mountain Winery, Israel (Cabernet Sauvignon, Merlot); Gamla, Israel (Cabernet Sauvignon, Merlot, Sauvignon Blanc); Tishbi Estate Winery, Israel (Cabernet, Cabernet Sauvignon, Chardonnay, Chenin Blanc, Emerald Riesling, Merlot, Sauvignon Blanc); Rashi, Italy (Moscato d'Asti, Prumasco Cortese white, Prumasco Barbera red); Villa Santero, Italy (Asti Spumante, Moscato d'Asti); Fortant de France, France (Chardonnay, Cabernet Sauvignon, Merlot); George Duboeuf, France (Beaujolais); Pays d'Oc, France (Cabernet Sauvignon, Merlot, Chardonnay, Sauvignon Blanc); Robert Cohen, France (Cru Beaujolais); Kijafa, Denmark (cherry and peach wines); Langer, Hungary (Muscat, Tokaj); Kolobarra Hills, Australia (Chardonnay, Shiraz-Cabernet); Alfasi, Chile (Cabernet Sauvignon, Chardonnay, Malbec/Syrah, Merlot, Sauvingnon Blanc); Mount Maroma, Rutherford, California (Chardonnay, Cabernet Sauvignon); Naveh Vineyards, Elgin, Arizona (Sonoita Sauvignon Blanc). California's Four Gates Winery, the country's only kosher winery using only organically grown grapes, produces a Chardonnay and a Merlot; not available in stores, they can be ordered by calling (831) 457-2673.

Kosher certification has been received by the following spirits, hard liquors, and beers: Stolichnaya vodka, Finlandia vodka, Cristall, Priviet, Godiva liquor, Ginjo Premium Sake, Sho Chiku Bai sakes, Takara Mirin beer, Coors beer and lager, Cherry Heering liqueur, Disaronno Amaretto liqueur, Sabra liqueurs, Leroux liqueurs and schnapps, Tio Pepe, Hungaro slivovitz, Old Williamsburg bourbon, Montaigne cognac, Hamashkeh scotch, Kisz Bier, Miller's beer, and Ramapo Valley Brewery beer and lager, including a gluten-free beer.

The following stores carry a wide selection of kosher wines:

Connecticut

Warehouse Wines and Liquors
808 East Main Street, Stamford
(203) 357-9151

New Jersey

Carlo Russo's Wine World
102 Linwood Plaza, Fort Lee
(201) 592-1655

New York

Skyview Wine and Liquors
5681 Riverdale Avenue, Bronx
(800) 472-1288; (718) 601-8222
Free catalogue and wine tastings

Chateau Shalom Wines and Liquors
446 Avenue P, Brooklyn
(718) 382-9463

Orlander's Fine Kosher Wines and Spirits
4821 Thirteenth Avenue, Brooklyn
(718) 436-1031
1781 Ocean Avenue, Brooklyn
(718) 377-0500
http://www.orlanders.com

Beacon Wines and Spirits
2120 Broadway, Manhattan
(212) 877-0028

Gotham Wines and Liquor
2517 Broadway, Manhattan
(212) 932-0990
http://www.gothamwines.com
orders@gothamwines.com

McCabe's Wines and Spirits
1347 Third Avenue, Manhattan
(212) 737-0790

Sherry-Lehman
679 Madison Avenue, Manhattan
(212) 838-7500
Offers Kosher wine tastings.

67 Wines and Spirits
179 Columbus Avenue, Manhattan
(212) 724-6767

Shuhag (Rame) Liquor
69-30 Main Street, Kew Gardens Hills, Queens
(718) 793-6629

Atlantic Bayview Wines and Liquors
380 Atlantic Avenue, Freeport (Long Island)
(516) 378-9421

Bottle Bargains
350 Glen Head Road, Glen Head (Long Island)
(516) 676-8400

Chateau de Vin
544 Central Avenue, Cedarhurst (Long Island)
(516) 374-WINE
http://www.chateaudevin.com

Great Neck Wines and Spirits
13 North Station Plaza, Great Neck (Long Island)
(516) 466-7585

Green's Wines and Liquors
216 Old Country Road, Hicksville (Long Island)
(516) 931-3290

Jacoves Liquors
20 Hempstead Turnpike, West Hempstead (Long Island)
(516) 489-5133

MAB Finer Wines and Spirits
385 Merrick Avenue, East Meadow (Long Island)
(516) 489-0303

National Liquors
125 Hempstead Turnpike, West Hempstead (Long Island)
(516) 539-1883

Peninsula Wines and Liquor
208 Franklin Place, Woodmere (Long Island)
(516) 374-0900

BevMax Wine and Liquor
513 Boston Post Road, Port Chester (Westchester)
(914) 937-2333

Wine Bazaar

2425 Palmer Avenue, New Rochelle (Westchester)

(914) 712-0260

Zachys Wine and Liquor

16 East Parkway, Scarsdale (Westchester)

(914) 723-0241

http://www.zachys.com

info@zackys.com

The California Winemakers Guild, (800) 858-9463; e-mail: cwg@napanet.net, can provide bimonthly shipments of wine produced by small kosher wineries around the world. Each shipment includes an informative newsletter.

A selection of kosher wines from around the world can also be found at http://www.kosherwine.com and http://www.kosherline.com.

🍃 Kosher Voices 🍃

"I was born in Poland, and my parents were very religious and of course kept kosher. I came to America as a very young girl and can still remember my mother teaching me how to cook kosher dishes, something that came in handy when I worked in a neighborhood kosher restaurant for a short while when I was seventy-five. It's a lot easier to buy kosher foods today; you don't have to travel too far to buy kosher meat, and there are lots of kosher products in the stores. It was much harder when I was starting my own family. I buy kosher foods now to keep up the tradition and in memory of my parents."

—*Phyllis, a vibrant ninety-two-year-old New Yorker*

Chapter 7

Kosher and Healthy

Are kosher foods healthier than nonkosher foods? Many people think so, but the answer to that apparently simple, straightforward question is "yes, no, sometimes." Junk food can be kosher; "natural" foods purchased in health food stores may contain nonkosher ingredients. And while a kosher diet eliminates fatty pork products including lard and bacon, it doesn't necessarily exclude fatty processed meats such as salami or bologna or baked goods made with coconut or palm oil, both high in saturated fats.

Although the original intent of the dietary laws set forth in the Bible and Talmud were religious and ethical, not medical, they may have given the people who followed them unexpected health benefits in the centuries before refrigeration, knowledge of germs and bacteria, and government inspection and regulation of food. Maimonides, in his *Guide for the Perplexed*, claimed that kosher foods were indeed healthier to eat. (Sounding more like a modern fitness guru than a medieval doctor, he advocated a diet that emphasized exercise, whole grains, and fresh fruit. He also advised moderation in the use of alcohol and warned about eating too much fat, pastries, and salty meat and cheese.)

Examples of the unintended and unexpected health benefits from "keeping kosher," still applicable today, might include the following:

1. Among the "unclean" animals prohibited by kosher laws are those that were frequently fed leftover, possibly moldy, food. Today

we know that some molds produce aflatoxins, which, when ingested by humans, can cause infections and diseases. There have also been reports of high aflatoxin concentrations in bacon and lard and in slaughtered pig carcasses. The ban against eating pork might also have led to a lower incidence of trichinosis. Undercooked pork and pork products are a major source of this serious disease, caused by eating foods infected by a parasitic roundworm.

2. The prohibition of shellfish, which sometimes grow and feed in polluted bottom waters, might also have had health benefits. Raw shellfish can contain naturally occurring toxins such as paralytic shellfish toxin; they can also cause illness from viruses, salmonella, and other bacterial infections. According to the National Academy of Sciences, "no other commercially available food poses a greater health risk." Raw shellfish, including oysters, mussels, and clams, account for 66 percent of the cases of food poisoning in the United States each year; more than one hundred thousand Americans become ill from contaminated shellfish yearly.

3. The koshering process—salting and washing—might have helped preserve meat in the days before refrigeration. (The ledger book of a cargo ship that sailed from Newport, Rhode Island, to the island of Jamaica in 1782 showed an entry for "Jew beef"—salted meat that had a kosher stamp on it.) Today we know that blood can carry disease. Kashering meat and poultry—draining it of blood— might also have lessened the incidence of blood-borne illness.

4. The fats forbidden by the dietary laws are those that surround vital organs and the liver. Scientists have discovered that there are differences between these kinds of fat and the permissible fats that occur around the muscles and under the skin.

Other beneficial effects may also come from kashering. One study, reported in *Food and Cosmetic Toxology* in 1976, indicated that the salting and soaking process appeared to lessen the risk of the formation of nitrosamines, cancer-causing agents. Salting can also reduce or eliminate some types of bacteria, especially campylobacter, a common contaminant of poultry. It also appears to reduce the risk of salmonella, a leading cause of food-borne illness, in chicken. The U.S. Department of Agriculture estimates that as many as five thousand deaths and five million illnesses result annually from the consumption of meat and poultry contaminated with four major bacterial pathogens: salmonella, campylobacter, *Escherichia coli*, and *Listeria monocytogenes*. Although the koshering process helps kill or reduce these pathogens, the only way to completely guarantee the safety of kosher and nonkosher meat products is to follow a few simple rules of handling and cooking.

All meat sold in the United States has become safer to eat when it comes to bacterial contamination. In the late 1990s, Congress agreed to provide money to underwrite major changes in the nation's meat and poultry inspection system, modernizing hundred-year-old procedures based on looking, touching, and smelling. In this so-called sniff-and-poke method, USDA inspectors had only a few seconds to spot obvious signs of disease or spoilage as animal and bird carcasses sped by them on a conveyor belt.

But some health hazards are invisible to the human eye. The new system, known as Hazard Analysis Critical Control Point, seeks to lessen the level of harmful bacteria, including salmonella. It also includes microbial testing (and quick computer analysis of the results) for *E. coli*, a potentially deadly side effect of fecal contamination. The new system and additional tests, however, do not completely eliminate the incidence of salmonella and campylobacter; they merely reduce it. A 2001 study by the Food and Drug Administration found that one in five samples of supermarket ground meat and poultry was contaminated with salmonella, and most of the strains were resistant to antibiotics.

Today, not only must kosher products meet safety standards set by the USDA and the FDA, but they must also adhere to the sometimes even stricter laws of kashrut. Kosher supervisors visit food-processing factories more often than federal inspectors do. In the case of meat and poultry, kosher supervisors may reject twice as many animals as their nonkosher counterparts, adding an extra level of health and safety protection for the kosher consumer.

Brave New World:
Are Genetically Altered Foods Kosher?

Is a kosher chicken still kosher if it is fed bioengineered grain?

Would the use of genetically engineered enzymes be enough to make a cheese nonkosher?

Is a tomato that has been genetically altered with a chromosome from a pig kosher?

In today's brave new world of DNA splicing, bioengineered food, and genetically altered crops, it is not far-fetched to ask such questions. Genetically altered food has been sold in the United States for well over a decade. About one-third of the corn crop in this country has been genetically altered, according to the *New York Times*, and scientists continue to mix and match the ingredients in the food we eat. A tomato with a pig gene—the Calgene Flavr Savr tomato—already exists and was approved for human consumption in 1994. For the most part, you can't tell by the labels if the food you are eating has been genetically altered. Current FDA guidelines do not mandate identifying ingredients that have been genetically engineered unless the product contains proteins from the eight most allergenic foods—milk, eggs, wheat, fish, shellfish, tree nuts, peanuts, or soy.

But what do the dietary laws have to say about bioengineered foods? Established Jewish traditions and contemporary rabbinic commentaries declare that if a substance is so chemically changed that it cannot be reconstituted into its original form, it is considered a "new thing," and therefore has lost the characteristics it once had. Also, if a substance is not visible to the human eye (such as pig DNA), it cannot be considered nonkosher, even if it originally came from a nonkosher source. According to the Orthodox Union, in the process of gene splicing, which can transfer virtually any characteristic of a living plant or animal to another organism, the new gene is introduced into tissue via bacteria. For example, the non-kosher pig gene is not implanted into the tomato itself but serves as a chemical formulation that is then reproduced onto material taken from yeast and then introduced into the plant via bacteria. The reproduced gene now in the tomato is therefore from a totally kosher source, the yeast, and not from the nonkosher pig. So the answers to our three questions are yes, no, and yes.

And if you are wondering whether cloning is kosher, contemporary Jewish law and commentaries have pondered the question and decided that there does not seem to be any substantive arguments to forbid it. However, as with most rabbinic discussion about modern medical and scientific miracles such as cloning, discussion continues.

Government Help for the Consumer

Whether you buy kosher or nonkosher foods, it is easier than ever to become a savvier, health-conscious consumer. New nutritional guidelines and recent changes in government labeling regulations are helping make it so.

The Food Guide Pyramid

Within the past few years, the USDA and the Department of Health and Human Services have revised their Food Guide Pyramid, a model of recommended daily food choices that emphasizes balance, variety, and moderation. With the wide range of kosher products available today, eating healthy while eating kosher is not a problem.

Did You Know?

Even with the government's new systems for reducing the bacterial contamination of meat and poultry, consumers should still follow the USDA's guidelines for safe food storage and preparation.

1. After purchase, perishable foods such as fresh meat or poultry should be taken home immediately and placed in a refrigerator (at 40°F. or below) or freezer (0°F.). Food-borne bacteria multiply rapidly in the danger zone between 40 and 140 degrees.

2. To avoid spreading bacteria (cross-contamination) from uncooked to cooked foods, after handling raw eggs, meat, fish, or poultry, wash hands and utensils with hot soapy water.

3. Cook or microwave meat to a high internal temperature to kill harmful bacteria and parasites. Beef, including ground beef mixtures such as meat loaf or hamburgers, should be cooked to 160°F. Steaks and roasts may be cooked to 145° (medium rare), 160° (medium), or 170° (well done). Meat that has been tenderized by pricking should be cooked to 160°. Lamb should be cooked to 170°; poultry, to 180–185° (juices should run clear); ground turkey or chicken, to 165°; whole chicken or turkey, to 180°; boneless turkey roast, to 170–175°; veal, to 170°F.; and fish to 140–145°F.

4. Before marinating raw meat, set aside some of the liquid to use for dipping the cooked meat. Throw out marinade after raw meat has been sitting in it.

For further information on food safety, consumers can call the USDA's Meat and Poultry Hotline at (800) 535-4555 or visit its Web site at http://www.fsis.usda.gov. Questions about the safety of other foods are handled by the Food and Drug Administration, (888) 723-3366. Information on handling food safely can also be found at http://www.foodsafetyanswers.org, a site run by the Iowa State University Extension.

The Food Guide Pyramid sets out the following recommended quantities for daily consumption by healthy adults:

Group	Servings per Day	Sample Serving
A (not a food group): Fats, Oils, and Sweets (salad dressing, cream, butter, margarine, soft drinks, candy)		Limit your servings. Also limit servings of high-calorie, high-fat pastries, cakes, cookies, and salty snacks.
B: Milk, Yogurt, and Cheese	2–3	1 cup low-fat milk or yogurt *or* 2 ounces processed cheese (preferably low-fat) *or* ½ ounces natural cheese (preferably low-fat)
C: Meat, Poultry, Fish, Eggs, Dry Beans, and Nuts	2–3	2–3 ounces cooked lean meat, poultry, or fish;[1] ½ cup cooked dry beans, 1 egg, *or* 2 tablespoons peanut butter is equivalent to 1 ounce lean meat
D: Vegetables	3–5	1 cup raw leafy vegetable *or* ¾ cup vegetable juice *or* ½ cup other vegetables, cooked or raw
E: Fruit	2–4	¾ cup fruit juice *or* ½ cup chopped, cooked, or canned fruit *or* 1 medium apple, banana, or orange
F: Bread, Cereal, Rice, and Pasta	6–11	1 muffin *or* dinner roll or slice of bread *or* 1 ounce ready-to-eat cereal *or* ½ cup cooked cereal, rice, or pasta

Food Labels

There are also federal labeling laws that help consumers make healthier choices in their food selections. These laws were revised jointly by the Food Safety and Inspection Service of the USDA, the agency responsible for labeling meat and poultry, and the FDA, which is in charge of all other packaged goods.

Since 1994, when the 1990 Nutrition Labeling and Education Act became law, all packaged and processed foods in the United States (including all kosher foods) have been required to display a detailed list of ingredients and specific information on their nutrient content.[2]

There are a few exceptions to the law. Some packages are allowed to have a short or abbreviated nutrition label. These include small or medium-size packages (less than 12 square inches available for labeling), which must then include an address or phone number of the manufacturer who may be contacted for information; plain coffee, tea, some spices, and other foods that are known to have no significant amount of any nutrient; foods that contain only a few of the nutrients that require listing; and infant formula. Also exempt are foods produced by some small companies; food served in restaurants, airplanes, hospitals, bakeries, delicatessens, and retail establishments; and food sold by vendors in malls, on the street, or from vending machines.

Nutritional information may also be voluntarily displayed at the point of purchase for fresh fruits and vegetables. If such information is posted and makes reference to the waxes and resins used to coat the produce, the laws mandate that the reference must indicate the *source* of the ingredients in the coating rather than just its name. This is important for both kosher and vegetarian consumers, who would want to know whether the coating was derived from animals or plants. In 2001, many of the country's largest food companies agreed to voluntary guidelines that would have them specify on processed food nutritional labels whether the product contains even tiny amounts of everyday ingredients that can cause potentially fatal reactions. Roughly seven million Americans have allergies to such common foods as milk, eggs, and nuts. Under current law, manufacturers can add very small amounts of such allergens as incidental ingredients without listing them on the label or identifying them as "natural flavors." The voluntary guidelines suggest that manufacturers list these ingredients on labels by their common names.

Nutrition Facts

Understanding nutritional labeling helps all consumers make knowledgeable choices about what they eat. The following is a brief look at labels and what important information can be gleaned from them. The labels, headed "Nutrition Facts," must, by law, give the following information:

1. *Serving Size*. Although it is not necessarily a "recommended amount," serving size is based on a typical portion as determined through consumer surveys by the U.S. government. The serving size is listed in both common household units, such as ½ cup, and in metric units—grams (g) and milligrams (mg). About 28 grams equals 1 ounce; 1,000 milligrams equals 1 gram. Serving sizes are the same for similar foods. For example, a serving of pretzels will be about the same size as a serving of potato chips. The amount of calories and the nutrients listed on the package are based on the serving size, so if you eat twice the serving size, you will get twice the calories and nutrients. Also be aware that many packaged foods that look like single servings are labeled as if they contain more than one serving.

2. *Calories*. This is expressed in two ways: the number of total calories in one serving and the number of calories derived from fat in that serving. Dietary guidelines recommend that people get no more than 30 percent of their calories from fat each day; some nutritionists think even that amount is too high.

3. *Percent Daily Values*. The label must state the amount, in one serving, of certain important nutrients including fat, cholesterol,

carbohydrates, fiber, sugar, protein, sodium, and vitamins. Amounts for two key vitamins and two minerals must be included: vitamins A and C, calcium, and iron. If vitamins and minerals other than these four have been added or the product makes a claim about other vitamins or minerals, their percentage must also be listed. The nutrients are listed in two ways: (1) in terms of the amount by weight per serving (given in grams or milligrams, rounded down to the nearest gram or half-gram) and (2) as a percentage of the daily value, a new nutrition reference tool. By using the Percent Daily Values, it is easy to determine whether a food contributes a lot or a little of a particular nutrient. A higher percentage means it contains a lot of that nutrient; a low percentage means it contains a little. If you eat twice the serving size indicated on the label, you are getting twice the *percentage* of daily value of nutrients.

The Percent Daily Value on all labels is based on a sample diet of 2,000 calories a day.[3] If your daily caloric intake is higher than 2,000, the food you eat adds a smaller percentage of daily value to your diet. If you eat less than 2,000 calories, the food you eat adds a greater percentage. Another part of the label shows recommended total daily amounts (in grams and milligrams) for total fat, saturated fat, cholesterol, sodium, total carbohydrates, and dietary fiber, based on two sample diets, one with 2,000 calories, the other with 2,500. (Beginning in 2006, the FDA will require food manufacturers to include the amount of trans fatty acid on nutrition labels, although they will not be listed as a percentage of a whole day's value.)

A note on the nutrition portion of the label explains the 2,000-calorie basis for the percentages given. An individual's daily caloric needs depend on many factors, including age, height, weight, and activity level. Whatever your caloric intake, the Percent Daily Value can be used as a reference to see how a particular food fits into the context of a total diet. For example, a diet of 1,500 calories a day is 75 percent of a 2,000-calorie diet; therefore, the Percent Daily Values for each of the nutrients in all the foods you eat should total 75 percent instead of 100 percent. If one food provides 25 percent of the daily value for fat, all the other foods you eat that day should add up to no more than 50 percent.

4. *Ingredients*. If a product contains more than one ingredient,[4] it must carry a list that states all the ingredients in descending order by weight. The ingredients that make up less than 2 percent of the product can be noted in any order at the end of the ingredient list. This list is now required on almost all foods, even standardized ones such as mayonnaise, peanut butter, and bread, which previously did not need to carry an ingredient list. Natural flavorings and colorings can be listed just as "flavorings" or "colorings," and their source does not have to be given (although it may be). However, artificial flavorings and colorings must be identified as such. The source of an artificial flavoring does not have to be given, but a source must be listed for an artificial color: for example, "yellow #5." Also, the total percentage of juice in juice drinks must be declared.

Front Label Claims

Many food labels and packaging carry health claims and claims about their nutritional content, such as "fat-free" or "high in fiber." The new labeling laws have placed specific and legal limits on what manufacturers can claim about their products. The FDA is now allowing claims linking a nutrient or food to the risk of a disease or health-related condition in only seven cases where the link has been supported by scientific evidence. Products making a health claim must contain a defined amount of nutrients.

The only allowable health messages that a manufacturer may make are claims that show a link between (1) calcium and a lower risk of osteoporosis; (2) fat and a greater risk of cancer; (3) saturated fat and cholesterol and a greater risk of coronary heart disease; (4) fiber-containing grain products, fruits, and vegetables and a reduced risk of cancer; (5) fruits, vegetables, and grain products that contain fiber and a reduced risk of coronary heart disease; (6) sodium and a greater risk of high blood pressure; and (7) fruits and vegetables and a reduced risk of cancer.[5]

In addition, terms that are used to describe a food's nutrient content are limited and now have strictly regulated definitions. Only certain terms are allowed. Standard serving sizes are assumed;

for products with small serving sizes (30 grams or less or 2 table-spoons or less), the amounts permitted are smaller.

Here are the legal definitions of terms manufacturers may use on food labels:

Free. The product must contain no amount or only a very small amount of the substance. For example, "calorie-free" means less than 5 calories per serving; "sugar-free" means less than 0.5 gram of sugar per serving; "fat-free" means less than 0.5 gram of fat per serving;[6] "cholesterol-free" means less than 2 milligrams of cholesterol and 2 grams (or less) of saturated fat per serving; "sodium-free" or "salt-free" means less than 5 milligrams of sodium.

Low, used in conjunction with *fat, cholesterol, sodium,* or *calorie.* "Low-fat" means 3 grams or less of fat per serving;[7] low saturated fat means 1 gram or less of saturated fat per serving and 15 percent or less calories from saturated fat. "Low-sodium" means 140 milligrams or less of sodium per serving; "very low sodium" means 35 milligrams or less sodium. "Low-cholesterol" means 20 milligrams or less cholesterol and 2 grams or less saturated fat per serving. "Low-calorie" means 40 calories or less per serving; a "low-calorie meal" has 120 calories or less per 100 grams.

Lean. This term may be used to describe the fat content of meat, poultry, or fish containing less than 10 grams of fat, less than 4 grams of saturated fat, and less than 95 milligrams of cholesterol per serving and per 100 grams.

Extra lean. This term may be used to describe the fat content of meat, poultry, or fish containing less than 5 grams of fat, less than 2 grams of saturated fat, and less than 95 milligrams of cholesterol per serving and per 100 grams.

High. The product must contain 20 percent or more of the daily value for that nutrient per serving. High-fiber means 5 grams or more of fiber. If a food is not "low-fat," the label must declare the level of total fat per serving and refer to the nutritional panel when a fiber claim is mentioned.

Good Source. A product may declare itself a "good source" of a nutrient if one serving of the product contains 10 to 19 percent of the Recommended Daily Value for that nutrient. A "good source of fiber" contains 2.5 to 4.75 grams per serving. If a food is not "low-fat," the label must declare the level of total fat per serving and refer to the nutritional panel when a fiber claim is mentioned.

Reduced or *less*. The product contains less than 25 percent of a nutrient or calories when compared to a similar product. If a claim is made for "reduced cholesterol," the product must also have 2 grams or less of saturated fat per serving than a comparison food. Consumers should be aware, however, that like fat-free products, those with less fat or reduced fat may contain more sugar or more sodium for taste and therefore may not be much lower in calories than comparable products.

Light or *lite*. The product contains at least one-third fewer calories or at least 50 percent less fat than the higher-calorie, higher-fat version or no more than half the sodium of the higher-sodium version. If a food derives more than half its calories from fat, fat content must be reduced by 50 percent or more. The adjective *light* can also be used to describe a food's texture or color, provided the intent is clear, as in "light brown sugar" or "light olive oil."

More. One serving provides at least 10 percent more of the Recommended Daily Value of a nutrient than a comparison food does.

Other familiar food packaging terms now also have specific meanings:

Enriched and fortified. The food has been nutritionally altered so that one serving provides at least 10 percent more of the Recommended Daily Value of a nutrient than the comparison food does.

Fresh. This designation may be used for food in its raw state; it cannot be used on food that has been frozen or cooked or that contains preservatives.

Fresh frozen. This description can be applied only to food that has been quickly frozen while still fresh.

Unsalted. No salt has been added during processing. To use this term, the product it resembles must normally be processed with salt and the label must note that the food is not a sodium-free food if it does not meet the requirements for the claim "sodium-free."

For further information on labeling laws consumers can contact the FDA or the USDA:

Food and Drug Administration
5600 Fishers Lane, HFE-88
Rockville, MD 20857
(800) 535-4555 (10 A.M. to 4 P.M., Eastern Time)

Food Safety Education
USDA Food Safety and Inspection Service
Fourteenth Street and Independence Avenue S.W.
Washington, DC 20250
(800) FDA-4010 (recorded information, 24 hours; agents,
    12 to 4 P.M., Eastern Time)
http://www.vm.cfsan.fda.gov

Additional Guidance

Health newsletters and healthy eating guides are also available from a variety of nongovernment sources. However, keep in mind that it is important that you always consult your doctor about your health concerns. Do not rely on newsletters or the Internet as your sole source of medical information.

Generally reliable information is available from the following sources.

Consumer Reports on Health
P.O. Box 52148
Boulder, CO 80322
(800) 234-2188

Harvard Health Letter
164 Longwood Avenue
Boston, MA 02115
(617) 432-1485

Harvard Women's Health Watch
(800) 829-5921
http://www.health.harvard.edu

Johns Hopkins Medical Letter/Health After 50
(800) 829-0422
http://www.hopkinsafter50.com

Mayo Clinic Health Letter
(800) 333-9037
http://www.mayoclinic.com

National Health, Lung and Blood Institute and National
 Cholesterol Education Program
National Institutes of Health
Bethesda, MD 20892

Nutrition Action Health Letter
Center for Science in the Public Interest
1875 Connecticut Avenue N.W. (Suite 300)
Washington, DC 20009
(202) 332-9110
http://www.cspinet.org

Tufts University Health and Nutrition Letter
50 Broadway
New York, NY 10004
(212) 668-0411
(800) 247-7581
http://www.healthletter.tufts.edu

University of California/Berkeley Wellness Letter
P.O. Box 412, Prince Street Station
New York, NY 10012
(212) 505-2255
(800) 829-9170
http://www.wellnewsletter.com

🌿 Kosher Voices 🌿

Although Ellen is Irish Catholic, she ate kosher food during her childhood on Long Island. "My mother wasn't a very good cook, and she often made hot dogs because they required no more than boiling water. She always bought kosher franks because she was concerned with the questionable 'meat products' found in non-kosher hot dogs. But the ones she made were terrible and tasted nothing like the ones I would eat at the homes of friends. The reason: my mother would boil them for at least forty-five minutes to make sure she eliminated the risk of trichinosis!"

Chapter 8

Kosher for Vegetarians

Vegetarianism[1] is as old as the Bible, a spiritual ideal of the Garden of Eden, where no meat was eaten. Adam and Eve may have been the first vegetarians. In Genesis 1:29–30, God tells them, "Behold, I have given you every seed-bearing grass upon the face of the earth and every fruit-bearing tree, these shall be for you to eat. And to every beast of the earth and every bird of the sky and every creeping thing, to everything that has the breath of life in it, I have given the green grass for food."

It was only after God saw the corruption of Noah's descendants that the killing of animals for consumption was permitted: "Every moving thing which lives shall be yours for food, just as I have given you the grasses, so do I give you all" (Gen. 9:3). Even then, several passages in the Torah assert that it would be better to eat no meat at all. The Talmud credits the longevity of the generations from Adam to Noah as being due to their vegetarian diet and also admonishes wise men not to live in a city where there are no green vegetables (Eruven 55b).

The German Rabbi Samuel Raphael Hirsch (1808–1888), a leading Orthodox thinker, concluded that perhaps vegetarianism was preferable to meat eating, since the human body and the human mind are connected by the food one consumes, and plants are "the most passive of substances." "Anything which gives the body too much independence or makes it too active in a carnal direction," he wrote in *Hoeb: A Philosophy of Jewish Law and Observances*, "brings it nearer to the animal sphere, thereby robbing it of its primary function, to be the intermediary between the soul of man and the world outside." Rav Kook, the first chief rabbi of Israel, was well known for his vegetarian beliefs. Rabbi Richard Schwartz, author of *Judaism and Vegetarianism*, argues that vegetarianism is a Jewish imperative, citing as one reason that the production and consumption of meat, which runs the risk of being unhealthy, violates Jewish teaching that one should preserve one's health above all else.

Others also think that the vegetarian lifestyle is a modern fulfillment of the goals of kashrut and Judaism, a way to follow the biblical and rabbinical imperatives of *tzaar baalei chayim* ("Do not cause another living being to suffer") and *bal tashchit* (Do not create waste").[2] If you must kill animals for food, the Jewish religion instructs, you must kill them humanely. Following this logic, not killing them is the most humane act of all. And since meat is a resource-intensive food, for ecologically minded vegetarians, not eating meat helps conserve, rather than deplete, our air, water, land, and energy.[3]

Whether you become a vegetarian out of concern for animals or the environment or because of a belief in nonviolence or for religious, spiritual, or other ethical reasons, kosher labeling and dietary laws can help all vegetarians better sort out the processed and packaged goods on supermarket shelves.

How Kosher Labeling Helps

Because milk and dairy products cannot be combined or eaten together with meat, kosher products marked with a "D" (for dairy) contain *no* meat or meat products. Products labeled "pareve" (neutral) contain neither dairy nor meat. However, vegetarians who want to avoid eggs and fish still need to check the ingredients list, since both those items are considered pareve.

For example, margarine sometimes contains animal fats or their derivatives. Margarine marked "pareve" would contain no such

Did You Know?

There are six common ways to practice vegetarianism:

- *Pescovegetarians* do not eat meat or poultry; they emphasize fish, plant foods (vegetables, fruits, grains).
- *Pollovegetarians* do not eat red meat or fish; they emphasize poultry, all plant foods (vegetables, fruits, grains).
- *Ovolactovegetarians* do not eat meat, fish, or poultry; they emphasize eggs, milk, milk products, all plant foods (vegetables, fruits, grains). (This is the most commonly practiced vegetarian regime.)
- *Ovovegetarians* do not eat any animal foods except eggs; they emphasize eggs, all plant foods.
- *Lactovegetarians* do not eat any animal foods except milk and milk products; they emphasize dairy products, all plant foods.
- *Vegans* do not eat any animal foods or foods derived from animals, such as honey—no meat, fish, poultry, eggs, milk, cheese, or other dairy products; they emphasize plant foods only.

(For a discussion of kosher dairy substitutes, soy milk, and tofu, see Chapter Nine.)

ingredients. Commonly used food dyes and flavoring agents may contain up to a hundred different chemicals and enzymes that do not have to be listed on the package. This includes flavors designated as "natural." Some of these chemically produced items are made from meat by-products, including such items as civet, an enzyme derived from extract of civet cat, or beaver secretions (castoreum). The bright-red coloring agent carmine is extracted from the ground-up bodies of female cochineal insects.

A long list of food products—including margarine, shortenings, cream fillings and toppings, cake mixes, doughnuts, puddings, coffee creamers, ice cream, frozen deserts, instant mashed potatoes, peanut butter, and breakfast cereals—contain emulsifiers, substances that allow two ingredients to mix together, making oil and water soluble. On labels, emulsifiers—or stabilizers, as they are sometimes called—may be listed as polysorbates, mono- and diglycerides, sorbitan monostearate, calcium stearol lactylate, magnesium stearate, or calcium stearate. Although emulsifiers may be derived from either animal or plant sources, federal laws do not mandate that their source be listed. Mention need only be made that emulsifiers have been added to the product. Pareve vegetarian kosher products would contain emulsifiers such as lecithin, which come from a nonanimal source.

Kosher dietary laws, which forbid the mixing of meat and dairy, do not allow the use of animal rennet in making cheese because it is derived from the lining of calves' stomachs. Kosher cheese is made with vegetable rennet, a highly concentrated derivative of plant material.

Kosher pareve or dairy products are not wrapped in plastic or paper that contains any animal product or was made with any chemicals or oils using any animal by-products. Some plastic packaging for food uses beef tallow as a surface coating material. This tallow can interact with the contents of the package, so packaging certified as kosher would not contain this coating.

The Question of Gelatin

Gelatin, a tasteless, odorless substance extracted from cattle or hog bones, hooves, and hides, is considered nonkosher by Orthodox dietary laws, even if the gelatin was derived from kosher animals (which itself is a very expensive process). Gelatin is an ingredient in many desserts, candies, frozen dairy products, baked goods, yogurt, sour cream, and cottage cheese. Kosher foods use vegetable gelatin substitutes, including agar-agar (also known as kantan or Japanese gelatin), a dried seaweed usually sold in powdered form or in long strips or sheets; carrageenan and Irish or Chinese moss, derived from algae; and vegetable gum, extracted from plants. Kosher pharmaceuticals may also use a new type of fish gel in place of animal gelatin.

🌿 Vegetarian Groups and Magazines 🌿

Here is a list of reliable sources of information on vegetarianism.

Vegetarian Resource Group
P.O. Box 1463
Baltimore, MD 21203
(410) 366-VEGG
http://www.vrg.org

A nonprofit group that will answer questions about vegetarian diet. Publishes books as well as a monthly magazine, *Vegetarian Journal*. Also maintains a list of vegetarian tour and travel services.

American Vegan Society
P.O. Box 369
Malaga, NJ 08328
(609) 694-2887

Publishes a quarterly magazine, *The American Vegan*.

Green Earth Travel
7 Froude Circle
Cabin John, MD 20813
(888) 246-8343
http://www.vegtravel.com

Maintains a database of bed and breakfasts, restaurants, tour operators, and spas that cater to vegetarians.

Natural Health Magazine
21100 Montgomery Street
Woodland Hills, CA 91367
(818) 884-6800
http://www.naturalhealth1.com

North American Vegetarian Society
P.O. Box 72
Dolgeville, NY 13329
(518) 569-7970
http://www.navs-online.org
Publishes a magazine, *The Vegetarian Voice*.

Vegetarian Times
9 Riverbend Drive South
Stamford, CT 06907
(203) 967-7266
http://www.vegetariantimes.com

Veggi Life
1041 Shary Circle
Concord, CA 94518
(925) 671-9852
http://www.vegilife.com

Vegetarian Nutrition and Health Letter
School of Public Health
Loma Linda University
1717 Nichol Hall
Loma Linda, CA 92350
(888) 558-8703
vegletter@sph.llu.edu

Did You Know?

The following famous people were vegetarians:

Pythagoras (c. 582–507 B.C.E): Greek philosopher and mathematician who favored a natural, meatless diet, for "the earth affords a lavish supply of riches."

Buddha (c. 563–483 B.C.E.): "To become a vegetarian is to step into the stream that leads to Nirvana."

Leonardo da Vinci (1452–1519): Tradition has it that this Florentine painter, engineer, and scientist loved animals so much that he would buy caged birds just to set them free.

Percy Bysshe Shelly (1792–1822): Romantic poet who published an 1813 treatise that claimed that plants were the only food suited to the human digestive system. "There is no disease, bodily or mental, which adoption of a vegetable diet and pure water has not infallibly mitigated wherever the experiment [vegetarianism] has been fairly tried."

Leo Tolstoy (1828–1910): Russian novelist who believed that since people could be healthy without eating meat, to do so was immoral.

George Bernard Shaw (1856–1950): Irish-born dramatist who gave up meat at age twenty-five, lived to be ninety-four.

Mohandas Gandhi (1869–1948): Indian statesman who believed that vegetarianism was not only a way of eating but a way of life that contributed to one's spiritual development.

Albert Einstein (1879–1955): The great scientist once proclaimed that "the vegetarian manner of living . . . would most beneficially influence the lot of mankind."

Isaac Bashevis Singer (1904–1991): Yiddish writer and Nobel Prize winner who often included vegetarian themes in his writings. Once asked if he was a vegetarian for health reasons, he replied, "Yes, for the health of the chickens."

And the following are some well-known contemporary vegetarians: Billie Jean King, Bob Dylan, Gloria Steinem, Jerry Seinfeld, Yoko Ono Lennon (so was John), Richard Gere, Brigitte Bardot.

Go to http://www.famousveggie.com for more on well-known vegetarians, past and present.

More information on vegetarianism can be found at the following Web sites:

http://www.jewishveg.com

http://www.jewishvegan.com

http://www.vegweb.com

http://www.vegsource.com

http://www.ivu.org

http://www.vegan.org

http://www.eatveg.com

http://www.veggievacations.com (maintains listings of vegetarian-friendly hotels, tours, and cruises)

http://www.vegdining.com (worldwide listings of vegetarian restaurants)

http://www.happycow.org (worldwide listings of vegetarian and health food stores)

🌿 Kosher Voices 🌿

"My Jewish roommate, also a vegetarian, told me how the dietary laws forbid mixing of meat and dairy, so we buy kosher products because we know that the labels will indicate any meat or meat by-products. It's important to know that the food I eat contains not even the slightest bit of meat. If the product is marked kosher and dairy, I know that's the case."

—*Matthew, a member of the noncreedal Unitarian Universalist Association and a vegetarian graduate student from Washington, D.C.*

Chapter 9

Kosher for the Lactose-Intolerant

Milk, in one form or another, is a hidden ingredient in thousands of different products, from processed foods such as TV dinners and canned tuna to candies and baked goods to vitamin pills and prescription drugs. But in the United States, millions of people have a problem with milk. This includes infants and children who are allergic to milk protein and exhibit such symptoms as respiratory distress, abdominal pain, skin rashes, and eczema after eating or drinking milk or milk products.

An estimated fifty million American adults are lactose-intolerant, suffering either from a lactose deficiency or from lactose maldigestion. Lactose deficiency results from a partial or complete lack of an enzyme (produced in the small intestine) called lactase, which the body requires to digest lactose, the sugar found in animal milk. The symptoms of lactose deficiency, which occur after consuming milk or milk products, include often painful intestinal cramping, bloating, excess gas, and diarrhea.

As they age, most people gradually lose, in varying degrees, the ability to digest lactose.[1] Some adults can have no dairy products at all. Others can eat dairy foods in moderation. Depending on the severity of their condition, some individuals can drink milk if it is consumed with a meal or if it contains bacterial cultures, such as yogurt. Cheese, which is low in lactose compared to milk (0.5 milligram per ounce versus 11 grams per ounce) can sometimes be eaten with no uncomfortable symptoms. Hard cheeses contain little or no lactose. Besides milk, the foods that cause the most problems are ice cream, cottage cheese, sour cream, ice milk, buttermilk, and frozen yogurt. Certain ethnic groups, including people of Asian, African, Native American, and Jewish descent, are more apt to have problems digesting milk as they grow older.

Lactose Intolerance

It is estimated that 70 percent of the world's adult population suffers from lactose intolerance to some degree. Different ethnic groups, however, exhibit the condition in varying percentages, according to the Wisconsin Department of Health and Social Services: Africans, 93 percent; Japanese, 92 percent; Greeks, 87 percent; Native Americans, 83 percent; Arabs, 80 percent; eastern European Jews, 78 percent; African Americans, 70 percent; South Americans, 65 percent; Hispanic Americans, 50 percent; Caucasian Americans, 20 percent.

Consumers who want to avoid milk or milk products need to read labels carefully, since milk and its derivatives can be listed under a number of different names, including whey (the liquid residue that remains when milk is curdled; it contains both milk sugar and milk protein), casein (a milk protein, sometimes used in processing canned foods, including tuna), sodium caseinate (a milk protein), lactalbumin (a milk protein), lactoglobulin (a milk protein), and calcium lactate (a crystalline salt, used in baking powder). Milk, lactose, whey, and curd may be found in products as diverse as bread and other baked goods, dry breakfast cereals, instant potatoes, margarine, canned tuna, and salad dressings. According to the American Dietetic Association, milk and its by-products can also be found in processed meats, drink mixes, commercial sauces and gravies, soups, frozen waffles, sugar substitutes, nondairy creamers, and some medications. Lactose fillers may be used in common additives such as monosodium glutamate (MSG).

> **Did You Know?**
>
> This is the lactose content of some common foods, expressed as approximate grams of lactose per 100 grams of food:
>
> Condensed milk, 11
>
> Ice milk, 8
>
> American cheese, 5
>
> Buttermilk, 5
>
> Cow's milk, (whole, low-fat, or skim), 5
>
> Feta cheese, 4
>
> Half-and-half or light cream, 4
>
> Ice cream, 3–8
>
> Yogurt, 3–6
>
> Cottage cheese, 3
>
> Ricotta, 3
>
> Whipping cream, 3
>
> Cream cheese, 2
>
> Sherbet, 1–2
>
> Swiss cheese, 1–2
>
> Butter or margarine, 1
>
> Muenster cheese, 1
>
> Parmesan, 0–3
>
> Mozzarella, 0–3
>
> Blue cheese, 0–2
>
> Brie, 0–2
>
> Cheddar cheese, 0–2
>
> Provolone, 0–2

The Kosher Option

Buying kosher products is one option for those who are lactose-intolerant, lactose-maldigestive, or allergic to milk protein,[2] allowing them to eat a variety of healthy foods safely.[3]

Since the kosher dietary laws prohibit the mixing of meat and milk, *all* kosher meat products are milk-free and do not contain even a trace of milk or milk products. For example, dried milk is a common ingredient in many nonkosher processed meats; some creamers labeled "nondairy" may in fact contain some dairy ingredients. With pareve or neutral foods such as fish, fruits, and vegetables, if the kosher certification symbol is followed by a "D," it means that the product contains *some* milk or milk product and is therefore considered dairy. The same would be true of those "nondairy" creamers. However, there are kosher nondairy creamers that are completely dairy-free. These (such as Rich's Non Dairy Creamer) would have the certifying symbol followed only by the word *pareve*.

Individuals who are lactose-intolerant or have lactose malabsorption can often eat yogurt (of which there are many kosher brands available) and acidophilus milk, which contains "cultures" that increase the bacterial count in the stomach and intestines and ease the digestion of lactose. Several companies—including Anderson Erikson Dairy, Dairy Maid Dairy, Dominick's Dairy, Louis Trauth Dairy, Muller Pinehurst Dairy, and Pensupreme—manufacture kosher acidophilus milk. Dynamic Health Laboratories of Brooklyn, New York, produces kosher (and pareve) liquid acidophilus in a variety of flavors. (Acidophilus milk tastes the same as regular milk, but it cannot be heated, as heat destroys the *Lactobacillus acidophilus* bacterium.) Ahava Food Corporation, (718) 972-8843, markets quart bottles of Goatrition, kosher goat milk which they say is suitable for those intolerant of or sensitive to cow's milk.

Kosher lactose-free or lactose-reduced milk (whole, skim, reduced-fat, and low-fat) is also available from a number of dairies. Among these products are Dairy Ease lactose-reduced and lactose-free milk, Dairyman's Cooperative Creamery lactose-reduced skim milk, McNeil Consumer Products' Lactaid milk, and Ultra Dairy's Bodywide lactose-reduced nonfat milk.

There is also a kosher over-the-counter product available that helps the body break down lactose, making it easier to digest by supplying the lactase enzyme the body lacks. Lactaid, which is available in caplet or liquid form, can be added to refrigerated skim or whole milk (it breaks down about 70 percent of the milk sugars after twenty-four hours in the refrigerator). Or it can be chewed along with the lactose-containing food. For further information and a sample caplet, call McNeil Nutritional Products at (800) LACTAID, 9 A.M. to 5 P.M., Eastern Time, or go to http://www.lactaid.com.

Additional sources for information on lactose intolerance include the American Dietetic Association, (800) 877-1600; the National Osteoporosis Foundation, (800) 223-9994, (202) 223-2226; and the National Dairy Council, http://www.nationaldairycouncil.org. For more information about calcium, call the Calcium Information Center, (800) 321-2681.

Dairy Substitutes: Soy Milk and Tofu

Many people consider soy a "wonder food" because it is the only common source of isoflavones, a class of hormones that appear to offer protection against a variety of ailments.[4] Soy milk and tofu, popular with vegetarians, are versatile lactose-free substitutes that are available with kosher certification.

Soy milk is a rich liquid extracted from soybeans. Nutritionally complete, it supplies many of the same important nutrients as milk. Soy milk contains protein and is also high in iron and vitamin B-12. Look for soy milk fortified or enriched with calcium, especially important for lactose-intolerant people who are also strict vegetarians and therefore never consume any animal products. Soy milk is available in low-fat and nonfat versions.

Tofu, also known as bean curd or soy cheese, is a relatively inexpensive yet complete and easily digestible food. A versatile form of high-quality protein, it is rich in calcium, vitamins, and minerals and is cholesterol-free. Tofu is made by heating soy milk to the boiling point, adding a curdling agent, and then separating the curds from the whey. The curds are then pressed together to make cakes of tofu.

Fresh tofu comes packed in water and will keep for four to five days in the refrigerator; the water should be changed every day or two. Tofu can be frozen for up to three months in a well-sealed container. Frozen tofu develops a chewy, meatlike texture. Tofu is also available freeze-dried. To rehydrate this product (which can last indefinitely), pour boiling water over it.

An 8-ounce serving of tofu (about 144 calories) provides substantial daily calcium and protein requirements for an adult, as well as the B vitamin choline, which is needed by the brain. Tofu contains all eight essential amino acids. It is low in fat compared to cheese and is free of cholesterol. A 1977 study cited in *The Lancet*, a British medical journal, reported that tofu actually lowered blood cholesterol in people who had high levels, perhaps because it provides lecithin, which helps dissolve the artery-blocking substance.

Tofu comes in a variety of styles. Depending on its water content, it is designated "extra firm," "firm," "regular," "soft," or "silken" (this last lends a creamy texture to sauces and desserts). Because it is porous and bland, tofu will absorb the flavors of whatever it is cooked or blended with. It can be prepared in a number of ways: broiled, deep-fried, sautéed, marinated, blended into sauces, or mashed into a spread. Kosher tofu can be served at any dairy meal.

Other soy-based products include soy flakes; soy flour; soy ice cream; soy powder; tamari (or shoyu), a rich, dark, naturally fermented soy sauce that contains no added flavorings or caramel; miso, a concentrated high-protein paste made from soybeans and grains that, like yogurt, is rich in lactobacilli; and tempeh, a fermented food (made from cooked soybeans inoculated with a mold starter) that has a high protein and B12 content.

There are also soy "cheeses" and soy ground "meats," so it is now possible to eat a kosher "cheeseburger."

A number of companies produce kosher soy and tofu based products. Among them are the following:

Carole's, Glen Cove, New York: soy crunch snacks

Eden Foods, Clinton, Michigan: soy milk (carob, vanilla, or regular flavor), dried tofu

Frieda's, Los Alamitos, California (http://www.frieda's.com): dessert tofu

GenSoy, Fairfield, California: soya flour, soy nuts

Glenny's, Freeport, New York: soy crisps, soy fudgies

Global Protein Foods, Valley Cottage, New York: tofu

Hain Celestial Group, Garden City, New York: Carbfit soy snacks, Soy Dream soy milk, Westbrae miso, WestSoy Plus soy milk

Leasa Tofu, Miami, Florida: fried and regular tofu

Lightlife Foods, Greenfield, Massachusetts: tofu, tempeh

Lumen Foods, Lake Charles, Louisiana: soy snacks

Mitoku, Tokyo, Japan: snow-dried tofu

Mu Tofu, Chicago, Illinois: tofu, tempeh, soy milk

Nasoya, Ayer, Massachusetts: tofu, tofu-based mayonnaise, tofu-based salad dressings

San-J International, Richmond, Virginia: tamari soy sauce, tamari low-sodium soy sauce

Soy Vay Enterprises, Felton, California: teriyaki sauces, marinades, salad dressings

Tofutti Brands, Cranford, New Jersey: nondairy frozen desserts and mixes, nondairy cream cheese and sour cream

White Wave, Boulder, Colorado: reduced-fat tofu, baked diced tofu

Note: The kosher status of products can change; always check the label for current kosher status.

For further information on soy and soy-based foods, here are some reliable contacts:

American Soybean Association
540 Maryville Center Drive
Saint Louis, MO 63140
(314) 576-1770

Soyfoods Association of America
1001 Connecticut Avenue N.W.
Washington, DC 20036
(202) 659-3520
http://www.soyfoods.org

United Soybean Board

(800) 989-8721

http://www.unitedsoybean.org

🍃 Kosher Voices 🍃

"I'm an observant Jew, and I've been keeping kosher since I was about thirteen, old enough to know the difference. It is simply what I do. In another sense, it is also imbuing an everyday, very basic, and even primitive act with spirituality. In addition, I'm lactose-intolerant, so knowing that a product is labeled pareve helps me know it is all right and it is safe [for me] to eat."

—*Sally, a lawyer from Connecticut*

Chapter 10

Cooking Kosher

> He who has fed a stranger, may have fed an angel.
>
> —*The Talmud*

Cooking kosher can be adapted to many cuisines, tastes, and budgets. The fifty-five recipes I've included here—longtime favorites from family and friends—represent dishes from Greece to Russia, from Israel to Portugal, from New York's Lower East Side to Louisiana's Cajun country.[1]

Most of these recipes are easy to prepare, although a few require some cooking expertise. I've included traditional Jewish foods (no collection of kosher recipes would be complete without one for chicken soup), adaptations from several international cuisines, and recipes that reflect today's health-conscious eating habits.

Note: When a recipe calls for a vegetable oil, I prefer to use canola, a polyunsaturated oil that has no discernible flavor. However, other vegetable oils can be substituted. But if a recipe calls for olive oil, do not make any substitution.

There is no festive occasion without eating and
drinking.

—*The Talmud*

🍃 Frittatas and Eggs 🍃

Italian Frittata   *Dairy*

Serves 2–4

This makes a quick, light lunch or dinner, prepared with ingredients that are usually at hand.

1 medium onion, peeled and sliced as thin as possible
3 tablespoons olive oil (divided)
1 clove garlic, peeled and crushed
4 eggs, lightly beaten
½ to ¾ teaspoon salt (or to taste)
⅛ teaspoon pepper
1 teaspoon dried basil
2 tablespoons grated Parmesan cheese

In a heavy 9- to 10-inch skillet, sauté the onion in half the oil over medium heat for 5 to 8 minutes until limp but not brown. Add the garlic and stir-fry for 1 minute.

Remove the onion and garlic from the skillet and add it to the eggs. Add the seasonings and cheese to the eggs and mix.

Add the remaining oil to the skillet and heat. Add the egg mixture and cook, without stirring, for 3 to 5 minutes until the bottom is browned and the top has just set. Cut into quarters and carefully turn to brown the other side for another 3 to 5 minutes or until cooked through.

Smoked Salmon (Lox) and Eggs   *Pareve*

Serves 1
I like to use a salty lox in this egg "soufflé."

> Vegetable oil for frying
> 1 slice of lox, cut into strips
> 2 whole eggs plus the white of 1 egg, beaten
> Pepper to taste

Heat the oil in a small skillet. Add strips of lox and sauté until they become opaque. Add pepper to the eggs and beat gently with a whisk. Add the eggs to the skillet and cook without stirring over low heat until the top begins to set. Carefully turn the eggs and cook until cooked through.

🌿 Soups 🌿

Fruit Soup   *Pareve*

Serves 6–8
This is a lovely, simple-to-prepare soup to start a warm-weather meal.

> 1 large cantaloupe
> 6 mint leaves (optional)
> 1 cup watermelon balls or cubes
> 1 cup honeydew balls or cubes
> 1 cup blueberries or sliced strawberries (optional)
> 1 cup diced peaches or diced mangoes (optional)

Cut the cantaloupe in half and remove the seeds. Scoop the flesh and any juice into a blender. Add mint leaves, if desired. Process until puréed. Set aside.

Combine the other fruits in a large serving bowl. Pour the puree over the fruit. Can be served at once or chilled.

Did You Know?

If you want to reduce or increase the size of recipes, these equivalent measurements will help.

3 teaspoons = 1 tablespoon

2 tablespoons = 1 fluid ounce

4 tablespoons = ¼ cup

5 tablespoons + 1 teaspoon = ⅓ cup

8 tablespoons = ½ cup

10 tablespoons + 2 teaspoons = ⅔ cup

12 tablespoons = ¾ cup

16 tablespoons = 1 cup

1 cup = 8 fluid ounces

2 pints = 1 quart

1 quart = 32 fluid ounces

4 quarts = 1 gallon

½ of ¼ cup = 2 tablespoons

½ of ⅓ cup = 2 tablespoons + 2 teaspoons

½ of ¾ cup = ¼ cup + 2 tablespoons

⅓ of ¼ cup = 1 tablespoon + 1 teaspoon

Mom's Good-for-What-Ails-You Chicken Soup   Meat
with Heavenly Light Matzo Balls

Serves 8

Practically every cuisine and culture has its own way of making chicken soup, but it is the version using kosher chickens that has come to be called "Jewish penicillin." Chicken soup's restorative and curative power has a long history. Centuries before modern scientific research suggested that hot chicken soup could indeed alleviate symptoms of colds and the flu, the twelfth-century Jewish physician and philosopher Maimonides recommended it both as a nourishing food and for its medicinal properties.

My mother's recipe makes, without prejudice, the best soup I've ever tasted (and also the best poached chicken). It is not difficult to prepare. I've also included her recipe for never-fail, heavenly light matzo balls. Both soup and matzo balls freeze well.

For the Soup

1 4- to 5-pound kosher pullet (stewing chicken), quartered
4 quarts water
1 tablespoon kosher salt
Salt and black pepper to taste
1 large onion, peeled
3 large carrots, peeled and cut into pieces 2 to 3 inches long
2 stalks celery, with tops, cut into pieces 3 to 4 inches long
3 large parsnips, peeled and cut in half cross-wise
A handful of flat Italian parsley
A bigger handful of fresh dill
4 low-sodium chicken bouillon cubes or dried bouillon
   packets

For the Matzo Balls

2 tablespoons vegetable oil

2 eggs, slightly beaten

½ cup matzo meal

Salt and pepper to taste

2 tablespoons chicken soup stock or water

1½ quarts water

2 low-sodium chicken bouillon cubes or dried bouillon
  packets

To Make the Soup. Wash and skin the chicken quarters. Trim off excess fat.

Put the water in a large enameled or stainless steel pot. Bring to a boil and then add the kosher salt. Add the chicken, cover, and simmer for about 1 hour. Every few minutes, skim off the foam that forms on top of the water—this will give you clear broth.

After the soup has simmered for about 1 hour, add the onion, carrots, celery, parsnips, parsley, and dill. Lower the flame and cook for approximately 45 minutes, covered. Then add the bouillon cubes and cook another 10 minutes, covered. Using a slotted spoon or tongs, remove the onion and discard. Remove the chicken and vegetables and set aside. Remove the dill and parsley and discard.

Let the soup cool a bit, then strain it into another pot. Put the carrots back in the pot. Add salt and pepper to taste.

Before serving, place the matzo balls (see recipe) in the pot and heat.

If you are going to freeze the soup, let it cool, uncovered, before storing in the freezer—covering warm soup can cause it to ferment. To serve, thaw and add some fresh parsley and dill when reheating to revive those flavors.

To Make the Matzo Balls. Mix the oil and eggs. Add the matzo meal and salt and pepper to taste. When well blended, add the 2 tablespoons chicken stock or water. Cover the mixture and place in the refrigerator for at least 1 hour, preferably 2. In a large pot, bring the 1½ quarts of water to a boil. Add the bouillon cubes. Reduce the heat.

With wet hands, form the dough into eight balls and drop them into the simmering water. Cover the pot and cook for a minimum of 45 minutes. The balls will expand as they cook. When they have achieved the desired softness, remove them from the water with a slotted spoon.

Freeze matzo balls separately from the soup. Place them on a flat pan or cookie sheet. Let cool, then cover with foil and set in the freezer.

Serving Suggestions

1. Serve the soup with matzo balls only. (This soup also goes well with rice or egg noodles.)

2. Before reheating the soup, return the chicken (on or off the bone), the matzo balls, and all the vegetables (except the onion) to the pot. Serve all together for a one-dish poached-chicken-in-the pot meal.

3. Serve the chicken and vegetables separately, either hot or at room temperature.

Did You Know?

Chicken soup has always had special meaning in Jewish culture. It has long been a traditional dish served at weddings, a custom derived from an old proverb, "Be fruitful and multiply like chickens." In eastern Europe, the soup itself had symbolic meaning—its golden color suggested prosperity.

Black Bean Soup   Meat

Serves 8

Served with a salad and a hearty peasant-type bread, this soup is perfect for a light dinner or lunch.

Note: Margarine can contain up to 12 percent dairy ingredients. Unless marked pareve, margarine should be considered dairy.

1 cup black beans, washed
5 cups cold water (divided)
2 medium onions, coarsely chopped
1 clove garlic, coarsely chopped
¼ cup pareve margarine, melted
½ teaspoon curry powder
¼ teaspoon turmeric
2 medium potatoes, peeled and cut into quarters
2 medium carrots, peeled and quartered crosswise
2 parsnips, peeled and quartered crosswise
1 cup stewed tomatoes
10½-ounces low-sodium kosher chicken broth
10½-ounces low-sodium kosher beef broth

Soak the beans overnight. Drain. In 4 cups of cold water, cook the beans for approximately 1 hour or until soft. Set the beans aside. In a large pot, sauté the onions and garlic in the margarine for about 5 minutes until soft. Add 1 cup of cold water and the curry powder, turmeric, potatoes, carrots, and parsnips. Cook until the vegetables are soft. Add the stewed tomatoes and the beans. Put the mixture into a blender and purée. Pour the puréed vegetables back into the pot. Add the chicken and beef broths. Stir, heat, and serve.

Vegetable Soup   Meat

Serves 4

This is my favorite all-season vegetable soup. And as an added health benefit, especially for those who need to restrict their salt intake, this soup is low in sodium.

1 tablespoon olive oil
1 cup diced onions
2 cups diced mushrooms (portobellos add a meatier taste to
    the soup, but white mushrooms are also fine)
1 cup diced zucchini, unpeeled
1 cup diced parsnips
1 cup diced carrots
1 14½-ounce can low-sodium stewed tomatoes
14 ounces low-sodium chicken broth (canned or from bouil-
    lon cubes or powder)
½ teaspoon dried oregano
½ teaspoon black pepper
1 15-ounce can great northern or cannellini beans, rinsed and
    drained

Heat the oil in a large pot. Add the onions, mushrooms, and zucchini and sauté for 5 minutes over medium heat. Add the parsnips and carrots and sauté 2 to 3 minutes more. Add the stewed tomatoes (with their liquid), chicken broth, oregano, pepper, and beans. Cover and simmer approximately 30 minutes until the vegetables are tender. This soup freezes well.

Note: If you substitute vegetable broth for chicken broth, this recipe becomes pareve. You may then want to top the soup with some grated Parmesan cheese. If you plan to freeze the soup, do not add cheese beforehand.

Some Cooking Tips

- Assemble all your ingredients and utensils before you begin.
- If a recipe calls for a number of spices to be added, one after another, mix them together beforehand.
- Be sure to preheat the oven if the recipe calls for it.
- Most professional cooks use kosher salt when cooking. Because its crystals are larger than those of table salt, you'll need almost twice as much to achieve the same level of saltiness. Add salt by the pinch, rather than directly from a salt shaker. You'll have a better idea of how much salt you are using.
- Water will come to a boil more quickly if you cover the pot. Unsalted water comes to a boil faster than salted water, so don't add salt until water is roiling.
- When heating oil, make sure your pan is hot before adding oil. This is the opposite of what most people do.
- When sautéing or stir-frying beef or chicken, be sure the oil is really hot before adding the meat. This ensures that the surface of the meat cooks quickly, sealing the juices in.
- When sautéing or stir-frying vegetables, be sure they are completely dry before adding them to the pan. Otherwise, you are in fact steaming them, and they will not be crisp or brown well.
- To prevent potatoes from discoloring after slicing or dicing, put them in a bowl of cold water until ready to use.
- Use the middle rack of the oven for general baking and roasting, unless a recipe specifically calls for the upper or lower level.
- Freezing cooked food tends to dilute the strength of some spices, so always taste a defrosted dish and add more seasoning if necessary.

🌿 Appetizers and Salads 🌿

Israeli Salad   *Pareve*

My grandfather, who was from Jaffa, Israel, introduced this salad to the family. It is still a Sunday morning breakfast tradition. It goes well with bagels, lox, and smoked fish and is equally delicious as a lunch, served in pita bread, or as a side dish with fried fish.

Diced ripe tomato
Diced green pepper
Diced red pepper
Diced cucumber
Thinly sliced scallion
Lettuce shredded into small pieces
1 tablespoon olive oil
Salt and pepper to taste
Lemon juice to taste
Lemon wedges

The exact proportions of tomatoes and other vegetables do not matter, although there should be proportionately more tomatoes.

Mix the tomato, peppers, cucumber, scallion, and lettuce with the oil. Add salt and pepper. Add lemon juice and toss. Serve at room temperature with lemon wedges on the side.

Gerry's Hummus   *Pareve*

Makes approximately 2½ cups
This is another Israeli dish, a snack food popular throughout the
Middle East.

    2 cups canned chickpeas (garbanzos), drained, liquid reserved
    2 cloves garlic, crushed
    1 tablespoon olive oil
    1 teaspoon lemon juice
    1 teaspoon salt
    Paprika
    Pita bread

Mix the chickpeas, garlic, oil, lemon juice, and salt in a blender. If
the mixture is too thick, add a few tablespoons of the reserved
chickpea liquid. Add more lemon juice to taste, if you wish. Place
in a bowl, sprinkle paprika on top, and serve with warm pita bread
wedges.

   This dip can also be garnished with chopped parsley and olives.

Carol's Tabbouleh   *Pareve*

Serves 6
Another Middle Eastern favorite, this mint-flavored cracked wheat
salad needs no cooking and is great for a picnic lunch.

    ½ cup bulgur (cracked wheat)
    4 ripe tomatoes, chopped, with their juice
    1 bunch each, cut fine with scissors: mint, scallions (white and
       green parts), Italian parsley
    2 teaspoons salt or to taste
    ½ cup olive oil
    ⅓ cup lemon juice

Place the bulgur in a bowl and cover with cool water. Set aside.

In a large bowl, place the chopped tomatoes with their juice and add the snipped mint, scallions, and parsley. Drain the bulgur and add to the tomato mixture. Add the salt, olive oil, and lemon juice and mix gently. Chill in the refrigerator for 6 hours or overnight. Return to room temperature before serving.

Greek Salad   *Pareve*

Serves 4–6
An easy-to-prepare salad that is perfect for buffets.

    1 small jar herring pieces in wine sauce (available in most
        supermarkets where kosher food is sold)
    1 large onion, sliced
    2 tomatoes, diced
    1 head cabbage, shredded
    4 radishes, thinly sliced
    1 cucumber, thinly sliced
    2 carrots, peeled and thinly sliced
    ¼ cup olive oil
    ¼ cup vinegar
    Salt and pepper to taste
    ¼ pound Greek olives

Drain herring pieces. Mix all the ingredients together and marinate in the refrigerator overnight. Garnish with the olives and serve.

Zena's Cajun Style Coleslaw *Dairy*

Serves 12

A slightly different way to prepare this popular side dish.

    1 head cabbage, sliced or shredded
    1 carrot, sliced
    1 red pepper, chopped
    1 small onion, diced
    ½ cup white vinegar
    1 teaspoon vegetable oil
    1 teaspoon sugar
    1 cup light mayonnaise
    2 tablespoons sour cream
    1 to 2 tablespoons Dijon mustard
    ½ to 1 teaspoon chili powder
    Parsley, dried or fresh, to taste
    Salt and pepper to taste

Mix all the ingredients in a large bowl. Chill for 3 hours before serving.

Eggplant au Claire   *Pareve*

Serves 8–12 as an appetizer

Claire was from Canada, but this dip has a decidedly Mediterranean flavor.

 1 large eggplant, peeled and cubed
 ½ cup plus 2 tablespoons olive oil (divided)
 2½ cups chopped onions
 1 cup chopped celery
 2 8-ounce cans plain tomato sauce
 ¼ cup wine vinegar
 2 tablespoons sugar
 2 tablespoons capers, drained
 12 black olives, pitted
 Salt and pepper to taste

Sauté the eggplant in ½ cup olive oil until lightly browned. Remove and set aside. Add the remaining olive oil to the pan and sauté the onions and celery until soft. Add the tomato sauce and simmer for 15 minutes. Add the eggplant and cook 15 minutes more. Add the vinegar, sugar, capers, olives, and salt and pepper to taste. Mash all the ingredients together. Serve with pita bread or crackers.

> Love is grand, but love with lukshen [noodles] is
> better.
>
> —*Yiddish proverb*

🌿 Pasta and Noodles 🌿

Summer Pasta with Uncooked Tomato Sauce   *Pareve*

Serves 3

An easy-to-prepare pasta, but use *only* very ripe tomatoes. I never
make this dish in winter or spring because it has no taste if pale winter tomatoes are used.

3 large, red vine-ripened tomatoes, skins removed
⅓ cup extra virgin olive oil
4 medium garlic cloves, peeled and halved
1 clove garlic, chopped fine (one plump garlic clove will yield
    approximately 1½ rounded teaspoons of minced garlic)
Red pepper flakes, to taste (up to ¼ teaspoon)
½ cup coarsely torn fresh basil leaves
2 or 3 sprigs fresh Italian parsley, coarsely chopped (optional)
Salt and pepper to taste
Penne or other tubular-shaped dried pasta such as rigatoni or ziti
Grated kosher Parmesan or Romano cheese (optional)

To remove their skins, cut a small X on the bottom of each tomato
before placing the tomatoes in a pot of boiling water for 15 to 20
seconds. Drain in a colander and pour cold water over them. They
should then peel easily.

Core the tomatoes and chop coarsely. Place the tomatoes and
their liquid in a large bowl. Add the olive oil, the halved garlic, the
chopped garlic, red pepper flakes, basil, parsley if desired, and salt
and pepper to taste. Mix. Cover the bowl with a paper towel and let
stand at room temperature for at least 4 hours, stirring once or
twice. (The mixture can also be put in the refrigerator overnight,

but be sure to bring it to room temperature before serving.) Before serving, remove the large pieces of garlic from the sauce.

Cook and drain the pasta. Add the sauce and toss. Add cheese, if desired, and toss again. Serve in soup bowls, with toasted garlic bread to sop up the extra sauce.

Note: If cheese is added to this dish, it becomes dairy, not pareve.

Spaghetti with Tuna Sauce   *Pareve*

Serves 4

This quick-cooking pasta sauce can be assembled with ingredients that people usually have in their cupboards and refrigerators.

    1 pound spaghetti
    2 tablespoons extra-virgin olive oil
    1 large onion, thinly sliced
    2 or 3 cloves garlic, minced
    1 small jar roasted red peppers, cut in strips
    1 small can pareve tuna, drained (oil-packed is preferred, but
        water-packed is fine)
    Pinch of crushed red pepper flakes
    2 teaspoons grated lemon zest
    ½ teaspoon black pepper
    Salt to taste
    1 tablespoon lemon juice
    Fresh parsley, chopped (optional)

Cook the spaghetti and drain. Heat the olive oil in a large skillet, and then add the onion and sauté about 5 minutes or until the onion is soft. Add the garlic, roasted peppers, tuna, red pepper flakes, lemon zest, pepper, salt, and lemon juice. Mix and cook 3 to 4 minutes. Pour over cooked spaghetti. Sprinkle with parsley and serve immediately.

Harry's Sweet Noodle Pudding (Lukshen Kugel)   *Dairy*

Serves 15–18

Kugel is a traditional dish of the Ashkenazim or Yiddish-speaking Jews from central and eastern Europe. This thick, rich noodle pudding is often served at the Jewish New Year, Rosh Hashanah, when sweet foods are eaten to symbolize a sweet year to come.

 3 eggs
 1 12-ounce can evaporated milk
 ¾ cup sugar
 1 teaspoon vanilla extract
 1 16-ounce package wide egg noodles, cooked, drained, and cooled
 1 pound cottage cheese
 ½–¾ cup raisins
 Cinnamon to taste
 ¼ pound (1 stick) butter

Preheat the oven to 350°F. Mix the eggs, evaporated milk, sugar, and vanilla. Add the noodles. Mix in the cottage cheese, raisins, and cinnamon. Melt the butter and add half of it to the noodle mixture. Pour the remaining butter into a lasagna-size baking pan and coat the pan. Pour in the noodle mixture and bake for 1 hour or until golden.

Kasha Varnishkes   *Pareve*

Serves 4–6

A traditional Russian dish, popular in Ashkenazic cuisine. Varnish-kes are bowtie noodles.

1 egg
1 cup uncooked whole kasha (buckwheat groats)
2 cups boiling water
2 tablespoons vegetable oil
1 onion, diced
1 cup diced mushrooms (optional)
1½ cups bowtie egg noodles, cooked and drained
1 cup steamed peas (optional)
Salt to taste
¼ teaspoon pepper

In a large bowl, beat the egg. Add the kasha and mix until all the grains are coated with egg. Heat a saucepan or skillet and add the kasha-egg mixture, stirring until the kasha grains are dry. Pour the boiling water over the kasha, cover, and simmer until all the liquid is absorbed and kasha is dry and fluffy.

In another saucepan, heat the oil and sauté the onion and mushrooms, if desired, until the onions are golden. Combine the bowties, kasha, onion and mushrooms, and steamed peas, if desired, and mix until well combined. Add salt and pepper and serve.

Note: Chicken bouillon can be substituted for the water, in which case this becomes a meat dish.

Tricolor Pasta with Broccoli,   Dairy
Garlic, and Bread Crumbs

Serves 2

I came up with this recipe when I had a yen for a vegetable pasta but the only vegetables on hand were some leftover steamed broccoli florets.

2 cups broccoli florets
3 tablespoons olive oil (divided)
Red pepper flakes, to taste
4 garlic cloves, sliced thin
¼ cup seasoned bread crumbs
½ pound tricolor fusilli or other similar pasta
Grated Parmesan cheese, to taste

Steam the broccoli and set aside to dry.

Heat 2 tablespoons of the oil in a large skillet. Add the red pepper flakes and garlic. Cook until the garlic just starts to turn brown. Quickly add the broccoli and mix so that the florets become coated with oil. Remove the skillet from the heat. In a small pan, heat the bread crumbs until browned. Shake the pan a few times and watch carefully because crumbs can go from brown to burnt very quickly. Set aside.

Cook the pasta al dente. Drain and add to the skillet containing the broccoli. Return the skillet to medium heat. Add the remaining tablespoon of olive oil, the bread crumbs, and grated Parmesan cheese. Mix and cook until heated through. Serve immediately.

🍃 Potatoes 🍃

Sephardic Potatoes   **Meat**

Serves 8–10

Sephardic or Ladino-speaking Jews trace their ancestry back to medieval Iberia (*Sepharad* is the Hebrew name for Spain). When King Ferdinand and Queen Isabella expelled the Jews from their country in 1492, many found safe refuge in North Africa and the lands of the Ottoman Empire. As a result, Sephardic cuisine reflects a number of cultures of the Mediterranean and Middle East, including Greece, Turkey, Syria, and Persia (Iran), as well as Spain and Portugal.

   1 large Spanish onion, sliced
   2 cloves garlic, minced
   ¼ cup olive oil
   1 stick pareve margarine
   6 medium potatoes, peeled and cubed
   3 large carrots, diced
   2 tablespoons diced red pepper
   2 tablespoons chopped parsley
   1¼ teaspoons salt
   ¼ teaspoon pepper
   1 15-ounce can clear low-sodium chicken broth

Sauté the onion and garlic in the olive oil and margarine until tender. Add the potatoes and carrots and sauté for 10 minutes. Add the remaining ingredients. Reduce the heat, cover, and simmer for 20 minutes until the vegetables are soft.

Spicy Potato Rounds   *Dairy*

Serves 8

I always think of these as potato chips for adults.

> 8 medium baking potatoes, peeled or not, thinly sliced in
>   rounds
> ½ teaspoon dry mustard
> ½ teaspoon paprika (sweet or hot)
> ¼ teaspoon chili powder
> 2 small onions, peeled and minced
> ½ cup butter, melted

Preheat the oven to 425°F. Place the potatoes in a single layer on nonstick cookie sheets. Mix the spices and onions in the melted butter and drizzle over the potatoes. Bake for about 45 minutes or until the potatoes are golden.

Herbed Potatoes   *Dairy*

Serves 4

Use an attractive baking dish, because the finished potatoes look so good, you'll want to bring them to the table directly from the oven.

> 4 large unpeeled baking potatoes
> ¼ cup melted butter
> ¼ cup olive oil
> 3 medium cloves garlic, minced
> Salt to taste
> ½ teaspoon dried rosemary or dried thyme

Preheat the oven to 400°F. Cut the potatoes into ¼-inch-thick slices. Place overlapping slices in a buttered oven-to-table baking dish or glass pie plate. Mix the butter and oil and brush the slices with the mixture. Pour any remaining mixture over potatoes. Sprinkle with the garlic, salt, and rosemary or thyme. Bake for 25 to 30 minutes or until the potatoes are done and browned at the edges.

Note: If pareve margarine is substituted for the butter, this recipe becomes pareve.

Oven "Fries"   *Pareve*

Serves 2–3
A healthier alternative to french-fried potatoes that's just as tasty.

  2 unpeeled baking potatoes, cut into lengthwise wedges, about
    ¼ inch thick
  Vegetable oil spray
  1 tablespoon olive oil
  ¾ teaspoon paprika
  1 teaspoon ground cumin
  Salt to taste

Preheat the oven to 425°F. Spray a baking sheet with vegetable oil.

Toss the potatoes with the olive oil. Add the remaining ingredients and toss. Bake the potatoes, turning once, until tender, about 20 to 25 minutes.

Sweet Potato Oven "Fries"   *Pareve*

Serves 2–3
Sweet potatoes make wonderful oven "fries" and contain a lot more nutrients than white potatoes.

> 2 large sweet potatoes, unpeeled, cut into wedges
> Vegetable oil spray
> 1 tablespoon olive oil
> ½ teaspoon ground ginger
> ½ teaspoon ground cumin
> ⅛ teaspoon black pepper

Preheat the oven to 400°F. Spray a baking sheet with vegetable oil.

Toss the potatoes with the olive oil. Add the remaining ingredients and toss. Bake for 10 minutes, turn the potatoes, and bake for 10 minutes more.

❧ Rice ❧

Baked Rice   *Dairy*

Serves 4
This dish makes a nice change from stove-top rice.

> 2½ tablespoons butter
> 2 tablespoon minced onion
> ½ teaspoon minced garlic
> 1 cup uncooked white rice
> 1½ cups water
> 3 sprigs parsley
> 1 sprig fresh thyme or ¼ teaspoon dried
> Salt and pepper to taste
> ½ bay leaf

Preheat the oven to 400°F. Melt half the butter in a casserole and sauté the onion and garlic, stirring until the onion is translucent. Add the rice and stir over a low flame until the rice is coated. Stir in the water, making sure there are no lumps in the rice. Add the parsley, thyme, salt, pepper, and bay leaf. Cover with a tight-fitting lid and bring to a boil. Remove the casserole from the flame and place in the oven. Bake for exactly 17 minutes (this is not an arbitrary number). After removing the casserole from the oven, discard the parsley, thyme sprig, and bay leaf. Stir in the remaining butter and serve.

Note: If pareve margarine is substituted for the butter, the recipe becomes pareve.

Chinese-Style "Fried" Rice   **Meat**

Serves 3

The rice must be cold when preparing this dish. Cook the rice the night before and chill it in the refrigerator.

   3 cups cold cooked white rice
   3 tablespoons vegetable oil
   4 scallions, minced
   ¼ cup low-sodium chicken broth
   1 tablespoon reduced-sodium soy sauce
   ¼ teaspoon sugar
   ⅛ teaspoon pepper
   Steamed vegetables—broccoli florets, baby carrots, peas, snow
      peas (optional)
   Thin strips of cooked, white meat chicken (optional)

Heat the oil in a nonstick skillet over moderate heat. Add the rice and stir-fry, pressing out any lumps in the rice, until it has taken on a pale golden color. Add the remaining ingredients, cover, and heat for 1 minute. Serve hot.

Brown Rice with Vegetables   Meat

Serves 6
This healthy dish is tasty yet low in fat.

    2 cups peeled, shredded carrots
    1 cup chopped onions
    1 cup brown rice
    2¼ cups low-sodium chicken broth
    1 teaspoon dried Italian seasoning
    ¼ teaspoon black pepper
    ⅔ cup peeled, shredded zucchini
    1 or 2 ripe tomatoes, sliced (optional)

Place the first six ingredients in a 2-quart pot. Stir well. Bring to a boil. Cover the pot, reduce the heat, and simmer for 35 minutes, stirring occasionally, until the rice is just tender.

Stir in the zucchini. Transfer to a serving bowl and serve hot.

Alternative: Place the rice-zucchini mixture in an ovenproof dish. Cover with tomato slices and place in a 350°F. oven until the tomatoes are hot. Serve immediately.

❦ Vegetables ❦

Acorn Squash with Peas   Dairy

Serves 2
A very attractive way to serve two vegetables at the same time.

    1 large acorn squash
    1 tablespoon butter
    1 tablespoon brown sugar
    2 cups fresh or frozen peas
    Fresh mint leaves (optional)

Preheat the oven to 400°F. Cut the squash in half and scoop out the seeds. Set the halves on a baking sheet, cavity side up. If they roll around a bit, cut away a small bottom portion so that the halves will sit upright.

Dot the rim and center cavity of each half with butter and sprinkle with brown sugar. Bake until fork-tender, about 45 minutes.

While the squash is baking, steam the peas (with mint, if desired). When the squash is ready, fill the cavities with peas and serve.

Note: If you substitute pareve margarine for the butter, this dish is pareve.

Chip's Carrot Pudding   *Dairy*

Serves 12

A perfect dish for carrot lovers with a sweet tooth. Carrots traditionally symbolize sweetness, and this dish is perfect for serving on Rosh Hashanah, the Jewish New Year, to usher in a sweet year.

1 pound carrots, cooked and riced
About ⅛ cup granulated brown sugar
1⅔ cups vegetable oil
3 eggs
2 teaspoons baking powder
½ cup Bisquick
1 11-ounce can crushed pineapple

Preheat the oven to 350°F. Mix all the ingredients together and pour into a greased baking dish or pan. Bake for 1 hour. This freezes well.

Warm Tomato Sauté   *Pareve*

Serves 4–6

I like to serve this dish in the winter, when the taste of vine-ripened tomatoes is a distant memory. Pints of cherry tomatoes are available all year round, as is fresh basil.

    1 tablespoon olive oil
    1 small or medium red onion, sliced
    1 or 2 cloves garlic, minced
    2 pints cherry tomatoes
    ½ cup julienned fresh basil leaves
    Salt and pepper to taste
    2 tablespoon balsamic vinegar

Heat a skillet and add the oil. Sauté the onions and garlic over medium heat until soft, about 3 minutes. Turn the heat to high and add the tomatoes and basil, tossing until the tomato skins begin to wrinkle. Remove the skillet from heat. Add salt and pepper to taste and then the balsamic vinegar. Toss gently to mix. Serve warm.

Slow-Cooked Apple-Carrot Pudding   *Pareve*

Serves 10–12

This festive, aromatic side dish is so delicious that it usually does not survive until mealtime. Although there are a lot of ingredients, it is worth the effort. One trick is to assemble and mix all the spices before starting.

Note: This recipe calls for cake meal. Cake meal, made from wheat flour and water, is a lactose-free vegetarian product available wherever kosher food is sold. It has the consistency of flour and is often substituted for it in Jewish cooking, especially for Passover baking. Five-eighths cup of cake meal is the equivalent of one cup of flour. Note that matzo meal, although it has similar ingredients to cake meal, has a much coarser texture and should not be substituted in recipes where cake meal is called for.

3 red apples, peeled and grated
8 large carrots, peeled and grated
1 cup raisins
½ cup chopped walnuts
½ cup diced candied orange peel
4 eggs
1 cup cake meal
⅔ cup vegetable oil
1 cup brown sugar
1 tablespoon cinnamon
½ teaspoon ground ginger
½ teaspoon allspice
Salt to taste (up to 1 teaspoon)
¼ cup brandy (optional)

Mix all the ingredients in a large bowl. Grease two loaf pans and divide the mixture between them. Cover tightly with aluminum foil and bake at 325°F. for 30 minutes. Reduce the oven heat to 150°F. (or the lowest setting) and bake for at least 8 hours or overnight.

Remove from the oven and let cool slightly before cutting in slices. Each loaf should make 6 or 7 slices, depending on the size of the slice.

Florence's Vegetarian Cutlets   *Pareve*

Serves 6

My aunt tells me that this recipe came from my grandmother, who started serving this dish during the Great Depression, when the family could not afford meat.

2 medium potatoes, peeled and cubed
2 onions, one cubed, one coarsely chopped
3 carrots, sliced
½ cup finely chopped celery
½ cup finely chopped green beans
½ cup peas
1 egg
½ cup matzo meal
Salt and pepper to taste
¼ cup vegetable oil

Boil a pot of water. Add the potatoes, the cubed onion, and the carrots and cook for 15 minutes. Add the celery, green beans, and peas and cook another 15 minutes.

Drain the vegetables and place them in a large chopping bowl. Add the chopped onion, and finely chop all the vegetables. Add the egg, matzo meal, and salt and pepper to taste. Mix. Cover and place in the refrigerator for 30 minutes.

Shape the mixture into six large patties and fry them in the vegetable oil until browned on both sides. Drain on paper towels.

These vegetable patties can be frozen and then reheated without thawing. Start the reheating process over a medium flame and be careful about spattering oil.

Sandy's Holiday Cranberry Compote   *Pareve*

Serves 8

This is a family Thanksgiving favorite and tastes like you spent a lot more time preparing it than you did.

    1 16-ounce can cranberry sauce (whole berry)
    1 package frozen strawberries, thawed and drained
    ½ cup walnut pieces
    1 cup applesauce

Mix all but ¼ cup of the walnut pieces in a large bowl. Refrigerate for a few hours so that the flavors have time to blend. Add the remaining walnuts as garnish.

Lynn's Spinach "Pie"   *Pareve*

Serves 12

An easy-to-prepare recipe—all you need to do is thaw, mix, and bake!

    4 10-ounce packages frozen chopped spinach, thawed, water
      squeezed out
    2 eggs
    4 tablespoons melted pareve margarine
    ½ cup matzo meal
    ½ cup kosher nondairy creamer
    Salt to taste

Preheat the oven to 350°F. Mix all the ingredients together. Pour the mixture into an 8-by-10-inch greased baking pan. Bake for 1 hour, until the top is lightly browned and the spinach mixture is firm.

Eggplant Stir-Fry   *Pareve*

Serves 2–4

Oriental eggplants (sometimes called Japanese or Chinese egg-plants) are long and slender and have a thin medium or light purple skin. They do not have to be salted or drained before cooking. Eggplant is often an important ingredient in Sephardic cooking, but this recipe is influenced by Eastern cuisines.

2 tablespoons sesame oil

1 tablespoon canola oil

4 Oriental eggplants, sliced on the bias, approximately ½ inch thick

2 medium red peppers, cored, seeded, and thinly sliced

1 to 1½ cups snow peas

5 scallions, cut on the bias into 1½-inch lengths (white and green parts)

¼ cup reduced-sodium soy sauce

2 teaspoons dark brown sugar

In a large nonstick skillet, heat the sesame and canola oils over medium-high heat until almost smoking. Add the eggplant and peppers and cook for approximately 4 to 6 minutes until softened. Add the snow peas and scallions.

Dissolve the sugar in the soy sauce and add this to the pan. Mix well and then cook covered for 2 minutes. Serve immediately, either as a side dish or over white rice.

Joyce's Zucchini Soufflé   *Dairy*

Serves 10–12
Even people who don't like vegetables like this dish. It's one of my most asked-for recipes.

3 large zucchini, unpeeled, grated (about 3 cups)
1 cup Bisquick
1 large onion, chopped
4 eggs or equivalent egg substitute
Fresh parsley, chopped, or dried parsley flakes, to taste
Pepper to taste
½ cup olive oil
Large chunk of cheese, grated

Preheat the oven to 350°F. Mix all the ingredients together. Pour into a greased baking dish and bake for about 1 hour, until the top is brown and crusty.

Note: Joyce uses part-skim Jarlsberg, but other cheeses will work as well.

🍃 Meat 🍃

My Favorite Chili   **Meat**

Serves 6

The use of whole cinnamon sticks and cloves in this recipe gives this chili a wonderful taste. Just remember to remove them before serving.

    1 pound lean chopped kosher beef (ground kosher turkey can be substituted for beef)

    2 tablespoons vegetable oil

    2 large onions, finely chopped

    4 medium garlic cloves, finely chopped

    3 tablespoons red chili powder

    2 teaspoons celery salt

    ½ teaspoon cayenne

    2 teaspoons ground cumin

    1 teaspoon dried basil

    1 teaspoon salt

    1 28-ounce can plum tomatoes

    2 small bay leaves

    6 cups water

    2 small cinnamon sticks

    4 whole cloves

    2 green bell peppers, cored, seeded, and coarsely chopped

    2 15½-ounce cans kidney beans, drained

Brown the ground beef or turkey in a skillet, draining off as much fat as possible. Set aside.

In the same skillet, heat the oil. Add the onions and garlic and cook until the onion is translucent. Add the meat. Stir in the remaining ingredients except the green peppers and the beans. Bring to a boil, then lower the heat and simmer, uncovered, for 2½ hours, stirring occasionally. Stir in the peppers and beans and simmer, uncovered, ½ hour longer. Remove the cinnamon sticks, bay leaves, and, if possible, the cloves. Taste and adjust seasonings if necessary. Serve over baked potatoes or rice.

Note: This chili freezes well. Use hot, mild, or a combination of chili powders, according to how spicy you like your chili.

Grandma Molly's Mishmosh   Meat

Serves 4

This recipe has been enjoyed by three generations of my family. It was first served by my grandmother, who passed the recipe on to my mother and aunt, who then served it to their children. I always think of it as "comfort food"; it's a wonderful, simple one-dish meal for a cold winter night. "Mishmosh" refers to the way the kids in my family always eat this dish, squishing and mashing the meat and potatoes together.

> 1 pound lean ground kosher beef (do *not* substitute ground
>   turkey in this recipe)
> Salt and pepper to taste
> 2 medium onions, coarsely chopped
> 2 medium carrots, peeled and cut into 1-inch chunks
> 4 or 5 medium potatoes, peeled and cut into thick slices
> 1 cup steamed green peas (optional)

Season the beef with salt and pepper and form it into little balls, about 1½ to 2 inches in diameter.

Bring a pot of water to a boil. Add the onions. Drop in the meatballs and bring the water to a boil again. Cover, reduce the heat, and cook for 10 minutes. Add the carrots and potatoes and cook until they are tender. Remove some of the liquid and set aside.

Drain the meatballs, add the peas if desired, and serve in large bowls. Pour a spoonful or so of the reserved liquid over each dish.

Note: Good accompaniments for this dish are rye bread and sour pickles.

Kufteles   **Meat**

Makes 7–8 patties

Given to me by my Aunt Florence, this is another of my Grandmother Molly's recipes. The recipe probably came into the family
via my grandfather, who lived in the Middle East as a young man.
Kufteh is Persian for "pounded," a way of preparing ground meat
into balls or patties, variations of which can be found in all the
cuisines of the Middle East, the Balkans, and western Asia: *keftes*
are Sephardic meat patties, *kaftas* are Lebanese meatloaves; and patties like these are called *keftedes* in Greece and *koftas* in Turkey and
India. *Kefte mi'leeye* is Arabic for fried meat patties. However, I've
not come across the term *kufteles* in any cookbook, so I think this
dish may have gotten its name because my grandmother, who came
from Poland, misheard the pronunciation and then gave it a Yiddish inflection.

   1 pound finely ground beef
   4 tablespoons minced garlic (divided)
   6 tablespoons coarsely chopped fresh Italian parsley (divided)
   1 egg, slightly beaten
   ¼ cup vegetable oil for frying (more if needed)
   ½ cup matzo meal
   1 28-ounce can whole tomatoes
   2 tablespoons sugar
   Salt to taste

In a large bowl, mix the meat, 2 tablespoons garlic, and 3 tablespoons parsley. Form this mixture into oval patties approximately
1 inch thick, 1 to 1½ inches wide, and 3 inches long. Dip each patty
into matzo meal and then into egg. Heat the oil in a large frying pan.
Fry the patties for 3 to 5 minutes on each side until lightly browned
all over.

While the patties are frying, coarsely chop the tomatoes and mix them with the remaining parsley, remaining garlic, sugar, and salt and bring to a boil in a large pot. Add the browned kufteles, including the oil they were fried in, to the tomato mixture. Stir gently, bring the pot to a simmer, cover it, and cook for 45 minutes. Taste the sauce and add more sugar or salt if needed.

Serve the kufteles and sauce over white rice.

Pot Roast with Lemon and Orange   **Meat**

Serves 6
The citrus fruits infuse this roast with a wonderfully aromatic flavor.

    1 cup chopped onions
    3 to 5 garlic cloves, minced
    ½ cup olive oil
    3- to 4-pound chuck roast, center cut, or brisket,
        with as much fat removed as possible
    1 28-ounce can Italian tomatoes, drained
    1 15-ounce can tomato sauce
    1 orange, sliced as thinly as possible
    1 lemon, sliced as thinly as possible
    ½ to 1 pound small button mushrooms

Preheat the oven to 350°F. In a large roasting pan on top of the stove, brown the onions and garlic in the olive oil. Add the beef and brown quickly on all sides. Add the other ingredients, placing the orange and lemon slices on top of the meat. Cover, place in the oven, and bake until the meat is soft and tender, about 2 hours.

Note: If fresh mushrooms are not available, canned mushrooms will work in this recipe.

Meat and Vegetable Stew   **Meat**

Serves 6
A delicious one-dish dinner.

> 1½ pounds ground kosher beef
> 1 tablespoon vegetable oil
> 1 large onion, chopped (about 1 cup)
> 1 10½-ounce can condensed beef broth
> 1¼ cups water (divided)
> Dash of cayenne
> 1 bay leaf
> 6 medium potatoes, peeled and quartered
> 1 tablespoon all-purpose flour
> 2 green peppers, seeded and chopped
>   (or 1 green and 1 red pepper)
> 1 16-ounce can tomatoes
> ¼ cup sliced green olives stuffed with pimientos
> Salt and pepper to taste

Shape the beef into 24 meatballs. Brown 12 at a time in a nonstick pot or one sprayed with kosher pan coating. Remove and set aside.

Add the oil to the pot and sauté the onions until soft. Add the beef broth, 1 cup water, cayenne, and bay leaf. Return the meatballs to the pot. Cover, lower the heat, and simmer for 10 minutes. Add the potatoes. Simmer for 20 minutes, or until the potatoes are tender. Remove the meatballs and potatoes with a slotted spoon. Remove and discard the bay leaf.

Combine the flour and remaining ¼ cup water in a cup, stir until smooth, and then stir into the cooking liquid. Cook, stirring, until thickened. Return the meatballs and potatoes to the pot. Add the peppers, tomatoes, and olives. Lower the heat, cover, and simmer for 5 minutes. Add salt and pepper to taste.

🌿 Fish 🌿

Portuguese Fish Bundles

Pareve

Serves 1

This Mediterranean-flavored dish is low in fat and calories, and serving the fish in its foil wrapper makes for a festive presentation.

Vegetable oil spray
3 slices onion
1 bay leaf, broken into pieces
1 4-ounce fillet of flounder, sole, fluke, or similar fish
3 slices peeled vine-ripe tomatoes, sliced (see the recipe
   for Summer Pasta on page 116 for directions on removing
   tomato skins)
Dried oregano to taste
Minced garlic to taste
Salt and pepper to taste
1 tablespoon dry red wine

Preheat the oven to 350°F. To make each bundle, use a square of aluminum foil, shiny side up, that is large enough to seal the packet loosely around the fish. Spray it lightly with vegetable oil. Place the onion slices and bay leaf pieces in the center of the foil. Place the fish fillet on top, and cover with the tomato slices. Sprinkle lightly with oregano, garlic, salt, and pepper to taste. Add the wine. Fold the foil loosely over the fish, crimping the edges so that the liquid will not leak out.

Place the bundle directly on an oven rack and cook undisturbed for 30 minutes. Transfer to a serving plate. Open the packet carefully; hot steam may come rushing out.

Cold Fried Fish   *Pareve*

Serves 4

Fish dipped in batter and fried in vegetable oil, not lard, and served cold or at room temperature is a legacy of the Sephardic and Marrano Jews from Holland who settled in England in the sixteenth century. Fish fried this way stays light and flavorful when served cold. Thomas Jefferson discovered "fried fish in the Jewish manner" when he visited London, and American cookbooks of the late seventeenth and eighteenth centuries often mention the dish. Tradition has it that the British national dish of fish and chips (fried potatoes) was "invented" by a Jewish immigrant, Joseph Malin, who had a fish business in London's East End in the 1860s and started selling his fish with potatoes from an Irish market next door.

    4 fillets or steaks of scrod, cod, flounder, or other firm white
        fish, cut into large serving pieces
    Salt and pepper to taste
    1 egg, lightly beaten
    ⅔ to 1 cup matzo meal
    ½ cup vegetable oil
    Lemon slices for garnish

Sprinkle the fish with salt and pepper. Dredge each piece in egg and then in matzo meal, making sure the entire piece is covered.

Heat the oil in a deep 9- or 10-inch frying pan. Fry the fish in a single layer until golden brown on both sides, 2 to 4 minutes on each side for thin fillets, 5 to 6 minutes a side for thicker pieces. Carefully remove the pieces from the oil with a slotted spatula and drain on paper towels.

Serve cold or at room temperature, garnished with lemon slices.

Note: I like to serve Israeli Salad (page 111) with this dish.

Did You Know?

When buying fresh whole fish, look for bright, clear eyes; bright pink or red gills; shiny skin; and firm flesh. There should be no fishy odor. When purchasing fillets or steaks, look for firm pieces with no sign of drying around the edges.

Salmon Teriyaki   *Pareve*

Serves 4

This dish tastes exactly like the salmon teriyaki you get in a Japanese restaurant.

  2 tablespoons reduced-sodium soy sauce
  1 tablespoon honey
  1 large clove garlic, minced
  1 teaspoon minced fresh ginger
  1 tablespoon sesame oil
  1 pound thin salmon fillets

Mix the first four ingredients in a small bowl until thoroughly blended. Set aside.

Heat the oil in a nonstick skillet. Add the fillets, flesh side down, and cook, without moving, 5 to 6 minutes until golden brown. Turn so that the skin side is down and cook another 3 to 4 minutes or until the fish is cooked through. Drizzle the honey mixture on top of the fish, and then turn fillets to coat both sides. Serve immediately.

Mustard Dilled Salmon   *Pareve*

Serves 4

An easy-to-prepare, elegant dish. I like to make enough to have some left over to eat cold the next day.

> 4 salmon steaks, about 1¼ inches thick
> Salt and pepper to taste
> 2 tablespoons olive oil
> 2 tablespoons lemon juice
> 1 teaspoon Dijon mustard
> 3 tablespoons minced fresh dill

Season the salmon with salt and pepper and place in a glass or ceramic dish.

Combine all the other ingredients and pour over the fish. Marinate in the refrigerator for at least 1 hour, turning the steaks a few times so that both sides are covered with the marinade.

Broil or grill the salmon on each side until cooked through.

❧ Chicken ❧

Herbed Chicken Rolls Stuffed with Mushrooms   Meat

Serves 4–6

An elegant dish that is worth the effort in its preparation.

> 6 chicken cutlets, skinless and boneless and of similar thickness
> Salt and pepper to taste
> 2 egg whites
> Unseasoned bread crumbs
> ⅓ cup vegetable oil
> ¼ teaspoon dried rosemary
> ¼ teaspoon dried sage
> 2 teaspoons chopped fresh parsley
> ¼ cup dry white wine

Filling

10 ounces fresh mushrooms, chopped

2 tablespoons vegetable oil

¼ teaspoon salt

A few tablespoons unseasoned bread crumbs

Preheat the oven to 350°F. To make the filling, sauté the chopped mushrooms in the oil until they are soft, about 8 to 10 minutes. Stir in the salt. Add the bread crumbs to absorb any liquid and to bind the mixture.

Season the chicken cutlets on both sides with salt and pepper to taste. Place 1 to 2 tablespoons of filling on each cutlet and roll up. Secure with a toothpick. Dip each rolled cutlet in egg white and then in bread crumbs. Place in a greased shallow baking pan.

Mix the oil, rosemary, sage, and parsley and pour over the chicken rolls. Place in the oven and bake uncovered for about 25 minutes. Pour the wine over the chicken and bake another 15 minutes, basting several times with the sauce.

Roasted Citrus Chicken   **Meat**

Serves 4–6

I always use the leftover chicken to make chicken salad.

1 medium roasting chicken, weighing about 4 to 5 pounds

4 teaspoons ground cumin (divided)

2 teaspoons dried oregano

1 to 2 teaspoons chopped garlic (divided)

1 bunch fresh parsley

2 oranges, sliced, rind intact

2 lemons, sliced, rind intact

2 medium onions, sliced thin

½ to 1 cup white wine

Preheat the oven to 350°F. Rub the inside of the chicken with cumin, oregano, and half the garlic. Layer fruit inside—one layer each of orange, then lemon, then onion and a bit of the parsley. Continue layering until the cavity is filled. Place slices of fruit and onion under the chicken's skin. Rub the skin with the remaining garlic and cumin.

Place the chicken in a roasting pan with the remaining fruit and onion around it. Sprinkle the fruit with the remaining parsley. Pour the wine around the bottom of the pan.

Roast the chicken for 1½ to 2 hours, until the skin is golden brown and the juices run clear.

Glazed Balsamic Chicken Breasts   Meat

Serves 3

This easy-to-prepare dish is low in both fat and calories.

3 boneless, skinless chicken breasts of similar thickness
1 tablespoon Dijon mustard
1 tablespoon olive oil
2 to 4 cloves garlic, cut in thin slivers
½ cup raisins
2 tablespoons balsamic vinegar
1 tablespoon brown sugar
¾ cup low-sodium chicken broth

Spread mustard on each breast and set aside.

Heat the oil over medium heat in a nonstick skillet. Add the garlic and cook, stirring, for 30 seconds. Add the chicken, mustard side up, and cook for about 3 minutes or until lightly browned. Turn and cook for another 3 minutes or until brown. Remove the breasts from the pan.

Add the raisins, balsamic vinegar, sugar, and chicken broth to the pan and bring to a boil. Reduce the heat, return the breasts to the pan, spoon some sauce over them, and simmer, covered, for 6 to 8 minutes or until the chicken is cooked through.

Orange Tarragon Chicken Meat

Serves 6–8

By removing the skin from the chicken parts, you greatly reduce the fat content of this dish.

1 cup orange juice
2 tablespoons reduced-sodium soy sauce
8 pieces kosher chicken, skin removed
1 cup unseasoned bread crumbs
2 tablespoons tarragon
½ teaspoon black pepper
3 tablespoons vegetable oil
2 onions, sliced
10 ounces fresh mushrooms, sliced
1 14½ oz. can undiluted kosher chicken soup
½ to 1 cup white wine

Preheat the oven to 375°F. Mix the orange juice and soy sauce and then marinate the chicken parts for 15 minutes. Combine the bread crumbs, tarragon, and black pepper, and roll the chicken pieces in the mixture to coat them evenly with crumbs.

Heat the oil in a large pan and fry the chicken until all sides are browned. Remove and place the pieces in a large baking dish.

In the same pan, brown the onions and mushrooms, then pour them over the chicken. Mix the chicken soup and wine and pour it over the chicken. Cover with aluminum foil and bake in the oven for 45 minutes.

Crispy Oven-Baked Lemon Ginger Sesame Chicken   Meat

Serves 6–8
Kids especially like the crunchiness of this dish.

⅔ cup lemon juice
⅓ cup light brown sugar
3 tablespoons canola oil
1 teaspoon ground ginger or 2 teaspoons slivered
    fresh ginger
¼ teaspoon dry mustard
2 broiler or fryer chickens, about 2½ pounds each,
    cut up, with skin removed
1⅓ cups matzo meal
½ cup sesame seeds
1 teaspoon paprika

In a large bowl, combine the lemon juice, brown sugar, oil, ginger, and mustard. Add the chicken pieces and toss until coated. Cover and refrigerate for several hours to marinate, turning the pieces occasionally.

Preheat the oven to 400°F. Line two roasting pans with aluminum foil, and set a wire rack in each pan.

In a plastic bag, combine the matzo meal, sesame seeds, and paprika. Shake the chicken pieces, a few at a time, in the crumb mixture. Place the pieces on the racks in the roasting pans and bake in the oven for approximately 50 minutes, until the chicken is tender. Serve hot or cold.

Lynn's Potted Chicken   Meat

Serves 4–6
A one-dish dinner that's even better the second day.

2 tablespoons vegetable oil
2 onions, diced
2 tablespoons hot paprika
Salt and pepper to taste
4 chicken breasts with skin and bone attached
3 boiling potatoes, peeled and cubed
2 large carrots, peeled and sliced
Cold water
1½ tablespoons garlic powder
1 cup fresh green beans or fresh peas (optional)

In a deep saucepan, heat the oil and brown the onions, adding a pinch of salt and pepper and 1 tablespoon paprika. Add the chicken, skin side down. Sauté the breasts until brown, then turn and brown other side. Continue until the chicken is almost cooked through. Add the potatoes and carrots. Cover with water. Add salt and pepper to taste, the remaining paprika, and the garlic powder. Cover and cook on a low heat, about 45 minutes.

Remove the chicken breasts and set aside. When cool enough to handle, remove and discard skin and bone.

Skim any fat from the potato-onion mixture. Add the green beans or peas, if desired. Then return the chicken to the pot, continuing to cook for 15 more minutes.

Cholent   Meat

Serves 6–8

The name *cholent* (traditionally pronounced "chulnt") may be derived from the French *chauffé lentement,* "heated slowly." This stew is a traditional midday Saturday meal because it could be cooked and served hot without violating the prohibition on performing work (including cooking) on the Sabbath. Cholent pots, placed in ovens before sundown on Friday, cooked slowly until the following midday. This recipe from my aunt differs from traditional recipes in that it uses chicken instead of beef, cooks on a stovetop instead of inside an oven, and can be ready in just a few hours.

1 cup dried lima beans
2 cups water, plus additional water as needed
2 tablespoons vegetable oil
1 cup onions, thinly sliced
1 clove garlic, chopped
3 chicken breasts on the bone
2 teaspoons salt
Pepper to taste
6 to 8 medium white potatoes, peeled and quartered
½ cup pearl barley
4 medium carrots, peeled, cut into chunks
2 tablespoons all-purpose flour
1 teaspoon paprika

Soak the lima beans. Either let them stand in 2 cups of cold water overnight or else place the beans and 2 cups of hot water in a pot, bring to a boil, and boil for 2 minutes. Turn off the heat and let the beans soak for 1 hour. Drain the beans—but whichever method you use, do not discard the water the beans have soaked in; it will be used later on in the recipe.

Heat the oil in a skillet. Add the onions and cook until soft. Remove the onions and set aside.

Season the chicken breasts with salt and pepper to taste. Place them in the skillet in which the onions were cooked and brown them on both sides, about 3 to 4 minutes per side.

Put the chicken breasts, the onion, and the chopped garlic in a 4-quart pot. Place the potatoes, carrots, and beans around the chicken. Put the barley around the chicken. Sprinkle the contents of the pot with the flour and paprika.

In a separate pot, heat the water from the beans to boiling, seasoned with salt and pepper to taste. Pour the boiling bean water onto the chicken and vegetables to cover them completely (you may have to add some additional water). Cover the pot and cook over low heat for 3½ to 4 hours. Do not uncover the pot during cooking.

Cookies and Pastry

My Sister's Mandelbrot   *Dairy*

Makes 36 cookies
The literal translation of *mandelbrot* is "almond bread." This twice-baked eastern European cookie bears a strong resemblance to Italian biscotti.

2¼ cups unsifted all-purpose flour
¾ cup sugar
Pinch of salt
½ teaspoon baking powder
½ cup vegetable oil
3 eggs
1 teaspoon vanilla extract
¼ cup slivered almonds
¼ cup chocolate chips

Preheat the oven to 375°F. Grease a cookie sheet. Combine the flour, sugar, salt, and baking powder. Make a hole in the middle of the mixture and add the oil, eggs, and vanilla. Stir until well combined and then stir in the almonds and chocolate.

With floured hands, form the dough into three long loaves. Place them on the cookie sheet and bake in the oven for 30 minutes (the loaves should be brown on top). Remove from the oven.

While the loaves are still hot, cut them on an angle into slices ½ to 1 inch thick. Lay the pieces flat on the cookie sheet. Return them to the oven and bake until the tops are browned, about 5 to 10 minutes. Turn the pieces over to brown on the other side if necessary.

Note: Because these cookies are baked twice, they will stay fresh for two weeks if kept in a tightly covered container. If they lose their crispness, reheat them in a 375°F. oven for 5 to 10 minutes.

Maren's Meringues   *Dairy*

Makes approximately 24 2-inch meringues
This easy recipe is fun to make with children.

> 2 egg whites
> ½ teaspoon peppermint extract or ½ teaspoon vanilla extract
> Dash of salt
> ⅛ teaspoon cream of tartar
> ¾ cup sugar (or less if you like your meringues less sweet)
> ½ cup chocolate bits

Preheat the oven to 325°F. Line a cookie sheet with plain brown paper. Combine the egg whites, extract, salt, and cream of tartar and beat until peaks form. Gradually add the sugar, beating until stiff. Fold in the chocolate bits. Drop by teaspoonfuls on the cookie sheet, 1 to 2 inches apart.

Bake in the oven for 20 to 25 minutes. Remove from the paper when cool.

Marcia's Toffee Squares   *Dairy*

Makes 8 squares

These cookies disappear fast—that's why Marcia tells me she always bakes a double batch.

    1 cup unsalted butter
    1 cup sugar
    1 teaspoon vanilla extract
    ½ teaspoon salt
    1 large egg
    1 cup cake meal (see note on page 128)
    8 ounces dark semisweet chocolate, melted
    1 cup chopped walnuts

Preheat the oven to 350°F. Cream the butter with the sugar, vanilla, and salt. Mix in the egg and beat well. Blend in the cake meal—the mixture should be stiff. Separately, mix the melted chocolate and nuts and set aside.

Spread the dough on a greased cookie sheet. Bake for 20 to 25 minutes. Allow to cool; then spread the chocolate-nut mixture on top. Cut into squares.

Note: The squares can be frozen. Thaw before serving.

Susan's Candy Kiss Surprise   Dairy

Makes 70–80 cookies, depending on how many Kisses there are in the package

This recipe is from my friend Susan, who calls it a surprise because there is no indication of the chocolate until you bite into the cookie.

2¼ cups all-purpose flour, sifted
½ cup sugar
1 egg
1 teaspoon vanilla extract
1 cup finely chopped walnuts
1 12- or 13-ounce package Hershey's Kisses
Powdered sugar

Preheat the oven to 350°F. In a large bowl, mix the flour, sugar, egg, and vanilla. Form the mixture into two balls, and wrap each in waxed paper. Refrigerate for approximately 30 minutes or until the dough is cold. You don't want the dough to be too soft; it should have a workable consistency. Remove the dough from the refrigerator and mix in the nuts so that they are evenly distributed.

Take a Hershey's Kiss and wrap just enough dough around it to cover the chocolate completely. Place the cookies on a nonstick cookie sheet and bake for 15 minutes.

Remove the cookies from the oven and immediately sprinkle them with powdered sugar. When they have cooled, sprinkle them again with powdered sugar.

Dad's Rugelach   *Dairy*

Makes 40–56 cookies

Rugelach means "little twists" in Yiddish. These pastries were a favorite of my father, an amateur baker renowned for his rugelach.

    1 cup unsalted butter, softened
    8 ounces cream cheese, softened
    2 cups all-purpose flour, sifted
    1 cup walnuts, finely chopped
    ½ cup raisins
    ½ cup sugar
    1½ teaspoons cinnamon

Cream the butter and cream cheese together in a large bowl. Mix in the flour until it is all incorporated. Knead gently if necessary. Refrigerate for 2 hours.

Preheat the oven to 350°F. Form the dough into 10 to 14 balls. Roll each ball out into a 6-inch circle. If the dough is sticky, dust it with some flour. With a sharp knife or a pastry wheel, cut each pastry circle into quarters.

Combine the walnuts, raisins, sugar, and cinnamon and place a teaspoonful of the mixture in the center of each quarter. Spread the mixture to cover the dough. Beginning at the wide edge of the quarter, roll the dough up toward the point. Place on an ungreased cookie sheet and bake in the oven for approximately 15 to 20 minutes or until golden brown.

Note: For a variation, use 1 cup chocolate bits instead of the walnuts, raisins, cinnamon, and sugar.

Chapter 11

Kosher Sources

These directories are by no means an all-inclusive list of kosher establishments and services, nor do they constitute an endorsement of any product or service by the author or publisher or an endorsement of the reliability of the kosher certification. Readers should also be advised that the kosher status of hotels, restaurants, markets, and products—and their addresses and telephone numbers—can change. If you have any questions about the kosher status of a particular listing, contact the certifying agency or speak with a local rabbi.

Hotels, Resorts, Travel Agents, and Tour Guides

United States

California

Bacara Resort and Spa
8301 Hollister Avenue
Santa Barbara
(877) 422-4245
http://www.bacararesort.com
Provides kosher meals if ordered in advance.

Florida

Catalina Inn Hotel Kosher Resorts
I-4 Exit 32 at John Young Parkway
Orlando
(800) 747-0013; (407) 238-9968

Days Inn Oceanside
4299 Collins Avenue
Miami Beach
(305) 673-1515
A kosher restaurant in the lobby can provide eat-in or carry-out food.

King David Resort and Spa
2901 North Federal Highway
Boca Raton
(561) 955-8500

Kosher Resort
8548 Palm Parkway
Orlando
(407) 238-7755

Kosher Vacation Club Orlando
7552 Universal Boulevard
Orlando
(407) 787-3400
http://www.kosherinorlando.com

Ramada Inn Crown Beach Resort
4041 Collins Avenue
Miami Beach
(800) 327-8163; (305) 531-5771
Offers a kosher meal plan between
   January and March.

Saxony Hotel
3201 Collins Avenue
Miami Beach
(305) 538-6211

Georgia

Omama's Kosher Bed and Breakfast
Toco-Hill
Emory (Atlanta)
(404) 633-9560

Massachusetts

Canyon Ranch Health Resort
165 Kemble Street
Lenox
(800) 742-9000
http://www.canyonranch.com
Offers kosher meals.

Four Seasons Kosher Bed and Breakfast
15 Madoc Street
Newton Centre
(617) 928-1128

Lilac Inn Bed and Breakfast
33 Main Street
Lenox
(413) 637-2172

New Hampshire

Arlington Hotel
33353 Main Street
Bethlehem
(845) 783-3464; (718) 486-6367
Summer: (603) 869-3353

New Jersey

Capitol Hotel
325 Seventh Street
Lakewood
(732) 363-5000

Seasons Resort
Route 517
P.O. Box 637
McAfee (Great Gorge)
(800) 742-8742

New York: Catskill Mountains

Adler Hotel Spa
Sharon Springs
(800) 448-4314
http://www.adlerhotelspa.com

Golden Acres Farm and Ranch
South Gilboa Road
Gilboa
(800) 252-7787 in New York;
   (800) 847-2151 elsewhere
http://www.goldenacres.com

Homowack Resort Hotel
Spring Glen
(800) 243-4567 or 243-4568;
   (845) 647-6800
http://www.homowack.com

Hudson Valley Resort and Spa
400 Granite Road
Kerhonkson
(800) 474-9627; (845) 371-0680

Kutsher's Country Club
1 Kutsher's Road
Monticello
(800) 431-1273; (914) 794-6000
http://www.kutshers.com

Oppenheimer's Regis Hotel
400 Lake Street
Fleischmann's
(800) 468-3598

Raleigh Hotel
Thompsonville Road
South Fallsburg
(800) 446-4003; (914) 434-7000
http://www.catskill.net/raleigh

Swan Lake Resort Hotel and Country
   Club
Briscoe Road
P.O. Box 450
Swan Lake
(877) 800-0705; (845) 292-8000;
   (845) 292-0323
http://www.swanlakeresorthotelcc.com

Zucker's Glen Wild Hotel and Country
   Club
Glen Wild
(845) 434-7470

New York:
New York City and Vicinity

Avenue Plaza Hotel
4624 Thirteenth Avenue
Brooklyn
(718) 552-3200

Levine's Washington Hotel
Beach 125th Street and Rockaway
   Beach Boulevard
Belle Harbor
(718) 634-4244; (718) 474-9671

Rocking Horse Resort Ranch
Highland Park
(800) 647-2624
http://www.rhranch.com

Pennsylvania

Block and Hexter Vacation Center
Route 370
Poyntelle
(800) 400-1924
http://www.bhvc.org

Tamiment Resort and Country Club
Bushkill Falls Road
Tamiment
(888) 682-7334; (800) 843-2144
http://www.tamiment.com

Wedgewood Inn Bed and Breakfast
111 West Bridge Street
New Hope
(215) 862-2570

Rhode Island

Admiral Weaver Inn/Kosher Bed
   and Breakfast
28 Weaver Street
Newport
(888) 465-0051
http://www.kosherbedandbreakfast.com

Virginia

Farbreng Inn/The Kosher Hotel of
   Virginia
212 North Gaskins Road
Richmond
(800) 733-8474; (804) 740-2000
http://www.farbrenginn.com

Other Countries

Canada

Holiday Inn
3450 Dufferin Street
Toronto
(416) 789-5161
Offers kosher meals if ordered two days
   in advance.

Hotel Le Chantecler
Saint Adele, Laurentians, Quebec
(888) 253-9167; (917) 753-5178

Montecassino Place Suite Hotel
3710 Chesswood Drive
Downsview (Toronto)
Has a kosher restaurant in the hotel,
   and kosher room service is available.

Dominican Republic

Playa Grande Beach Resort
Rio San Juan

England

Croft Court Kosher Hotel
44 Ravenscroft Avenue
Golders Green, London
(020) 8458-3331

Golders Green Hotel
147–49 Golders Green Road
Golders Green, London
(020) 8458-7127

Menorah Hotel and Caterers
54-55A Clapton Common
London
(44181) 806-4925

Normandie Hotel
Manor Road, East Cliff
Bournemouth
+44 (0) 1202-552246

France

Art Hotel
98, rue d'Hauberville
Paris
(01-45) 23.85.00

Hotel Aida
17, rue du Conservatoire
Paris
(01-45) 23.11.11

Hotel Alpha
11, rue Geoffroy Marie
Paris
(01-45) 23.10.59

Hotel Lebrun
4, rue Lamartine
Paris
(01-48) 78.75.52

Hotel Touring
21, rue Buffault
Paris
(01-48) 78.09.16

Hungary

Kings Hotel and Restaurant
Nagydiofea U. 25–27
Budapest
++ (36) 1352-7675

Italy

Geneve
Via della Mattonaia 43
Florence
(39-55) 247.79.23

Grand Hotel Michelacci
61011 Gabricce
Rimini
0541-95-4361

Hotel Dei Giovannella
Plaza Trieste 1
Rome

Ruth's
Via Farini 2/A
Florence
(39-55) 248.08.88

Mexico

Hacienda de los Morales
Vazques de Mella 525
Mexico City
(525) 281-0545

Hyatt Regency
Acapulco
(800) 233-1234

Marquis Las Cabos Hotel
Las Cabos, Baja Mexico
(877) 238-9399
Kosher meals available on request.

Marquis Reforma Hotel
Paseo de la Reforma, 465 Col.
   Cuauhtémoc
Mexico City
(800) 235-2387

Spain

Hotel N.CH
Torremolinos
(43-952) 37.37.80

Switzerland

Dan Hotel
Lugano

Levin's Hotel Metropole
Arosa
(0011-4181) 377-4444

Turkey

Khan Hotel
Antalya
(972-9) 748.48.46

Kosher for Passover Package Tours

Check with your travel agent about resort hotels that host special "Kosher for Passover" package tours. The following is a selection of hotels around the world that have been "Kosher for Passover."

United States

Arizona: Arizona Biltmore Resort and Spa, Phoenix; Wigwam Resort and Golf Club, Phoenix; Fairmont Princess, Scottsdale; Double Tree Paradise Valley Resort, Scottsdale; Orange Tree Suites Golf Resort, Scottsdale

California: Western Diplomat Resort, Spa and Country Club, Hollywood; Rancho Mirage, Palm Beach; Coronado Island Marriott Resort and Spa, San Diego; La Costa Resort and Spa, Carlsbad; Hyatt Regency, Irvine; Westin Mission Hills Resort, Palm Springs; Hilton Torrey Pines, La Jolla; Rancho Bernardo Inn, San Diego; Sunny Lake Tahoe, Squaw Creek

Florida: Ritz-Carleton Grande Lakes Resort and Spa, Orlando; Walt Disney World Swan Resort, Orlando; Sheraton World Resort and Spa, Orlando; Ramada Crown Beach Resort, Miami Beach; Castillo del Mar, Miami Beach; Fontainebleau Hilton, Miami Beach; Eden Rock Resort, Miami Beach; Radisson Deauville Resort, Miami Beach; Boca Raton Resort, Boca Raton; Bonaventure Wyndham Resort and Spa, Fort Lauderdale; Coral Springs Hotel, Fort Lauderdale; Ritz-Carleton, Sarasota; Registry Resort and Club, Naples; PGA National Resort and Spa, Palm Beach; Ritz-Carleton Resort and Spa, Palm Beach

Hawaii: Turtle Bay Resort, Hawaii

Nevada: Rio Suites Resorts, Spa and Casino, Las Vegas; Ritz-Carleton Lake Las Vegas Resort and Spa, Las Vegas

New Hampshire: Mount Washington Resort, White Mountains

New Jersey: Doubletree Resort, Somerset; Howard Johnson Hotel, Atlantic City; Legends Resort and Country Club, McAfee

New York: Rye Town Hilton, Westchester; The Sagamore, Lake George; Villa Roma Resort, Callicoon; Friar Tuck Inn, Catskill; Nevele Grande, Fallsview

Pennsylvania: Lancaster Host Resort, Lancaster

Vermont: The Equinox, Manchester Village

Other Countries

Aruba: Wyndham Beach Resort and Casino

Canada: Fairmont Chateau Whistler, Whistler, British Columbia

France: Noga Hilton, Cannes

Mexico: Gran Melia, Cancun; Moon Palace, Cancun; Western Regina, Cancun

Italy: Hotel Luna, Capri; Sheraton's Hôtel des Bains, Venice; Regina Palace, Lake Maggiore

Puerto Rico: Caribe Hilton, Old San Juan; Hyatt Dorado Beach Resort, Dorado; Ritz-Carleton San Juan Hotel, Spa and Casino, Isla Verde

Spain: Hotel Maritim, Barcelona; Sea Golf Luxury Hotel, Andalusia

For further information on kosher hotels worldwide, go to http://www.totallyjewishtravel.com, http://www.jewishpeople.net, and http://www.kosherdelight.com. The Jewish Travel Guide at http://www.aish.com provides kosher travel information for ten major cities in North America.

Travel Agents and Tour Guides

The following travel agents and tour guides specialize in domestic or foreign kosher tours or kosher holiday packages.

Afikoman Tours
(888) 234-5662
http://www.afikomanTours.com.
info@afikomanTours.com

Club Kosher
(866) KOSHER2; (203) 799-7791
http://www.clubkosher.com

Elite Dimensions Tours
(718) 454-5778; outside New York:
   (800) 228-4525
Organizes tours during Passover
   season only.

Exquisite Kosher Tours
(866) 843-3585

ISRAMWorld Tours
(877) 477-2622; (212) 661-1193
http://www.isram-k.com
Organizes individual and group tours
   to Eastern Europe, Russia, Spain,
   Portugal, Mediterranean, Africa,
   Latin America, South Pacific.

Jewish Heritage Tours
(718) 851-2469; (888) 253-9167
http://www.ahavathtorah.com
Jewishheritagetours@hotmail.com

Jewish Journeys
(888) 273-9384
Organizes tours to Thailand, Vietnam,
   China, Hong Kong, India, Russia,
   Europe, South America, Australia,
   and New Zealand.

Kesher Kosher Tours
370 Lexington Avenue
New York, NY 10017
(212) 949-9580; outside New York:
   (800) 847-0700
http://www.keshertours.com
Organizes tours in the United States,
   Europe, and Russia.

KMR Tours
(888) 567-0100
http://www.kmrtours.com
Organizes tours in the Rocky Mountains
   and the western United States.

Kosher Expeditions
(800) 923-2645
Organizes tours of the United States,
   Central and South America, the
   Caribbean, Asia, Africa, and Europe.

Kosher Flyaway
http://www.kosherflyaway.com
Organizes individual and group tours
   of the United States, Canada, the
   United Kingdom, Ireland, and
   Continental Europe.

Kosher Konnections
(888) 790-8999

Kosher Tours to Scandinavia
626 Montgomery Street
Brooklyn, NY 11225
(718) 773-0440
scandiatrio@aol.com

Kosher Tours Worldwide
http://www.koshertoursworldwide.com

Kosher Travels Unlimited
(800) 832-6676
http://www.koshertravelsunlimited.com

Kosher Treks
http://www.koshertreks.com
(972-2) 563-3218
Organizes hiking trips around the world.

Lasko Family Kosher Tours
2699 Stirling Road, Suite C-405
Fort Lauderdale, FL 33312
(800) 532-9119; (954) 894-6000
http://www.laskotours.com
laskotours@aol.com

Leisure Time Tours
(718) 528-0700; outside New York:
    (800) 223-2624
http://www.leisuretimetours.com
info@leisureTT.com
Organizes tours during the Passover
    season only.

Mendy Vim's Holidays and Vacations
(718) 998-4477; outside New York:
    (800) 464-VIMS
Organizes tours during the Passover
    season only.

Norman's Wholesale Travel
1641 East Thirteenth Street
Brooklyn, NY 11229
(718) 339-3141

Palace Tours
(866) 448-6577; (305) 672-0226
http://www.palacetours.com

Presidential Kosher Holidays
(718) 332-3900; outside New York:
    (800) 950-1240

Pruzansky Family
5521 Fifteenth Avenue

Brooklyn, NY 11219
(718) 436-4405
mpruzansky@aol.com

Seven Star Kosher Tours
(866) 782-7470
http://www.sevenstartours.com

Sunburst Kosher Tours
1555 East Nineteenth Street
Brooklyn, NY 11230
(800) 875-7574; (845) 436-9212
Organizes domestic package tours for
    groups and individuals.

TAL Tours
(800) 825-9399; (516) 825-0966

Teva Adventures/Jewish Outdoor
    Education
(718) 576-1302
http://www.tevaadventure.org
Organizes backpacking and wilderness
    programs for teens and adults in the
    Rocky Mountains, Alaska, and New
    Hampshire.

World Wide Kosher Tours
(800) 525-0035; (323) 525-0015

Kosher Cruises

In 2003, the world's first fully kosher luxury cruise ship, the *Wind Surf*, was launched by Holland-America's WindStar Line. The 308-room motorized sailing yacht offers six- and seven-day cruises. The *Wind Surf* is used by Chosen Voyage, a kosher cruise company, for voyages to the Caribbean, the Baltic Sea, the Mediterranean, the Great Lakes, and Bermuda. The *Queen Elizabeth II* can provide a variety of frozen kosher foods prepared in microwave ovens and served still in their seals. The Orient Line's *Marco Polo* has one galley dedicated to preparing fresh kosher dishes and one dining room for kosher diners, with silverware, dishes, and glassware newly unpacked.

Several travel agencies specialize in kosher cruises:

Chosen Voyage
(866) 462-4673
http://www.chosenvoyage.com
http://www.kosherboat.com
Organizes cruises in the Baltic, the
    Greek isles, and Russia.

Kosher Cruise Enterprises
http://www.KCEcruises.com

Kosherica Cruises
(877) 724-5567; (305) 695-2700
http://www.kosherica.com
Organizes cruises to Alaska, the Greek
    isles, and Italy.

Suite Life Kosher Cruises
(866) 604-9838
http://www.slkosher.com
Organizes cruises to Alaska,
    Scandinavia, Russia

Kosher Food When Traveling

Some resort hotels that do not have their own kosher dining rooms can make arrangements for kosher meals to be served to guests. If you wish to bring your own kosher food, you have a number of options. There are several companies that provide prepared kosher meals that require no refrigeration or cooking. Meals from La Briute, (866) 432-8522, http://www.labriutemeals.com, come with a self-heating unit or can be heated in a microwave or by immersion in boiling water; entrees include instant soup, cookies, and disposable cutlery. Tasty Bite, (888) 827-8900, http://www.TastyBite.com, offers dishes that are all-natural and MSG-free. Meals feature Indian cuisine that can be heated or served at room temperature; dairy and nondairy selections are available. My Own Meals, (847) 948-1118, http://www.myownmeals.com, has a line of glatt kosher meat, dairy, and pareve meals that do not need refrigeration. This company, which in the mid-1990s was the first to provide certified kosher meals as U.S. military rations, can also fill special requests for vegetarians and those who are lactose-intolerant or suffer from celiac disease (and need wheat- or gluten-free dishes). Other options include http://www.koshermeal.com (frozen microwavable kosher food delivered overnight anywhere in the United States); http://www.kosherflyaway.com (glatt kosher meals delivered anywhere in the United States, Canada, United Kingdom, Ireland, or Continental Europe); and http://www.kosher line.com, (888) 567-4378 (meals shipped overnight in the United States). Kosher on Wheels, (323) 933-0089, will deliver kosher meals from Los Angeles restaurants to hotels and airports throughout the United States overnight.

Airline Food

Since 9/11, many airlines have changed or amended their meal services, so it is best to check if your flight features meals. In 2002, most major domestic carriers eliminated most free food service in coach on most domestic flights, replacing that service with food for sale. Carriers that do offer in-flight meals can provide kosher meals. They generally need twelve to twenty-four hours' notice that such meals are required.

All airline meals services are contracted out to large food-service caterers, which are responsible for other special-request meals such as vegetarian, lactose-intolerant, and salt-free diets, as well as kosher meals. Generally, airline food is not prepared fresh at an airport kitchen but is brought in frozen. On some flights, the food is cooked on board; other flights serve preheated food. Cold kosher meals come sealed in plastic; hot kosher meals are double-sealed. Exceptions are the meals service on El Al, Israel's national airline (http://www.elal.com), on international flights from New York's John F. Kennedy Airport. They are prepared fresh at the airline's airport commissary, which is certified kosher.

There is also a kosher restaurant at JFK. Berso's Caterers operate Erwin's Glatt Kosher Restaurant, Terminal 4, Food Court, East Wing, (718) 428-5000.

Kosher Camps

All camps are coed unless otherwise indicated.

Adult Camps

Berkshire Hills-Emanuel (ages 60+)
Copake, New York
(718) 828-8952
http://www.bhecamps.com
info@bhecamps.com

Block and Hexter Camp (ages 55+)
Poyntelle, Pennsylvania
(800) 400-1924
http://www.bhvc.org
information@bhvc.org

Isabella Freedman (ages 55+)
Falls Village, Connecticut
(212) 242-5586
http://www.isabellafreedman.org
campifreed@aol.com
Also offers spring and fall Elderhostel
  programs in the Berkshires.

Kislak (Ages 55+)
Lake Como, Pennsylvania
(973) 575-3333
http://www.njycamps.org
kislak@njycamps.org

Children's Day Camps

Beth Sholom Day Camp (ages 3–15)
Roslyn Heights, New York
(516) 621-9257

Camp Gan-Eden of the Five Towns
  (toddlers and nursery school age)
703 West Broadway
Cedarhurst, New York
(516) 295-0067

Camp Moed (ages 6–14)
SUNY-Maritime Campus
Bronx, New York
(212) 627-8442
Campmoed@aol.com
Offers a 9 A.M.–4 P.M. day camp plus a
  weekday sleepaway camp.

Camp Zemer (grades 2–7)
Hewlitt, Long Island
(866) 869-3637
http://www.campzemer.com

Central Queens Y Camps (ages 5–15)
67-09 108th Street, Forest Hills,
  New York
(718) 268-5011, ext. 202

Educational Alliance Day Camp
  (ages 5–14)
Manhattan (preschool and kindergarten)
Staten Island
(212) 780-2300
http://www.edalliance.org

Hillcrest Jewish Center Day Camp
  (ages 4–14)
183-02 Union Turnpike
Flushing, Queens, New York
(718) 380-4145

JCC Metrowest/JCC Camp Deeny
  Riback (age 3 to grade 10)
Flanders, New Jersey
(973) 428-9300
http://www.jccmetrowest.org
jccriback@aol.com

Machane Devora Day Camps
  (ages 5–14)
Queens, New York
(718) 575-8760

Ma-Tov Day Camp (ages 5–11)
1170 Sussex Road
Teaneck, New Jersey
(201) 692-1027 winter;
  (201) 768-4955 summer
http://www.ma-tov.com
Orthodox camp serving Northern New
  Jersey, Manhattan, Westchester, and
  the Bronx.

Ninety-Second Street Y Camps
  (ages 5–15)
Pearl River, New York
(212) 415-5600
http://www.92ndsty.org
A dozen different camps divided by age
  and interests.

Ruach Summer Camp (ages 4–12)
Uniondale, New York
(516) 565-5640
Also offers a Teen Tour program.

Samuel Field/YM and YWHA Day
  Camps (kindergarten through
  grade 11)
58-20 Little Neck Parkway
Little Neck, New York
(718) 225-6750
http://www.samuelfield.org
Samfield@aol.com

Suffolk Y Camps (ages 3–16)
Huntington, New York
(631) 462-9800
http://www.suffolkyjcc.org/
Includes sports camp, teen travel,
and theater camp.

Westchester Day School Summer
Program
856 Oriental Avenue
Mamaroneck, New York
(914) 698-8900, ext. 153

Children's Overnight and Sleepaway Camps

Berkshire Hills-Emanuel Camps
(ages 7–14)
Copake, New York
(718) 828-8952
http://www.bhecamps.com
bhecamps@aol.com

B'nai Brith Perlman (ages 7–16)
Starlight, Pennsylvania
(202) 857-6532; (800) 270-7375
(winter only)
http://www.perlmancamp.org
bbyobbpc@aol.com

Camp Dina for Girls (ages 7–15)
Dingmans Ferry, Pennsylvania
(718) 437-7117
http://www.campdina.com
info@campdina.com

Camp Dora Golding for Boys
(ages 7–15)
East Stroudsburg, Pennsylvania
(718) 437-7117
http://www.campdoragolding.com
info@campdoragolding.com

Camp Horei Maarav for Boys
(grades 7–9)
(866) 700-9378; (303) 629-8200, ext. 33
http://www.horeimaarav.com
Travel and hiking in Colorado and the
Rocky Mountains.

Camp Kanfei Nesharim
(201) 833-0310
http://www.kanfei.com
Organizes teen tours of the South
Pacific and California and winter ski
tours in Vermont.

Camp Kunatah
Kosher Boy Scouts
(718) 376-2585

Camp Louemma (ages 7–15)
Sussex, New Jersey
(718) 631-3747
camplouemma@aol.com

Camp MaRabu (boys, ages 13–15)
(301) 681-3411
CampMaRabu1@juno.com
Three-week travel camp in the western
United States and along the Pacific
Coast.

Camp Monroe
Monroe, New York
(845) 782-8695

Camp Nagella (ages 9+)
Fallsburg, New York
(616) 374-1528
http://www.jepli.org
campnagella@jepli.org

Camp NuYu for Girls (fitness and
weight management, ages 10–17,
18–24)
Killington, Vermont
(718) 645-6399; outside New York:
(866) 366-8948
http://www.campnuyu.com
info@campnuyu.com

Camp Poyntelle-Lewis Village
(ages 6–16)
Poyntelle, Pennsylvania
(718) 279-0690
http://www.poyntlle.com
summers@poyntelle.com

Camp Ramah in the Berkshires
(ages 8–16)
Wingdale, New York
(212) 279-0754
http://ramahberkshires.org
info@ramahberkshires.org

Camp Sternberg for Girls/Camp Anna
Heller for Girls (ages 8–14)
Narrowsburgh, New York
(212) 691-5548

Edward Isaacs (ages 7–16)
Holmes, New York
(718) 268-5011
http://www.campedi.com
director@campedi.com
A division of the Queens YM/YWHA.

Glatt Sports Camp
(888) 848-1629

IBA-IHA Camp (ages 11–17)
Sidney, New York
(888) IBA-CAMPinfo@ibacamp.com
Orthodox sports camp.

Meytiv Camp Ramah in California
(high school juniors and seniors)
Sacramento and San Francisco
(310) 476-8571
http://www.meytiv.org
meytiv@ramah.org

Mogen Avraham (boys, ages 7–15)
Avraham Chaim Heller (boys, ages
13–16)
Swan Lake, New York
(212) 691-5548
http://www.campmogenav-heller.org
info@campmogenav-heller.org

Morasha (Modern Orthodox/Zionist)
(ages 9–16)
Lake Como, Pennsylvania
(718) 252-9696
cmpmorasha@aol.com
http://www.campmorasha.com

Moshava (Zionist) (grades 3–9)
Honesdale, Pennsylvania
(212) 683-4484
http://www.moshava.org
cmosh@atdial.net

Na'aleh (Labor Zionist/kibbutz lifestyle)
Holmes, New York
(212) 255-1796
http://www.naaleh.org
naaleh@aol.com

New Jersey Y—Cedar Lake (grades 7–9)
New Jersey Y—Nah-Jee-Wah
(grades 1–6)
New Jersey Y—Teen Camp
(grades 10–11)
Milford, Pennsylvania
New Jersey Y—Nesher (sports and
creative and performing arts; ages
8–16)
Lake Como, Pennsylvania
(973) 575-3333
http://www.njycamps.org
info@njycamps.org *or*
nesher@njycamps.org
The New Jersey Y also runs Mountain
Top Camp (ages 7–16) with sessions
that last one to two weeks.

Shomria (Zionist) (ages 9–16)
Liberty, New York
(212) 627-2830
http://www.hashomerhatzair.org/camp
shomria.htl
mail@hashomerhatzair.org

Sportstar Academy (boys, ages 9–16)
Swan Lake Resort and Country Club
Swan Lake, New York
(888) 848-1629
http://www.sportstaracademy.com
joseph@sportstaracademy.com

Surprise Lake Camp (ages 7–15)
Cold Spring, New York
(212) 924-3131
http://www.supriselake.org
slcamp@aol.com

Tel Yehudah (ages 14–18)
Barryville, New York
(800) 970-2267
http://www.youngjudea.org
telyehudah@youngjudea.org
Sponsored by Hadassah.

Welmet (grades 3–11)
Putnam Valley, New York
(718) 882-4000
http://www.campwelmet.com
campwelmet@aol.com

Young Judea-Sprout Lake (ages 7–14)
Verbank, New York
(201) 487-2448
http://www.cyjsl.org
campsprout@aol.com

Oakhurst (ages 8–20, 21–60)
Oakhurst, New Jersey
(212) 533-4020
http://www.campchannel.com/camp
 oakhurst
For individuals with physical handicaps
 without mental retardation.

New Jersey Y–Round Lake Camp
 (ages 7–18)
Lake Como, Pennsylvania
(973) 575-3333
http://www.njycamps.org
For individuals with attention deficit
 disorder or learning disabilities.
ric@njycamps.org

Special Needs Camps

Camp HASC (ages 3–21 and adult)
Parksville, New York
(718) 851-6100
For individuals with mental retardation.

The Association of Jewish Sponsored Camps offers a wealth of information about kosher camps, including a free yearly listing of member adult, children's, and special needs camps. The AJSC can be reached at (212) 751-0477; http://www.jewishcamps.org; info@jewishcamps.org.

Some Things to Consider Before Choosing a Camp for Your Child

- Is your child physically and emotionally ready for camp?
- What type of camp would be best for your child? Day camp or sleepaway? A traditional-style camp with many activities? One that specializes in the arts or sports or weight loss? A travel camp?
- What is the tuition, and what does it cover? Are there any extras not included in the basic fee?
- What are the session lengths?
- What is the background of the director and counselors?
- What is the ratio of staff to campers? What percentage of counselors are trained and certified in CPR or first aid?
- At speciality camps, are there professional teachers instructing campers?
- How are emergencies and medical care handled? Ask to see the camp's written safety plan (which describes not only staff qualifications and training but also camper supervision, safety requirements for specific activities, and fire safety and medical requirements).
- What provisions are made for children with special dietary needs, such as food allergies?

If you are considering a day camp:

- What are the hours?
- Does the camp provide lunch or snacks?
- Does the camp provide transportation, and if so, is it included in the tuition or is it extra?

If you are considering a sleepaway camp:

- How often may parents visit?
- What is the condition of the facilities, equipment, and living quarters?

The American Camping Association, (800) 428-CAMP, http://www.acacamps.org, offers information on choosing a camp, tips on packing for camp, and advice on helping kids cope with the camping experience.

Kosher by Mail

A & B Famous Gefilte Fish
(866) GEFILTE
http://www. Gefiltefish.com
Shipped frozen overnight.

Avi Glatt Kosher
(866) AVIGLATT
orders@avilglatt.com
Meat, poultry.

Bagelboss.com
400 Willis Avenue
Rosyln Heights, NY 11577
(888) BOSSTIME
Appetizing baked goods, bagels, and coffee; ships throughout the United States.

Benson's Gourmet Seasonings
(800) 325-5619
All-natural, salt-free, sugar-free, preservative-free, MSG-free seasonings. Free catalogue.

Bon Appetit Kosher Diet Programs
381 Willis Avenue
Rosyln Heights, NY 11577
(516) 621-0402
Free shipping.

Broadway Basketeers
Brochures and custom orders: (888) 599-GIFT (24 hours); orders: (800) 378-7173
Gift baskets. Ships throughout North America. Free color brochure.

Challah Connection
(866) 242-5524
http://www.challahconnection.com
Plain, cinnamon, raisin, chocolate chip, and honeyed whole wheat challah, rugelach, babka, cookies, and Russian coffeecake. Delivers from Maine to Washington, D.C.

Chocolate Emporium
(888) 246-2528
http://www.choclat.com
Chocolates and confections, hard candy, sugar-free candy, flavored cordials, ice cream (regular and lactose-free). Free catalogue.

Confection Collection
6754 Route 9 South
Howell, New Jersey
(732) 905-3039
http://www.confectioncollection.com
Chocolates, nuts, dried fruit, candy, gift baskets; ships nationwide.

If You Are Buying Food by Mail . . .

Consumer Reports suggests the following tips:

- Ask if there are any limitations on when and where the seller ships.
- Specify how you want your purchase shipped. The difference in cost between overnight delivery and standard ground shipping can be enormous.
- Does the company guarantee that perishable foods, such as meat or fish, will arrive safely (still frozen or cold) regardless of how it is shipped?
- Would the seller substitute a similar item if the one you ordered was not available without letting you know beforehand?

Creative Basket
(718) 380-4326
Food and gift baskets; delivery
　throughout the United States.

Delancey Street Dessert
　Company/Gertil's Bakery
New York City
(212) 254-0977; (800) 254-5254
http://www.babka.com
Babka, rugelach, mandelbrot, and other
　baked goods; also sugar-free products.
　Free catalogue.

Dr. B's Kosherlite Meals
(718) 591-3447; (877) 622-8500
　outside New York
http://www.drblite.com
Diet, low-carb, and low-fat meals; ships
　nationwide.

Endangered Species Chocolate
　Company
http://www.chocolatebar.com
Belgian chocolates, described as child-
　and environment-friendly—beans
　bought from cooperative farms that
　do not use child labor, company
　donates 10 percent of its profits to
　environmental causes.

Fairytale Brownies
Scottsdale, Arizona
(800) 324-7982
Belgian chocolate brownies. Free
　catalogue.

Food4Thought
http://www.food4tht.com
Gift baskets.

Freeda Vitamins
(800) 777-3737
Kosher vitamins containing no sugar,
　starch, sulfates, salt filler, coal tar dyes,
　or animal stearates. Free catalogue.

FreshDirect.com
(866) 2U-FRESH
http://www.freshdirect.com
Custom-cut glatt kosher meat, cold
　cuts, fish, and groceries. Delivers in
　the New York City area.

Global Products and Distribution
2480 Briarcliff Road, Suite 285
Atlanta, GA 30329
(800) 435-1755
Holiday gift baskets. Ships throughout
　the United States and to Israel.

Godiva Chocolatier
(800) 9GODIVA (8 A.M.–11 P.M.,
　Eastern Time, seven days a week)
http://www.godiva.com
Chocolate gift boxes and baskets. Most
　Godiva products are kosher and are so
　indicated in the company's catalogue.

Guss's Pickles
(516) 569-0909
Delanceypickle@aol.com
Pickles, pickled peppers, olives,
　sauerkraut, and horseradish. Ships
　overnight.

Hamakor Judaica, "The Source for
Everything Jewish"
P.O. Box 48836
Niles, IL 60714
(800) 426-2567 (24 hours)
http://www.jewishsource.com
Kosher snack foods, chocolates,
delicatessen, gift baskets, and
cookbooks. Free catalogue.

Herman Glick's Sons Kosher Food
Emporium
100-15 Queens Boulevard
Forest Hills, New York
(800) GLICKSS; (718) 896-7736
Meat and nonperishable items.

H&H Bagels
639 West Forty-Sixth Street
New York City
(212) 765-7200
2239 Broadway
New York City
(212) 595-8000
http://www.hhbagels.com
Open 24 hours. Ships worldwide.

Howard Lane Gift Baskets
(800) 261-3848
http://www.howardlane.com
Gourmet gift baskets.

Jinil Au Chocolat
444 Central Avenue
Cedarhurst, New York
(516) 295-2550
238 Madison Avenue
New York City
(212) 679-7415
1371 Coney Island Avenue
Brooklyn, New York
(718) 758-0199
(800) 645-4645
http://www.Jinil.com

Kariba Farms
5A Stewart Court
Denville, NJ 07834
(800) 442-1969; (973) 537-8500
http://www.karibafarms.com

Natural organic dried fruits and
vegetables, nuts, and condiments;
gift packs available.

Kohn's Kosher Market Online
http://www.kohnskosher.com
(314) 569-0727
Meat, including bison, poultry, homemade pastrami, corned beef, and
smoked fish. Ships throughout the
United States.

Kosher Bison
http://www.kosherbison.com
Bison meat.

Kosher Club
5225 Wilshire Boulevard
Los Angeles, California
(323) 939-9377
http://www.kosherclub.com
Kosher food superstore. Ships
nationwide.

Kosher Connections
Portland, Oregon
(800) 950-7227
http://www.thekosherconnection.com
Kosher gourmet foods from the Pacific
Northwest and Israel: willow gift
baskets, alder-smoked salmon, fresh
berry preserves, dried Oregon cherries,
chocolates, low-fat delicacies. Ships
to the United States and Canada.
Illustrated brochure and price list
available.

Kosher Cornucopia/Gifts Direct
P.O. Box 326, Beechwoods Road
Jeffersonville, NY 12748
(800) 756-7437; (845) 482-3118
http://www.koshercornucopia.com
sales@koshercornucopia.com
Gift baskets and gourmet foods,
including smoked salmon, smoked
trout, smoked turkey, dried salami,
knishes, candies, chocolates, popcorn,
fruit, nuts, cookies, brownies, cakes,
and pastries. Ships throughout the
United States and to Canada and
Israel. Free catalogue.

Kosher Delight
(212) 541-GIFT
Kosher delicacies: hand-dipped
  chocolates, Alaskan smoked salmon,
  gourmet coffee, nuts, candy, baked
  goods, cider.

Kosher Diet Delivery
(800) 354-3122
http://www.kosherdietdelivery.com
Low-calorie meals; delivers throughout
  New York City, Westchester, and
  Long Island.

Kosher King
(877) 567-4546
http://www.kosherking.com
Frozen meat.

Kosher Maven
(800) 229-2677; (413) 436-0506
Gift baskets, including fruit, nuts,
  chocolates, pasta, and sauces; some
  products fat-free or sugar-free.

Kosher on Wheels
(323) 933-0089
Kosher meals delivered to hotels and
  airports nationwide.

Kosher Pets
6278 North Federal Highway, Suite 567
Fort Lauderdale, FL 33308
(954) 938-6270
http://www.kosherpets.com
All-natural kosher pet food for cats and
  dogs.

Kosher Supermarket
http://www.koshersupermarket.com

Kosher Vitamins
(800) 645-1899
http://www.koshervitamins.com
Discount vitamins. Catalogue available.
  Worldwide shipping.

Kossar's Bialys
(212) 473-4810
mail@kosssarsbialys.com

Lake Champlain Chocolates
(800) 634-8105
http://www.lakechamplainchocolate.com
Truffles, pralines, chocolate bars, gift
  baskets.

Le Chocolate
(845) 352-8301
http://www.finestchocolate.com

Le Chocolatier Extraordinaire
1711 Avenue M
Brooklyn, NY 11230
(718) 258-5800; (800) 877-GIFT

Long Island Kosher Meat and Poultry
829 West 181st Street
New York City
(212) 795-0248
Fresh and frozen meat; delivery
  throughout the United States.

Maxi-Health Research
(800) 544-MAXI; (718) 645-2222
Vitamins and supplements.

Mill Basin Deli
http://www.pastrami.net
Pastrami.

Musicon Deer Farms
Goshen, New York
(914) 294-6378
Freshly frozen kosher venison raised free
  of hormones, steroids, chemicals, and
  additives.
Ships individually wrapped butchered
  cuts throughout the United States.
  Call for price list and recipes.

Negev Foods
(718) 258-8440
http://www.negev.com
Kosher for Passover foods. Ships
  nationwide.

Northwest Smoked Salmon
(800) 645-FISH
http://www.seabear.com

N.Y. Flying Pizza Pies
(800) 969-6974
http://www.flyingpizzas.com
Fresh kosher pizza. Ships throughout the United States.

O'Bissenger's
http://www.bissengers.com
Candy, chocolate covered matzo.

Organic Provisions
P.O. Box 756
Richboro, PA 18954
(800) 490-0044
http://www.orgfood.com;
 http://www.goodeats.com
info@organicfoods.com
Natural foods, health and beauty supplies, pet food, kitchenware and home care products, organic clothing, books and magazines; over two thousand items in all. Specializes in organic, kosher, macrobiotic, environment-friendly, and cruelty-free products. Catalogue is $3.00, refundable with first purchase. Minimum purchase: $20.00.

Our Sweet Delights
(443) 562-6006
http://www.oursweetdelights.com
Gourmet candy, baked goods, party favors. Ships nationwide.

Pepperidge Farm Holiday Gift Collection
P.O. Box 917
Clinton, CT 06413
(800) 243-9314 (8 A.M.–11 P.M., Eastern Time, seven days a week)
Baked goods, cookies, brownies, chocolates, candies, gift baskets, and decorated tins. A number of products are kosher and are so labeled in the catalogue.

Pino's
13 North Fourth Avenue
Highland Park, New Jersey
(732) 242-5421
Kosher gift baskets; kosher wines from the United States, Australia, France, Italy, Hungary, and Israel.

Royal Palace Foods
http://www.koshermeal.com
info@koshermeal.com
Frozen microwavable kosher and halal meals; entire kosher menus, including banquets and room service, for hotels that do not have kosher kitchens. Overnight delivery to all fifty states.

Sarabeth's Kitchen
2291 Second Avenue
New York, NY 10035
(800) PRESERVE
Naturally flavored, preservative-free preserves, including orange-apricot marmalade, cherry-plum preserve, strawberry-peach preserve, peach-apricot preserve, apricot-pineapple-current preserve. Free catalogue.

Scharffen-Berger Chocolates
(800) 930-4528
http://www.scharffen-berger.com
Called the finest American chocolate maker by *House and Garden, Bon Appetit,* and *Gourmet* magazines.

Second Avenue Deli by Mail
156 Second Avenue
New York, NY 10003
(800) 692-3354; (212) 677-0606
http://www.2ndavedeli.com
Kosher salamis and other deli items; rugelach. Ships anywhere in the United States. Free color catalogue.

Shaklee Food Supplements
(888)-874-5533
Kosher vitamins and natural personal-care products. Free delivery throughout the continental United States. Catalogue: $2.00.

Start Fresh Weight Control Program
4813 Twelfth Avenue
Brooklyn, NY 11219
(800) 226-5000; (718) 851-0081
Kosher diet foods low in fat, calories, and sodium. Ships anywhere in the United States. Free brochure.

Sugar Plum
(800) 44-SUGAR
Chocolates, gifts.

Sweet Odyssey
(718) 258-2534
http://www.sweetodyssey.resqnet.com/so
Gift baskets, chocolates, nuts, dried
fruits. Ships nationally.

Tropical Source
http://www.nspiredfoods.com
Flavored chocolate bars and chocolate
cooking chips that are dairy-free,
contain no refined sugar, and are
vegan-friendly.

Well-Bread Loaf
Congers, New York
(800) 937-9252
Brownies, baked goods. Free brochure.

Wolsk's Gourmet Confectioners
81 Ludlow Street
New York, NY 10002
(212) 475-0704
Gift baskets, dried fruit, nuts, hand-
dipped chocolates, international
candies, coffee, tea, fresh baked
goods; sugar-free and low-calorie
items available. Ships nationwide.

World of Chantilly
(718) 859-1110
http://www.chantilly.com
Cakes, pies, pastries, chocolates. Ships
nationwide.

http://www.a1steaks.com
Beef, salmon, and baked goods.

http://www.aaronsgourmet.com
Meat (including buffalo), poultry, fish,
entrees, desserts.

http://www.boutarque.org
Kosher Mediterranean caviar. Free
shipment within the United States
and Canada.

http://www.chulon.com
info@holon foods.com
Israeli foods.

http://www.kosher.com
(866) 567-4379
Groceries, baked goods, pizza, smoked
fish, meat, wine and spirits, chocolates, travel meals, cosmetics. Ships
all products throughout the United
States and, except for wine and
perishable goods, worldwide.

http://www.kosherline.com
(888) 567-4378
Food, gifts, gift baskets, wine, travel
meals. Ships overnight.

http://www.koshermania.com
(866) KOSHER1
kosherfood@koshermania.com
Groceries, fish, candy, chocolate,
gourmet tea and coffee, gift baskets,
travel meals.

http://www.kosherstyle.com
Gift baskets, chocolate.

http://www.mykosherfood.com
Groceries, frozen food, baked goods,
wine. Delivers throughout the United
States.

http://www.mykoshrmarket.com
Meat, wine, dairy products.

http://www.123kosher.com
Meat, poultry, and fish; freezer-packed
overnight shipments.

Yonah Schimmel
http://www.yonahschimmel.com
Knishes.

Yossi's Sweethouse
(718) 234-7629
http://www.yossisweethouse.com
Chocolate, candies, nuts, gift baskets.
Ships nationwide.

Zabar's
2245 Broadway
New York, NY 10024
(212) 787-2000
info@zabars.com

One of New York City's largest and best-known gourmet markets with a wide selection of gourmet kosher items, including baked goods, coffee, and smoked salmon. Catalogue available.

Restaurants and Caterers

Many hotels in large metropolitan areas either maintain separate kosher kitchens or can have their kitchens koshered for kosher caterers. A number of those hotels are listed in this directory. (An asterisk indicates that the restaurant also does catering.)

Arizona

Phoenix

Cactus Kosher
5017 South Central Avenue
(602) 265-6870

King Solomon Pizza
4810 North Seventh Street
(602) 870-8655

Segal's Kosher Deli
4818 North Seventh Street
(602) 263-9377

Taster's Vegetarian
3407 North Seventh Street
(602) 230-2466

Valley Kosher Deli
1331 East Northern Street
(602) 371-0999

Yaffa Restaurant
3527 West Bethany Home Road
(602) 973-8110

California

Los Angeles

*Afshan Restaurant
306 East Ninth Street
(213) 622-1010 (Persian)

Aria Catering
(818) 342-7000

Bagel Factory
3004 South Sepulveda Boulevard
(818) 477-8460

Beverly Hills Chinese Cuisine
9025 Wilshire Boulevard
(310) 247-1239

Brami's Pizza
17735½ Sherman Way
(818) 342-0611

Café Elite/City Café au Lait
7115 Beverly Boulevard
(323) 936-2861 (dairy)

Catering by Brenda
(310) 203-8365

Cellar Café
6505 Wilshire Boulevard
(213) 852-1234

Chana's Cuisine Catering
(310) 659-2834

Chick-A-Deli
7170 Beverly Boulevard
(213) 932-0674

Chick'N Chow Chinese Food
9301 West Pico Boulevard
(310) 274-5595

Chinese and Kabob
11330 Santa Monica Boulevard
(310) 914-3040
9180 West Pico Boulevard
(310) 274-4007

City Deli
7119 Beverly Boulevard
(323) 930-1303

*Classic Raphy's
12454 Magnolia Boulevard
North Hollywood
(818) 487-9531 (Chinese Morrocan
   Sushi)

Coffee Bean and Tea Leaf Coffee
   Houses
various locations

Cohen's Restaurant
316 East Pico Boulevard
(213) 742-8888

Creations by Chumie (Mrs. Vann)
   Catering
(818) 225-1405

Dan Michael's
7777 Sunset Boulevard
(213) 851-7557

David's
9303 West Pico Boulevard
(213) 859-7633

Dizengoff Restaurant
8107 Beverly Boulevard
(213) 651-4465

Drexler's Restaurant
12519½ Burbank Boulevard
(818) 984-1160

Elat Burger
9340 West Pico Boulevard
(310) 278-4692

Elegant Caterers
9030 West Olympic Boulevard
(310) 274-8856

*Elite Cuisine Restaurant
7119 Beverly Boulevard
(323) 930-1303

Embassy Caterers
(323) 937-1374

Fairfax Pizza
453 North Fairfax Avenue
(213) 653-7200

Falafel Village
16060 Ventura Boulevard
(818) 783-1012

Fish Grill
7226 Beverly Boulevard
(323) 937-7162

Fishing Well
8975 West Pico Boulevard
(213) 859-9429

Flora Falafel
12450 Burbank Boulevard
(818) 766-6567

*Glatt Hut
9303 West Pico Boulevard
(310) 246-1900

*Golan Restaurant
13075 Victory Boulevard
(818) 763-5375

Grill Express Restaurant
501 North Fairfax Avenue
(323) 655-0649

HaBayit Restaurant
11921 West Pico Boulevard
(310) 479-5444

Hadar
12514 Burbank Boulevard
(818) 762-1155

Haifa Restaurant
8717 West Pico Boulevard
(310) 888-7700

I'm-a-Deli
8930 West Pico Boulevard
(213) 274-2452

Jeff's Gourmet Kosher Sausage
8930 West Pico Boulevard
(310) 858-8590

Jerusalem Pizza
17942 Ventura Boulevard
(818) 758-9595

*Judy's La Petite
129 North La Brea Avenue
(323) 934-7667

Kabob and Chinese Food
9503 West Pico Boulevard
(310) 274-4407

Kinaret
18046 Ventura Boulevard
Encino
(818) 609-0599

Kolah Farengi Kabob and Chinese Food
9180 West Pico Boulevard
(310) 274-4007
11330 Santa Monica Boulevard
(310) 914-3040

Kosher Bite
8626 West Pico Boulevard
(310) 659-5982

Kosher Kettle
17614 Ventura Boulevard
Encino
(818) 995-1484

Kosher Kolonel
9301 West Pico Boulevard
(213) 858-0111

Kosher Nostra
365 South Fairfax Avenue
(213) 655-1994

Kosher on Location
11852 Vose Street
(818) 759-5222 (mobile kitchens)

Kosher Pizza Nosh
8844 West Pico Boulevard
(213) 276-8708

La Brea Bagel Company
7308 Beverly Boulevard
(323) 965-1287

La Gondola Ristorante Italiano
6405 Wilshire Boulevard
(323) 852-1915

La Mamounia
370 North Fairfax Avenue
(213) 930-1891 (Moroccan)

La Pizza
12515 Burbank Boulevard
(818) 760-8198

Lax Catering
(213) 934-1638

Le Chaim Catering
(323) 654-1683

Little Israel
18038 Ventura Boulevard
(818) 609-1001

Little Jerusalem
8971 West Pico Boulevard
(213) 858-8361

Magic Carpet Restaurant
8566 West Pico Boulevard
(310) 652-8507

Maison Gourmet Restaurant and Bakery
9618 West Pico Boulevard
(310) 248-4822

Menorah Restaurant
306 West Fifth Street
(213) 489-3954

Metro Glatt Restaurant
8975 West Pico Boulevard
(310) 275-4420

*Micheline's
2627 South La Cienega Boulevard
(310) 204-5334

*Milk N' Honey
8837 West Pico Boulevard
(310) 470-4860 (dairy)

Milky Way
9108 West Pico Boulevard
(310) 859-0004 (dairy; owned and
    managed by Steven Spielberg's
    mother Mrs. Adler)

Mrs. Pickles Kosher Deli
13354 Washington Boulevard
(310) 823-8156

Nagila Meating Place
9407 West Pico Boulevard
(310) 788-0119

Nagila Pizza
9411 West Pico Boulevard
(310) 788-0111

Narkiss
509½ Fairfax Avenue
(213) 655-0332

Nathan's Famous
9216 West Pico Boulevard
(310) 273-0303

*Nessim's
8939 West Pico Boulevard
(310) 859-9429

Noah's Bagels
9618 West Pico Boulevard
(310) 288-0319

Nosh N'Rye
12422 Burbank Boulevard
(818) 760-7694

Olé
7912 Beverly Boulevard
(213) 933-7254

Pacific Pizza
12460 Oxnard Street
(818) 760-0087

Pasha Restaurant
112 West Ninth Street
(213) 622-7578

*Pat's
9233 West Pico Boulevard
(310) 205-8705

Perfect Pizza
415 North Fairfax Avenue
(213) 651-5330

Pico Café
8944 West Pico Boulevard
(310) 385-0592 (dairy
vegetarian)

Pico Deli
8826 West Pico Boulevard
(310) 273-9381

Picolo
8706 West Pico Boulevard
(310) 854-3030 (Middle Eastern)

Pizza Delight
435 North Fairfax Avenue
(323) 655-7800

Pizza Maven
140 North La Brea Avenue
(323) 857-0353

Pizza Station
8965 West Pico Boulevard
(310) 276-8708

Pizza World
365 South Fairfax Avenue
(323) 653-2896

Rami's
17736½ Sherman Way
(818) 342-0611 (Middle Eastern,
    Mexican, Italian)

Rimini
9400 West Olympic Boulevard
(310) 552-1056

Royal Glatt
855 South Santee Street
(213) 623-0033

Serravalle
8837 West Pico Boulevard
(213) 550-8372

Shady Sason Catering
(310) 659-5982

Shalom Hunan
5651 Wilshire Boulevard
(213) 934-0505

Shalom Pizza
8715 West Pico Boulevard
(310) 271-2255

*Sharon's
18608½ Ventura Boulevard
(818) 344-7472

Sharon's II
306 East Ninth Street
(213) 622-1010

*Shimon's La Glatt
446 North Fairfax Avenue
(323) 658-7730

Shula and Ester
519 North Fairfax Avenue
(323) 653-9024

Simon's Catering
(323) 961-7271; (323) 961-7272

Simon's Restaurant
17614 Ventura Boulevard
Encino
(818) 995-1484
8706 West Pico Boulevard
(310) 657-5552
914 South Hill Street
(213) 627-6535

Sinai Catering
12233 Santa Monica Boulevard
(310) 820-0048

Solomon's Kitchen
934 South Los Angeles Street
(213) 623-3653

Star Restaurant
1335 South Santee Street
(213) 746-4464

Tami's Fish House
533 North Fairfax Avenue
(213) 655-7953

Tiberias Restaurant
18046 Ventura Boulevard
Encino
(818) 343-3705 (Middle Eastern)

Unique Café
18381 Ventura Boulevard
(818) 757-8100

Kosher kitchens and catering are available at the Beverly Grand Hotel, 7257 Beverly Boulevard, Los Angeles (213) 939-1633; the Four Seasons Hotel, 300 South Doheny Drive, Los Angeles, (310) 273-2222; and Loew's Santa Monica Beach Hotel, 1700 Ocean Avenue, Santa Monica, (310) 458-6700.

Mendocino

Ravens at the Stanford Inn by the Sea
44850 Comptche Ukiah Road
(707) 937-5615

Oakland/Berkeley

Holyland Deli
677 Rand Street
(510) 272-0535

Oakland Kosher Deli and Take Out
3419 Lakeshore Avenue
(510) 839-0177

Oakland Kosher Foods and Deli
5640 College Avenue
(510) 653-8902

*Ristorante Raphael
2132 Center Street
Berkeley
(510) 644-9500

Palo Alto

Izzy's Brooklyn Bagels
477 California Avenue
(650) 329-0700

Meekk's
655 Arastradero Road
(650) 424-3900

San Diego

Del Mar University City Garden Taste
1237 Camino del Mar
(858) 793-1500 (vegetarian)

Eva's Fresh and Natural
6717 El Cajon Boulevard
(619) 462-5018 (vegetarian)

Glatt Kosher B.B.Q.
3813 Governor Drive
(858) 455-1670

Lang's Loaf Take Out and Bakery
6165 El Cajon Boulevard
(619) 287-7306

Le Marais
8861 Villa de la Jolla Drive
La Jolla
(858) 658-9445

Mossarello's Pizza Restaurant
6663 El Cajon Boulevard
(619) 668-0643

*Sheila's Café and Bakery
4577 Clairmont Drive
(858) 270-0251 (also supplies kosher
   meals to local hotels)

Shmoozers Kosher Dairy
6366 El Cajon Boulevard
(619) 583-1636 (pizza, Mexican,
   Italian, Israeli)

Western Kosher New York Deli
7739 Fay Avenue
La Jolla
(619) 454-6328

San Francisco

Café de la Terrace
5217 Geary Boulevard
(415) 379-9588

Lotus Garden
532 Grant Avenue
(415) 397-0707

Sabra Grill
419 Grant Avenue
(415) 982-3656 (Israeli,
Middle Eastern)

Shangri-La Chinese Vegetarian
   Restaurant
2026 Irving Street
(415) 731-2548

Shirat-Ha-Ya Fish Grill
420 Geary Street
(415) 776-2683

Tella's Pastry Café
446 Columbus Avenue
(415) 986-2914

This Is It
430 Geary Street
(415) 749-0201 (Israeli)

San Jose

Isaac's Kosher Catering and Take Out
1504 Meridian Avenue
(408) 623-2384

Willow Glen Deli
1185 Lincoln Avenue
(408) 297-6604

Colorado

Denver

East Side Kosher Deli
5475 Leetsdale Drive
(303) 322-9862

Elegance by Andrew
745 Quebec Street
(303) 388-8883

JCC Snack Bar
4800 East Alameda Avenue
(303) 399-2660

Johnny's Pizza
934 South Monaco Parkway
(303) 399-6666

Mediterranean Health Café
2817 East Third Avenue
(303) 399-2940

Pete's Kosher Pizza
5606 East Cedar Street
(303) 355-5777

Connecticut

New Haven

Claire's Corner Copia
1000 Chapel Street
(203) 562-3888 (natural foods,
  vegetarian)

Edge of the Woods
379 Whalley Avenue
(203) 782-1055 (health food)

*Westville Kosher Deli
95 Amity Road
(203) 389-1166

Stamford

Delicate-Essen
111 High Ridge Road
(203) 316-5570

Garelick and Herb Thyme for Kosher
1035 Newfield Avenue

West Hartford

JCC Snack Bar
1035 Newfield Avenue
(860) 329-7862

Paul's Kosher Café/JCC Snack Bar
335 Bloomfield Avenue
(860) 236-4571

District of Columbia and Vicinity

Archives
1101 Pennsylvania Avenue N.W.
(202) 639-0400

Ben Yehuda Pizza
1370B Lamberton Drive
Silver Spring,
Maryland
(301) 681-8900

Center City Café Express
Washington JCC
Q Street Lobby
(202) 387-3246

East Side Kosher Deli
2161 Industrial Parkway
Silver Spring,
Maryland
(301) 622-9300

Max's Kosher Café
2319 University Boulevard West
Silver Spring,
Maryland
(301) 949-6297

*Stacks Delicatessen
1101 Pennsylvania Avenue
N.W.
(202) 628-9700

The following Washington area hotels maintain separate kosher kitchens for group reservations and catered events: Capital Hilton, Sixteenth and K Streets, N.W., (202) 393-1000; Washington Hilton and Towers, 1919 Connecticut Avenue, N.W., (202) 483-3000; Grand Hyatt, 1000 H Street, N.W., (202) 582-1234; Park Hyatt, Twenty-Fourth and M Streets, N.W., (202) 789-1234; Holiday Inn Bethesda, 8120 Wisconsin Avenue, Bethesda, Maryland, (301) 352-4525; Fairview Park Marriott, 3111 Fairview Park Drive, Falls Church, Virginia, (703) 849-0730; Washington Renaissance, 999 Ninth Street, N.W., (202) 898-9000; Stouffer Renaissance Mayflower, 1127 Connecticut Avenue, N.W., (202) 347-3000; Sheraton Washington, 2600 Woodley Road, N.W., (202) 328-2000.

Florida

Boca Raton

Café Haifa (in the King David Hotel and Spa)
2901 North Federal Highway
(561) 955-8500

City Deli and Grill
7158 North Beracasa Way
(561) 417-8986

Eilat Café International
6853 S.W. Eighteenth Street
(561) 368-6880

Essen Essen Peking
15200 Carter Road
(561) 495-8661

Jerusalem Grill
19635 State Road 7
(561) 470-1120

Jon's Place
22191 Powerline Road
(561) 338-0008

Mahzon Tov Mandarin
5046 West Atlantic Avenue
(561) 496-6278

Sagi's Falafel Armon
22767 State Road 7
(561) 477-0633

Sara's Dairy Restaurant
1898 West Hillsboro Boulevard
(954) 427-2272

Fort Lauderdale

Bagelmania
7632 West Commercial Boulevard
(305) 748-5088

Baraka Restaurant
3025 North Ocean Boulevard
(954) 567-2525

Fressor's Pizza and Pasta
3327 East Oakland Boulevard
(954) 564-0730

JCS/Gourmet Kosher Meals
3260 S.W. Eleventh Avenue

Kosher Café
5485 North University Drive
(305) 572-3010

Sunrise Kosher
8330 West Oakland Park Boulevard
(954) 741-0855

Thai Taste
2430 North University Drive
(954) 748-7782

Hollywood

Jerusalem II
5650 Stirling Road
(954) 964-6811

My Favorite Café
3369 Sheridan Street
(954) 965-0111

Pinati Restaurant
2832 Stirling Road
(954) 929-2290

Miami Beach and Vicinity

Aroma Kosher Restaurant
9415 Hardy Avenue
Surfside
(305) 805-0693

Aviva's Kitchen
16355 West Dixie Highway
North Miami Beach
(305) 944-7313

Bagel Time Restaurant
3915 Alton Road
(305) 538-0300

Beethoven Restaurant (in the Sasson
    Hotel)
2001 Collins Avenue
(305) 531-0761

Bissaleh's Café
17608 Collins Avenue
North Miami Beach
(305) 682-2224

Cine City Café
9544 Harding Avenue
(305) 866-8688

Coifiocchi
9477 Harding Avenue
Surfside
(305) 866-7415

Crown Buffet and Dairy Bar (in the
    Crown Hotel)
4041 Collins Avenue
(305) 531-5771

David's Glatt Kosher Deli
1790 N.E. Miami Gardens
Miami
(305) 944-4068

David's Shai King
5599 North University Drive
North Miami Beach
(305) 572-6522

Embassy Peking Tower Suite
4101 Pinetree Drive
(305) 538-7550

Embassy 41
534 Forty-First Street
(305) 534-7550

Europa Grill (in the Castle Beach Club)
5445 Collins Avenue
(305) 865-5757

Famous Pita Hut
1728 Collins Avenue
North Miami Beach
(305) 945-6573

Frieze
1626 Michigan Avenue
(305) 538-0207 (homemade ice cream)

Galleria Restaurant (in the Versailles
    Hotel)
Thirty-Fourth Street and Collins Avenue
(305) 672-4233

Getty's Hungarian Kitchen
6565 Collins Avenue
(305) 865-4893

Giuliana's Café
3439 N.E. 163rd Street
North Miami Beach
(305) 940-8141

Giusseppe Goldberg's (in the Sans
    Souci Hotel)
3101 Collins Avenue
(305) 531-8261

Hamifgash Restaurant
17044 West Dixie Highway
North Miami Beach
(305) 947-4946

Harissa Café (in the Ramada Marco
    Polo Hotel)
19201 Collins Avenue
North Miami Beach
(305) 932-2233

Issac's Kosher Kitchen
16460 N.E. Sixteenth Avenue
North Miami Beach
(305) 944-5222

Jerusalem Peking (in the Days Inn)
4299 Collins Avenue
(305) 532-2263

Jerusalem Pizza
761 N.E. 167th Street
North Miami Beach
(305) 653-6662

Kaifeng Chinese
18117 N.E. Nineteenth Avenue
North Miami Beach
(305) 940-6500

Kikar Tel-Aviv (in the Carriage Club)
5005 Collins Avenue
(305) 866-3316

King David Restaurant
1339 Washington Avenue
(305) 534-0197

Kosher Kingdom
3715 Aventura Boulevard
North Miami Beach
(305) 792-7988

Kosher Ranch
740 Forty-First Street
(305) 856-7437

Kosher Treats
1682 N.E. 164th Street
North Miami Beach
(305) 947-1800

Kosher World
514 Forty-First Street
(305) 532-2210

Mexico Bravo Glatt Kosher
16850 Collins Avenue
Sunny Isles Beach
(305) 945-1999

Miami Pita
175 Sunny Isles Boulevard
North Miami Beach
(305) 940-4007

My Chosen Delight
7146 S.W. 117th Avenue
(305) 596-5223

New Time Moroccan and Spanish
   Restaurant
2120 N.E. 123rd Street
North Miami Beach
(305) 891-6336

Noshery (in the Saxony Hotel)
3201 Collins Avenue
(305) 538-6811

Ocean Terrace Restaurant and Grill
   (in the Crown Hotel)
4041 Collins Avenue
(305) 531-5771

Original Pita Hut
534 Forty-First Street
(305) 531-6090

Original Steakhouse
530 Forty-First Street
(305) 534-4144

Pianeta Kosher Argentine Style Steak
   House
3207 N.E. 163rd Street
North Miami Beach
(305) 947-8711

Pinati Restaurant
2520 N.E. 186th Street
North Miami Beach
(305) 931-8086

Pineapple's Natural Health Food
   Restaurant
530 Forty-First Street
(305) 523-9731

Pita King
343 East Flagler Street
(305) 358-0386

Pita Loca
601 Collins Avenue
(305) 673-3388

Pita Plus
20103 Biscayne Boulevard
North Miami Beach
(305) 935-0761

Royal Hungarian Kosher Restaurant
3425 Collins Avenue
(305) 532-8566

Sara's Natural Food Restaurant and
     Kosher Kitchen
2214 N.E. 123rd Street
North Miami Beach
(305) 891-3312

Sara's Pizza
1127 N.E. 163rd Street
North Miami Beach

Shalom Haifa
18533 West Dixie Highway
Aventura
(305) 936-1800
1330 N.E. 113th Street
North Miami Beach
(305) 945-2884

Shalom Tokyo
501 Collins Avenue
(305) 866-6039

Shem Tov's Pizza
514 Forty-First Street
(305) 538-2123

South Beach Pita
1448 Washington Avenue
(305) 534-3706

Subrific
1688 N.E. 164th Street
(305) 949-7811

Surfside Café
9490 Harding Avenue, Surfside
(305) 867-3151

Surfside Kosher Deli
9517 Harding Avenue, Surfside
(305) 868-0559

Tasti-D-Lite Café
4041 Royal Palm Avenue
(305) 673-5483

Tea for Two
1205 Seventeenth Street
(305) 672-0565

Thai Treat
2176 N.E. 123rd Street
North Miami Beach
(305) 892-1118

*Toni Guichi's Place Japanese
     Restaurant
2224 N.E. 123rd Street
North Miami Beach
(305) 892-6744

Wing Wang
1640 N.E. 164th Street
North Miami Beach
(305) 945-3585

Yonni's Italian Restaurant and Bakery
19802 West Dixie Highway
North Miami Beach
(305) 932-1961

Yo Si Peking (in the Eden Roc
     Resort and Spa)
4525 Collins Avenue
(305) 532-9060

Yummi Miami
18090 Collins Avenue
Sunny Isles Beach
(305) 792-5500

Orlando

Elaine's Café
3716 Howell Branch Road
(407) 679-9000

*Kosher Korner
4944 West Irlo
Bronson Memorial Highway
Kissimee
(407) 787-3344
http://www.kosherkorner.com

Lower East Side Glatt Kosher Restaurant
4846 Palm Parkway
(407) 465-0565
http://www.kosherOrlando.com

Saint Petersburg

Jo-El's Café
1619 Twenty-Third Avenue North
(727) 321-3847

West Palm Beach

Four Seasons Restaurant
2800 South Ocean Boulevard
(561) 582-2800

Georgia

Atlanta

Atlanta JCC
1745 Peachtree Road
N.E.
(404) 875-7881

Bagel Break
6444 Roswell Road
Sandy Springs
(404) 255-6055

Bijan Catering
3130 Raymond Drive N.E.
(770) 457-4578

*Broadway Café
2166 Briarcliff Road
(404) 329-0888 (vegetarian)

Café Ofi
5342 Tilly Mill Road
(770) 396-3250

Chai Peking (in the Toco Hills Kroger)
2205 La Vista Road
(404) 633-8694

Elegant Essen Catering
425 Pleasant Hill Road
Liburn
(770) 925-3105

Pita Palace
1658 Lavista Road
(404) 781-PITA

Pizza Palace
2157 Briarcliff Road
(404) 477-4992

Quality Kosher Emporium
2153 Briarcliff Road
(404) 636-1114

Wall Street Pizza
2470 Briarcliff Road
(404) 633-2111

The following Atlanta hotels have kosher catering facilities: Atlanta Marriott Perimeter, 246 Perimeter Center Parkway, N.E., (770) 698-6433; Doubletree Hotel, 7 Concourse Parkway, N.E., (770) 395-3900; Crown Plaza Ravina, 4355 Ashford Dunwoody Road, N.E., (770) 395-7700; Sheraton Colony Square, 188 Fourteenth Street, N.E., (404) 892-6000; Swishotel, 3391 Peachtree Road, N.E., (404) 365-0065; Westin Atlanta North at Perimeter, 7 Concourse Parkway, N.E., (770) 395-3937.

Illinois

Chicago and Vicinity

*A Beautiful Taste Take Out
3411 Dempster Street
Skokie
(847) 677-3663

Bagel Country
9306 Skokie Boulevard
Skokie
(847) 673-3030

Best's Kosher Express Deli/Sinai Kosher
  Foods
1000 Pershing Road
(773) 650-6330

Bugsy's Charhouse
3353 Dempster Street
Skokie
(847) 679-4030

Da'Nali's
4032 Oakton Street
Skokie
(847) 677-2782

Danziger Kosher Caterers
(847) 982-1818

*Delectables Unlimited
2732 West Farwell Street
(773) 761-9613

Falafel King
4507 West Oakton Street
Skokie
(847) 677-6020

Goldman-Segal Kosher Caterers
Evanston
(847) 338-4060

Great Chicago Food and Beverage Co.
3149 West Devon Avenue
(773) 469-9030

Hy Life Bistro
4120 West Dempster Street
Skokie
(847) 674-2021

Jerusalem Café
3014 West Devon Avenue
(773) 262-0515

Ken's Diner
3353 Dempster Street
Skokie
(847) 679-2850

King Solomon
3445 Dempster Street
Skokie
(847) 677-0700

*Kirshner Cuisine/Sabta's Kitchen
2839 West Touhy Avenue
(773) 465-3636
2905 West Fitch Street
(773) 465-6247

Kosher City Deli and Grill
3353 Dempster Street
Skokie
(847) 679-2850

Kosher Gourmet
3552 Dempster Street
Skokie
(847) 679-0432 (Chinese)

Kosher Gourmet Caterers
Skokie
(847) 679-0597

Main Pizza
4209 Main Street
Skokie
(847) 568-9920

Marrakesh
3334 West Dempster Street
Skokie
(847) 676-1948

Mi Tsu Yan Restaurant
3010 West Devon Avenue
(773) 262-4630

Polski Kosher Caterers
2732 West Farwell Street
(773) 539-2288

Ronnie's
3517 West Dempster Street
Skokie
(847) 763-8181

Selig's Kosher Deli
209 Skokie Valley Road
Highland Park
(708) 831-5560

Shallots
2324 North Clark Street
(773) 755-5205

Slice of Life
4120 West Dempster Street
Skokie
(847) 674-2021

Ta'boun Grill
6339 North California Street
(773) 381-2606

Tel Aviv Kosher Pizza and Dairy
Restaurant
6349 North California Avenue
(773) 764-3776

The following Chicago hotels have their own kosher kitchens: Chicago Hilton and Towers, 720 South Michigan Avenue, (312) 922-4400; Fairmont Hotel, 200 North Columbus Drive, (312) 565-8000; Hyatt Regency, 151 East Wacker Drive, (312) 565-1234; North Shore Hilton, 9599 Skokie Boulevard, Skokie, (708) 679-7000; Palmer House Hilton, 171 East Monroe Street, (312) 726-7500.

Kansas

Overland Park (Kansas City area)

Irv's Kosher Deli and Market
10334 Metcalf Avenue
(913) 385-7474

JCC Snack Bar
5801 West 115th Street
(913) 451-1660

Louisiana

New Orleans

Casablanca
3030 Severn Avenue
Metairie
(504) 888-2209

Creole Kosher Kitchen
115 Chartres Street
(504) 529-4120

*Kosher Cajun Deli and Grocery
3520 North Hullen Street
(504) 888-2010

Maryland

Baltimore

Brasserie at Pomona/Pomona Square
Chapps
1700 Reisterstown Road
(410) 484-0476

Café Shalom (in Sinai Hospital)
2401 West Belvedere Avenue
(410) 601-5000

Camden Yards
(410) 539-5077 (kosher food stand)

Caramel's
700 Reisterstown Road (gourmet ice
cream and coffee bar)

Catering by Yaffa
4311 Old Milford Mill Road
(410) 486-3325

Daniell's Cuisine
401 Reistertown Road
(410) 486-1487

David Chu's China Bistro
7105 Reisterstown Road
(410) 602-5008

Ester Catering
6312 Benhurst Road
(410) 358-2306

Goldberg's N.Y. Bagels
708-10 Reisterstown Road
(410) 415-8001

KB Szechuan
6309 Reisterstown Road
(410) 358-6349

Knish Shop
508 Reisterstown Road
(410) 484-5850

*Kosher Bite
6309 Reisterstown Road
(410) 358-6349

Liebes Kosher Deli and Take Out
607 Reisterstown Road
(410) 613-1977

Mama Leah's Gourmet Pizza
1852 Reisterstown Road
(410) 653-7600

Metro Stop Deli
105 East Baltimore Street
(410) 727-6224

*Milk and Honey Bistro
1777 Reisterstown Road
(410) 486-4344

O'Fishel Restaurant and Caterers
509 Reisterstown Road
(410) 764-3474

Orly Caterers
3130 Northbrook Road
(877) ORLY-TLC

Ravens Stadium (kosher food stand)

*Royal Restaurant
7002A Reisterstown Road
(410) 484-3544

Sabra Grill
102 Reisterstown Road
(410) 580-9477

Tov Pizza
6313 Reisterstown Road
(410) 358-5238

Weiss Acquisition Caterers
Owings Mills
(443) 394-8338

Kosher catering services are available at the Hyatt Regency on the Inner Harbor, 300 Light Street, (410) 528-1234, and at the Sheraton Inner Harbor Hotel, 300 South Charles Street, (410) 962-8300.

Rockville

Katz's Café
4860 Boiling Brook Parkway
(301) 468-0400

Royal Dragon
4830 Boiling Brook Parkway
(301) 468-1922

Wheaton

Nuthouse and Pizza
11419 Georgia Avenue
(301) 942-5900

Shaul's Deli
2503 Ennalls Avenue
(301) 949-8477 (dairy)

Massachusetts
Boston and Vicinity

Café Eilat
406 Harvard Street
Brookline
(617) 277-7770

*Café Shiraz
1030 Commonwealth Avenue
Brookline
(617) 566-8888 (Persian and Middle
  Eastern cuisine)

Catering by Andrew
404A Harvard Street
Brookline
(617) 731-6585

G & T Catering
42 Pines Road
Worcester
(508) 791-8443

Hain's Kosher Deli
1657 Beacon Street
Brookline
(617) 734-8350

Hurwitz Deli
326 Concord Street
Framingham
(508) 733-7375

Kosher Cuisine by Tova
80 Brook Road
Sharon
(781) 784-5162

JCC Snack Bar (Sweetberry Café)
333 Nahanton Street
Newton
(617) 965-8513

JCC Snack Bar
65 Nahant Avenue
Revere
(617) 284-8395

Meyer's Kosher Kitchen
176 Shirley Avenue
Revere
(617) 289-2063

Milk Street Café
50 Milk Street
(617) 542-2433
Congress and Franklin Streets
(617) 350-7275

NRM Catering
160 Herrick Road
Newton
(617) 559-8822

Ora Catering
310 Summit Avenue
Brighton
(617) 566-2147

Pastry Land 'N' More
417 Harvard Street
Brookline
(617) 278-2400 (sandwiches, baked
  goods)

Provender Caterers
(781) 871-1364

Rami's Restaurant
324 Harvard Street
Brookline
(617) 738-3577

Rami's II Restaurant
341 Cochiute Road
Framingham
(508) 370-3577

Rubin's Kosher Delicatessen and
  Restaurant
500 Harvard Street
Brookline
(617) 566-8761

Ruth's Kitchen
401 Harvard Street
Brookline
(617) 734-9810

Shalom Hunan
92 Harvard Street
Brookline
(617) 731-9760

Taam China
423 Harvard Street
Brookline
(617) 264-7274

The following Boston hotels have kosher kitchens available for catered events: Four Seasons Hotel, 200 Boylston Street, (617) 338-4400; Hyatt Regency Cambridge, 575 Memorial Drive, (617) 492-1234; Westin Hotel, Copley Place, (617) 262-9600.

Springfield

Harvest Tyme
1312 Memorial Avenue
(413) 733-7375

Michigan
Detroit and Vicinity

Café Katon
23005 Coolidge Road
Oak Park
(810) 547-3581

JCC Restaurant and Snack Bar
6600 West Maple Road
West Bloomfield
(810) 661-1000

New York Pizza World
15280 Lincoln (10.5 Mile Road)
Oak Park
(810) 968-2102

Sara's Deli
15600 West 10 Mile Road
Southfield
(810) 443-2425

Taste of Class
25254 Greenfield Road
Oak Park
(248) 967-6020

Unique Kosher Carryout
25270 Greenfield Road
Oak Park
(810) 967-1161

Minnesota
Minneapolis

Breadsmith
3939 West Fiftieth Street
(952) 920-2278

Kosher in the Park (inside Chi's Market)
4000 Minnetonka Boulevard
(612) 920-4144

Newkirk's Calypso Café
3238 West Lake Street
(612) 929-6245

Saint Paul

JCC Snack Bar
1375 Saint Paul Avenue
(612) 698-0751

Old City Café
1571 Grand Avenue
(612) 699-5347

Missouri
Saint Louis

Adventures Unlimited Catering
(314) 426-4477

Empire Steak Building
8600 Olive Street Road
(314) 993-9977

Kohn's Kosher Deli
10405 Old Olive Street
(314) 569-0727

Kosher Hangar Restaurant (inside the
  Marriott Airport Hotel)
Lambert International Airport
(314) 423-9700

Lazy Susan Catering
(314) 291-6050

No Bull Café
10477 Old Olive Street Road
(314) 991-9533 (vegetarian)

Peking II
8206 Delmar Boulevard
(314) 727-3387

Reservations Catering
(314) 205-2900

*Simon Kohn Enterprises
10424 Old Olive Street Road
(314) 569-0727

*Sol's
8627 Olive Street Road
(314) 993-9977

The following Saint Louis hotels are available for kosher catering: Adam Mark Hotel, Fourth and Chestnut Streets, (314) 241-7400; Frontenac Hilton, 1335 South Lindbergh Street, Frontenac, (314) 993-1100; Hyatt Regency, 1 Saint Louis Street, Union Station, (314) 231-1234; Marriott Airport Hotel, Lambert International Airport, (314) 423-9700; Ritz-Carleton, 100 Carondelet Plaza, Clayton, (314) 863-6300.

Nevada

Las Vegas

Adar Kosher Pizza and Restaurant
318 West Sahara Avenue
(702) 385-0006

Casba
855 East Twain Avenue
(702) 791-3344

Haifa Restaurant
855 East Twain Avenue
(702) 791-1956

Jerusalem Kosher Restaurant and Deli
1305 Vegas Valley Drive
(702) 696-1644

Las Vegas Deli and Internet Café
3317 Las Vegas Boulevard
(702) 892-9080

Shalom Hunan
4850 West Flamingo Road
(702) 871-3262

New Jersey

Atlantic County

Jerusalem Kosher Restaurant
6410 Ventnor Avenue
Ventnor
(609) 822-2266

Shari's Steakhouse (at the Clarion
  Hotel)
6821 Black Horse Pike
Egg Harbor
(609) 272-8822

Bergen County

Al's Kosher Deli
209 Marin Street
Fort Lee
(201) 461-3044

Chopstix
172 West Englewood Avenue
Teaneck
(201) 833-0200

Dougie's BBQ and Grill
184 West Englewood Avenue
Teaneck
(201) 833-6000

Eighth Day Caterers
396 Newbridge Road
Bergenfield
(201) 214-0803

EJ's Pizza
1448 Queen Anne Road
Teaneck
(201) 862-0611

Fish Grill
16 West Palisades Avenue
Englewood
(201) 227-6182

Five Star Kosher Caterers
117 Fort Lee Road
Leonia
(201) 585-9781

*Foster Village Kosher Deli
469 South Washington Avenue
Bergenfield
(201) 384-7100

Grill Street
184 West Englewood Avenue
Teaneck
(201) 833-0001

Fliegels
456 Cedar Lane
Teaneck
(201) 692-8060

Foremost Glatt Kosher Caterers
58 Jefferson Avenue
Westwood
(201) 664-2465

Hunan Teaneck
515 Cedar Lane
Teaneck
(201) 692-0099

JC Pizza
14-20 Plaza Road
Fair Lawn
(201) 703-0801

JC Pizza at Jerusalem
24 West Palisades Avenue
Englewood
(201) 569-5546

Jerusalem Pizza
496 Cedar Lane
Teaneck
(201) 836-2120

Kosher Designers Caterers
Fair Lawn
(201) 791-0518

Kosher Memories Caterers
172 State Street
Teaneck
(201) 837-0111

Kosher Nosh
894 Prospect Street
Glen Rock
(201) 445-1186

Lazy Bean Café
1404 Queen Anne Road
Teaneck
(201) 837-BEAN

Ma'bat Steak House
540 Cedar Lane
Teaneck
(201) 836-4115

Main Event Caterers
26 West Forest Avenue
Englewood
(201) 894-8710

New Wave Café
22-08 Morlot Avenue
Fair Lawn
(201) 791-8810

*Noah's Ark
493 Cedar Lane
Teaneck
(201) 692-1200

On the Grill
1409 Palisades Avenue
Teaneck
(201) 837-1111

Perfect Platters Caterers
260 Grand Avenue
Englewood
(201) 227-1661

Plaza Pizza and Restaurant
1431 Queen Anne Road
Teaneck
(201) 837-9500

Piccanti
1409 Palisade Avenue
Teaneck
(201) 837-1111

Pizza Cave
439 Cedar Lane
Teaneck
(201) 836-1700

Pizza Pros
1448 Queen Anne Road
Teaneck
(201) 862-0611

PK Café and Pizza at the JCC
411 East Clinton Avenue
Tenafly
(201) 894-0801

Rabica Restaurant Café
192 West Englewood Avenue
Teaneck
(201) 837-7558

Sergi's Café at the Bergen Y/JCC
605 Pascack Road
Washington Township
(201) 666-6610

Shelly's Vegetarian Restaurant
482 Cedar Lane
Teaneck
(201) 692-0001

Sol and Sol
34 East Palisades Avenue
Englewood
(201) 541-6880

Sushi Metsuyan
102 West Englewood Avenue
Teaneck
(201) 837-8000 (Japenese fusion
    steakhouse and sushi)

*Tenafly Kosher Deli
22 Washington Street
Tenafly
(201) 567-3033

Veggie Heaven Chinese Restaurant
473 Cedar Lane
Teaneck
(201) 836-0887

Essex County

David's Decotessen
555 Passaic Avenue
West Caldwell
(201) 808-3354

Jerusalem Restaurant
99–101 West Mount Pleasant Avenue
Livingston
(973) 533-1424

Reuben's Glatt Spot
659 Eagle Rock Avenue
West Orange
(973) 736-0060

Hudson County

Kosher Kiosks
Giants Stadium
Secaucus (located at Gate D on both
    upper and lower levels)

Middlesex County

Elite Caterers
271 U.S. Highway 1 South
Edison
(732) 985-6363

Jerusalem Pizza
231 Raritan Avenue
Highland Park
(908) 249-0070

Mei Garden
229 Raritan Avenue
Highland Park
(732) 418-1881

Orchid
455 Main Street
Metuchen
(732) 321-9829

Monmouth County

Bagel Nosh
380 Clifton Avenue
Lakewood
(732) 363-1115

Bistro Entre Nous
2680 Norwood Avenue
Deal
(732) 660-0076

Chang Mao Sakura Chinese/Japanese
Restaurant
214 Roosevelt Avenue
Oakhurst
(732) 517-8889

Grill House
100 Route 9 North
Manalapan
(732) 863-7339

J Café
100 Grant Avenue
Deal
(732) 531-9100

Jerusalem Restaurant
106 Norwood Avenue
Deal
(732) 531-7936

Kosher Chinese Express
335 Route 9 South
Manalapan
(732) 866-1677

Levy's Kosher Pizza and Pasta
335 Route 9 South
Manalapan
(732) 683-9978

Little Israel
116 Norwood Avenue
Deal
(732) 531-1404

Poppy's
65 Monmouth Road
Monmouth
(732) 263-9100

Slices
250 Norwood Avenue
Monmouth
(732) 531-6811

Morris County

Beck's Best Deli
76 North Beverwyck Road
Lake Hiawatha
(973) 263-9515

Passaic County

China Pagoda/Chopstix of Passaic
227 Main Avenue
Passaic
(973) 777-4900

Kosher Kitchen
224 Brook Avenue
Passaic
(973) 614-0026

Somerset County

*East Side Deli and Restaurant
6 West Main Street
Somerville
(908) 927-0270

Lin's Kosher Chinese Restaurant
244 South Main Street
Manville
(908) 722-8668

Union County

Burgers and Bites
157 Elmora Avenue
Elizabeth
(908) 354-6777

New Kosher Chinese
163 Elmora Avenue
Elizabeth
(908) 353-1818

Reuben's Glatt Spot Kosher Deli
155 Elmora Avenue
Elizabeth
(908) 354-0448

The Newark Airport Hilton, 1170 Spring Street, Elizabeth, (908) 351-3900, has separate kosher catering facilities.

New York

Buffalo/Niagara Falls

Bert's Deli at University of Buffalo
3 Talbert Hall
(716) 645-2334

Juicery at the JCC
2640 North Forest Road
(716) 688-4033

Top's Kosher Deli and Grocery
North Bailey-Maple Road
(716) 515-0075

Long Island

Ackerstein Caterers
338 Hempstead Avenue
West Hempstead
(516) 538-6655

Aderet
726 Old Bethpage Road
Old Bethpage
(516) 293-3144 (dairy,
Middle Eastern)

*Ahava Fine Foods Café
82 Main Street
Westhampton
(631) 288-9800

Andel's of Roslyn Catering
350 Roslyn Road
Roslyn
(516) 621-9858

Anise
600 Central Avenue
Cedarhurst
(516) 797-2793

*Bagel Boss Café
432 South Oyster Bay Road
Hicksville
(516) 935-9079

for catering, (888) BOSSTIME

10 Jericho Turnpike
Jericho
(516) 334-0300

405 Merrick Road
Oceanside
(516) 766-1581

2101 Merrick Road
Merrick
(516) 379-2836

43 Old Country Road
Carle Place
(516) 248-1155

400 Willis Avenue
Roslyn Heights
(516) 626-5599

1011 Oyster Bay Road
East Norwich
(516) 624-0406

1941 Jericho Turnpike
East Northport
(631) 462-3922

10 Mayfair Shopping Center
Commack
(631) 864-2233

119 Alexander Avenue
Lake Grove
(631) 979-2233

Bagel Delight Restaurant
598 Central Avenue
Cedarhurst
(516) 374-7644

Bagel Mensch
176 Middle Neck Road
Great Neck
(516) 487-2243

*Bagel Town
488 Hempstead Avenue
West Hempstead
(516) 505-5556

Banim
135 Cedarhurst Avenue
Cedarhurst
(516) 374-4646

B.B.Q. Al Aish Steak House
76 Columbia Avenue
Cedarhurst
(516) 791-7085

Bellcrest Kosher Deli
2793 Merrick Road
Bellmore
(516) 785-8691

Bellcrest 3 Kosher Deli
1282 Hicksville Road
Seaford
(516) 797-0600

*Ben's Kosher Delicatessen
Wheatley Plaza
Greenvale
(516) 621-3340

95 Old Country Road
Carle Place
(516) 742-3354

235 Alexander Avenue
Lake Grove
(631) 979-8770

933 Atlantic Avenue
Baldwin
(516) 868-2072

7971 Jericho Turnpike
Woodbury
(516) 946-4236

*Ben's Kosher Restaurant
437 North Broadway
Jericho
(516) 939-2367

*Bistro Grill
132 Middle Neck Road
Great Neck
(516) 829-4428 (French,
    steakhouse, sushi)
1034 Broadway
Woodmere
(516) 829-4428

*Bon Appetit II Gourmet and Diet
    Cuisine
381 Willis Avenue
Rosyln Heights
(516) 621-0402

Burger Express
140 Washington Avenue
Lawrence
(516) 295-2040

Cedar Club
564 Central Avenue
Cedarhurst
(516) 374-1714

Central Kosher Deli
488 Central Avenue
Cedarhurst
(516) 374-3296

Central Perk Café
105 Central Avenue
Cedarhurst
(516) 374-6400 (dairy)

*Centro
564 Central Avenue
Cedarhurst
(516) 374-1714

*Chap-a-Nosh
410 Central Avenue
Cedarhurst
(516) 374-5100

Chattanooga
37 Cutter Mill Road
Great Neck
(516) 487-4455 (Persian)

*Cho-Sen Island
367 Central Avenue
Lawrence
(516) 374-1199

Colbeh Restaurant
75 North Station Plaza
Great Neck
(516) 466-8181

Dairy King
1564 Union Turnpike
New Hyde Park
(516) 437-7100

Dairy Revue
143 Washington Avenue
Cedarhurst
(516) 295-7417

Danny's Restaurant
624 Middle Neck Road
Great Neck
(516) 487-6666

David's Famous Pizza and Borekas
580 Central Avenue
Cedarhurst
(516) 295-6925

Deli Grill
136 Middle Neck Road
Great Neck
(516) 829-4426

Deli King
1570 Union Turnpike
New Hyde Park
(516) 437-8420

Del-Mir Caterers
96 Jerusalem Avenue
Massapequa
(516) 795-5900

Elite Pizza and Sushi
94 Middle Neck Road
Great Neck
(516) 466-2233

*5 Towns Deli
274 Burnside Avenue
Lawrence
(516) 239-1103

Four Winds
223 Commack Road
Commack
(516) 858-3920

Fressen Bombay Express
107 Broadway
Hicksville
(516) 939-6626 (Israeli, Indian,
    vegetarian)

*Great Neck Glatt Deli
501 Middle Neck Road
Great Neck
(516) 773-6328

Great Neck Kosher Pizza
770 Middle Neck Road
Great Neck
(516) 829-1660

Hapina
128 Cedarhurst Avenue
Cedarhurst
(516) 295-1800

Hunan
507 Middle Neck Road
Great Neck
(516) 482-7912

Hunki's Pizza
338 Hempstead Avenue
West Hempstead
(516) 538-6655

Jem Prestige Caterers
200 Southwoods Road
Woodbury
(516) 364-2000

Jerusalem Famous Pizza
244 Central Avenue
Cedarhurst
(516) 569-0074

Kay Caterers
111 Irving Place
Woodmere
(516) 374-5657

King David Delicatessen and Caterers
550 Central Avenue
Cedarhurst
(516) 569-2920

King Kosher Pizza
605 Middle Neck Road
Great Neck
(516) 482-0400

Kosher World Caterers
177 Hempstead Avenue
West Hempstead
(516) 489-2700

Kotimsky and Tuchman Catering
(516) 599-1330

K-Roasters
9 Cuttermill Road
Great Neck
(516) 487-3573
72 Columbia Avenue
Cedarhurst
(516) 791-5100

LaMaLo Grill
128 Cedarhurst Avenue
Cedarhurst
(516) 791-1216

La Pizzeria/Sushi Metsuyan
114 Middle Neck Road
Great Neck
(516) 466-5114

L'Chaim Catering
(845) 354-2626

Lido Deli
641 East Park Avenue
Long Beach
(516) 431-4411

Mauzone of Lawrence
341 Central Avenue
Cedarhurst
(516) 569-6411 (take-out only)

Max's Gourmet Kosher Appetizing
1016 Broadway
Woodmere
(516) 374-0617

Meir Kosher Pizzeria
426 Hawkins Avenue
Lake Ronkonkoma
(631) 467-3278

Millennium Catering
North Woodmere
(516) 791-3555

Mister Bagel
159 East Park Avenue
Long Beach
(516) 432-4242

Mitch's Grill
169 Hempstead Avenue
West Hempstead
(516) 505-4500

Model K Caterers
3445 Lawson Boulevard
Oceanside
(516) 766-2318

Mr. Omelette Caterers
3445 Lawson Boulevard
Oceanside
(516) 766-1884; (800) 625-6474

Natural Gourmet/Gourmet Grill
546 Central Avenue
Cedarhurst
(516) 374-1199
(516) 569-7609

Off the Grill
600 Central Avenue
Cedarhurst
(516) 569-4140

Pastrami 'n Friends
110A Commack Road
Commack
(631) 499-9537

Perfect Impressions Caterers
472 Mulberry Lane
West Hempstead
(516) 286-8633

Pizza Cave
580 Central Avenue
Cedarhurst
(516) 295-6925

Pizza Pious
18 East Park Avenue
Long Beach
(516) 431-1777
1063 Broadway
Woodmere
(516) 295-2050

Pizza Professor
684 Central Avenue
Cedarhurst
(516) 569-5000

President Caterers
1400 Prospect Avenue
East Meadow
(516) 483-4991
2860 Brower Avenue
Oceanside
(516) 536-6387

*Primavera
357 Central Avenue
Cedarhurst
(516) 374-5504 (dairy)

Prime Grill
10 Beach Road
Westhampton Beach
(516) 631-6970

*Ruven's Kosher Deli and Restaurant
357 South Oyster Bay Road
Plainview
(516) 931-8787

Sabra Kosher Pizza
560 Central Avenue
Cedarhurst
(516) 569-1563

Scharf Caterers
597A Willow Road
Cedarhurst
(516) 295-5959

*Schwartz 11 Appetizing
130 Cedarhurst Avenue
Cedarhurst
(516) 295-2957

Sharmel Catering
(516) 766-2700

Shish Kabob Palace
90 Middle Neck Road
Great Neck
(516) 487-2228

Shish Kabob Steak House
3216 Long Beach Road
Oceanside
(516) 766-0097

Shula's Pizza and Catering
60 Central Avenue
Cedarhurst
(516) 569-7408

Silver Caterers of the Five Towns
Broadway and Locust Avenue
Cedarhurst
(516) 791-2046
410 Hungry Harbor Road
North Woodmere
(800) 7-SILVER

Soprano's
1034 Broadway
Woodmere
(516) 792-9800
113 Middle Neck Road
Great Neck
(516) 482-0000

Starks Chinese Dynasty
2831 Merrick Road
Bellmore
(516) 221-1414

Sushi Metsuyan
488 Central Avenue
Cedarhurst
(516) 295-2700 (Japanese fusion
    steakhouse and sushi)

Toddy's Appetizers
436 Central Avenue
Cedarhurst
(516) 295-1999

*Traditions Restaurant
302 Central Avenue
Lawrence
(516) 295-3630

*Wing Wan
248 Hempstead Avenue
West Hempstead
(516) 292-9309

Wok
72-26 Columbia Avenue
Cedarhurst
(516) 791-5100
9 Cuttermill Road, Great Neck
(516) 487-3573

Wok Tov
594 Central Avenue
Cedarhurst
(516) 295-3843

Woodbury Glatt Kosher Catering
428 South Oyster Bay Road
Hicksville
(516) 681-7766

Woodro Kosher Restaurant and
    Caterers
1342 Peninsula Boulevard
Hewlett
(516) 791-4033
302 Cedarhurst Avenue
Cedarhurst
(516) 486-8181

Yossi's Grill
140 East Washington Avenue
Cedarhurst
(516) 295-2040

*Zan's Kosher Delicatessen
135 Alexander Avenue
Lake Grove
(631) 979-9970

Zenith Vegetarian Cuisine
517 Cedarhurst Avenue
Cedarhurst
(516) 792-9755

Zen Palate
477 Old Country Road
Westbury
(516) 333-8686 (vegetarian)

The Best Western Hotel, 80 Clinton Street, Hempstead, (516) 486-4100, has a kosher kitchen for catered events.

New York City: Bronx

Cira
430 West 238th Street
(718) 432-2046 (Chinese, Japanese,
    sushi)

Corner Café and Bakery
3552 Johnson Avenue
(718) 601-2861

Ginger Grill
3717 Riverdale Avenue
(718) 601-7763

*Main Event
3708 Riverdale Avenue

(718) 601-3013; for catering: (718)
    601-MAIN

Mr. Bagel of Broadway
5672 Broadway
(718) 549-0408

Riverdelight Restaurant
3534 Johnson Avenue
(718) 543-4270

Second Helping Deli
3532B Johnson Avenue
(718) 548-1818

Yankee Stadium has a kosher food stand.

New York City: Brooklyn

Adelman's Deli
1906 Kings Highway
(718) 336-4915

A-Kosher Delight
4600 Thirteenth Avenue
(718) 435-8599
1223 Avenue J
(718) 377-6873

Amazon Café
1123 Quentin Road
(718) 382-8360

Amnons Pizza
4814 Thirteenth Avenue
(718) 851-1759

Asia Restaurant
4813 New Utrecht Avenue
(718) 972-3434 (Russian)

Back to Nature
535 Kings Highway
(718) 339-0273 (natural foods
   and juice bar)

Bagel Hole
1431 Coney Island Avenue
(718) 377-9703
1423 Avenue J
(718) 377-9700

Bamboo Garden
904 Kings Highway
(718) 336-4915

Bella Luna
557 Kings Highway
(718) 376-0666 (dairy)

Bella Stella
1725 East Eighth Street
(718) 376-0666 (dairy)

Benny's Famous Pizza Plus
4514 Thirteenth Avenue
(718) 438-2369

Bernie's Place
1217 Avenue J
(718) 677-1515 (vegetarian)

Bertolini's Italian Restaurant
1969 Coney Island Avenue
(718) 382-5559

Big Fleishigs Express
5508 Sixteenth Avenue
(718) 435-2779

Bissaleh Café
1922 Coney Island Avenue
(718) 998-8811

Broadway J-2 NYC Pizza
926 Third Avenue
(718) 768-7437

Cachet Glatt Kosher Restaurant
815 Kings Highway
(718) 336-8600

Café Au Lee
193 Lee Avenue
(718) 384-2379

Café K
1111 Avenue K
(718) 677-3033
4110 Eighteenth Street
(718) 438-1859

Café Napoli
1636 Coney Island Avenue
(718) 627-6077

Café Paris
4424 Sixteenth Avenue
(718) 853-2353

Café Renaissance
802 Kings Highway
(718) 382-1900

Café Shalva
1305 Fifty-Third Street
(718) 851-1970

Carmel
523 Kings Highway
(718) 375-8501

Chadash Pizza
1919 Avenue M
(718) 253-4793

Chap-a-Nosh
1424 Elm Avenue
(718) 627-0072 (Chinese)

*Chef-Ah Glatt
4810 Thirteenth Avenue
(718) 972-0133

Cheskel's Shwarma King
3715 Thirteenth Avenue
(718) 435-7100

*China Glatt
4413 Thirteenth Avenue
(718) 438-2576

China Meharin
1202 Avenue J
(718) 677-5536

*Circa-NY Restaurant
1505 Avenue J
(718) 758-9500

Class Kosher Catering
(718) 692-3100

Crawford's Café
1209 Kings Highway
(718) 382-0474

Crown Bagel
333A Kingston Avenue
(718) 493-4270

Culinary Creations by Sharon
(718) 951-1873

Dagan Dairy
4820 Sixteenth Avenue
(718) 435-5711

Dagan Pizza
6187 Strickland Avenue
(718) 209-0636

Dairy Delight
82 Kings Highway
(718) 236-8111
549 Kings Highway
(718) 627-9668

Dalya and Zion Restaurant
4102 Eighteenth Avenue
(718) 871-9467 (Middle Eastern)

David's Restaurant
539 Kings Highway
(718) 998-8600 (Middle Eastern,
    Sephardic)

Deli 52
5120 Thirteenth Avenue
(718) 436-4830

Donut Man Soup and Sandwiches
4708 Thirteenth Avenue
(718) 436-7318

Dougie's
4310 Eighteenth Avenue
(718) 686-8080 (meat and barbecue)

D. Zion Burgers
4102 Eighteenth Avenue
(718) 853-9000

*Essex on Coney Restaurant
1359 Coney Island Avenue
(718) 253-1002

Esther Grill and Delicatessen
463 Albany Avenue
(718) 735-4343

Estihana
1217 Avenue J
(718) 677-9052 (Asian,
sushi)

Estihana Express
819 Kings Highway
(718) 645-0717

Expresso Café
1218 Kings Highway
(718) 339-0054

Famous Pita
935 Coney Island Avenue
(718) 284-0161

Flavors Homemade Ice Cream
6001 Strickland Avenue
(718) 241-0969

Fontana Bella
2086 Coney Island Avenue
(718) 627-3904 (Italian, Middle
   Eastern)

Fuji Hana Japanese Restaurant
512 Avenue U
(718) 336-3888

Gan Orly
3911 Thirteenth Avenue
(718) 435-5108

Garden 13
4905 Thirteenth Avenue
(718) 437-1962

Garden by the Courts
151 Remsen Street
(718) 222-3900

Garden of Eat-In
1416 Avenue J
(718) 252-5298

Gio Caffe
448 Avenue P
(718) 375-5437

Glatt a La Carte
5502 Eighteenth Avenue
(718) 621-3697 (French Italian)

*Glatt Galore
4305 Fifteenth Avenue
(718) 686-0042
412 Avenue M
(718) 336-1570

Glatt Kosher Family
4305 Eighteenth Avenue
(718) 972-8085 (Chinese)

Glatt Kosher #1
1411 Avenue M
(718) 336-3888

Golden King Restaurant
595 Bedford Avenue
(718) 384-6577

Gottlieb's Deli
352 Roebling Street
(718) 384-6612 (Hungarian, American)

Gourmet on the Bay
8501 Bay Parkway
(718) 621-4492

Greens
128 Montague Street
(718) 246-1288 (Chinese vegetarian)

Greens Restaurant
216 Ross Street
(718) 384-2540 (dairy, Hungarian,
   Italian)

Hall Street Kosher Café
7 Hall Street
(718) 923-6000

Hamilton Kosher Gourmet
4521 Fort Hamilton Parkway
(718) 740-1362

Haossan
1387 Coney Island Avenue
(718) 252-6969 (Southeast Asian)

Hot Bagels
1218 Kings Highway
(718) 339-0054

Island Grill
2279 Coney Island Avenue
(718) 382-8999

Itzu's
45 Lee Avenue
(718) 302-3548 (French, Turkish, sushi)

*Jay and Lloyd's Kosher Deli
2718 Avenue U
(718) 891-5298

Jerusalem Steak House
533 Kings Highway
(718) 336-5115

Jerusalem Steak House II
1319 Avenue J
(718) 258-8899 (Moroccan,
  Mediterranean)

Jerusalem II Pizza
1312 Avenue J
(718) 338-8156
1424 Avenue M
(718) 645-4753

Joey's Glatt Kosher Palace
936 Kings Highway
(718) 382-2527

Josef's Organics
1712 Avenue M
(718) 336-9494 (pasta, juice bar, baked
  goods, ice cream)

Kaosan Kosher Bistro
1387 Coney Island Avenue
(718) 252-6969 (Thai, Vietnamese)

Kennereth Glatt Kosher Caterers
1920 Avenue U
(718) 743-2473

Kingsbay Caterers
3692 Nostrand Avenue
(718) 891-7178

Kingston Pizza
395 Kingston Avenue
(718) 773-7154

Kingsway Caterers
2902 Kings Highway
(718) 338-5000

Kinneret Steakhouse
521 Kings Highway
(718) 336-8888

Kosher Delight
4600 Thirteenth Avenue
(718) 435-8500
1223 Avenue J
(718) 377-6873

*Kosher Haven at Brooklyn College
2900 Bedford Avenue
(718) 434-6852

Kosher Hut
709 Kings Highway
(718) 376-8996

Krechme
411 Troy Avenue
(718) 493-4370 (pizza, vegetarian)

Le Chateau/Pruzansky Family Caterers
431 Avenue P
(718) 339-0200

Locker Caterers
(718) 258-7088

Lou's Delicatessen
514 Kings Highway
(718) 627-3180

Mabat Steakhouse
1807 East Seventh Street
(718) 339-3300 (Middle Eastern)

Mama's Red
906 Kings Highway
(718) 382-7200

Masihani Japanese
816 Avenue U
(718) 376-8086

Matamim Dairy Restaurant
5001 Thirteenth Avenue
(718) 437-2772

McDaniel's Pizza
549 Kings Highway
(718) 627-9668

Meisners
2924 Avenue I
(718) 338-7888
5410 New Utrecht Avenue
(718) 436-5592

Mendel's Pizza
4923 Eighteenth Avenue
(718) 438-8493

Mendelsohn's Pizza
4418 Eighteenth Avenue
(718) 854-0600

Mermelstein Kosher Deli
351 Kingston Avenue
(718) 777-3100

*Mr. Wok
597 Flushing Avenue
(718) 387-0056

Naim Pizza
3904 Fifteenth Avenue
(718) 438-3569

Napoli to Go Take Out
1018 Avenue M
(718) 627-6077

Nathan's Famous
825 Kings Highway
(718) 627-5252

Natanya Pizza
1506 Avenue J
(718) 258-5160

Nesher Fine Foods
4023 Thirteenth Avenue
(718) 437-3631 (Hungarian)

Nosh Express
2817-19 Nostrand Avenue
(718) 677-3600

Olympic Pita
1419 Coney Island Avenue
(718) 258-6222

Oneg Take Out and Caterers
4911 Twelfth Avenue
(718) 438-3388

Orchidea
4815 Twelfth Avenue
(718) 686-7500

Paradise Manor Catering
5802 New Utrecht Avenue
(718) 438-3388

Pardes Kosher Pizza
4001 Thirteenth Avenue
(718) 633-0138

Pastrami Box
82 Livingston Street
(718) 246-7089

Pita Corner
419 Avenue P
(718) 627-3373

Pizza Natanya
1506 Avenue J
(718) 258-5160

Pizza Nosh
2807 Nostrand Avenue
(718) 253-3200

Pizza Planet
3005 Avenue K
(718) 692-2800

Pizza Time
1324 East Fourteenth Street
(718) 252-8801

Plaza Dining Restaurant (in the Avenue
    Plaza Hotel)
4644 Thirteenth Avenue
(718) 552-3200

Rishon Pizza
5114 Thirteenth Avenue
(718) 438-9226

Ruthy's Catering
547 Kings Highway
(718) 339-1201

Schwarma Hatikvah
1510 Avenue K
(718) 339-8686

Schwarma King
3715 Thirteenth Avenue
(718) 435-3700

Schwartz Appetizing and Catering
4824 Sixteenth Avenue
(718) 851-1011

Sea Dolphin
2096 Coney Island Avenue
(718) 627-3904

Shalom Chai
2189 Flatbush Avenue
(718) 377-6100

Shalom Hunan
1619 Avenue M
(718) 382-6000

Shalom Pizza
1621 Kings Highway
(718) 339-7884

Shang Chai
2189 Flatbush Avenue
(718) 377-6100

Shawarma Hamacabim
1510 Elm Street
(718) 382-0410

Shemtov Restaurant
5326 Thirteenth Avenue
(718) 438-9366

Sixteenth Avenue Bagel and Pizza
4303 Sixteenth Avenue
(718) 853-5395

Subsational Sandwiches
992 East Fifteenth Street
(718) 677-6987
1928 Coney Island Avenue
(718) 998-4545

Sunflower Café
1223 Kings Highway
(718) 336-1340 (vegetarian)

Taam Mevorach
815 Avenue U
(718) 336-3368

Tam Tov Pizza
509 Avenue P
(718) 998-5200

Tea for Two Café
547 Kings Highway
(718) 998-0020

Think Sweet Café
546 Kings Highway
(718) 645-3473

Third Avenue
274 Forty-Seventh Street
(718) 492-2000 (dairy, fish)

Tov U'Maitiv
2668 Nostrand Avenue
(718) 258-7991

Tropper Ltd. Caterers
(718) 258-9006

Viva Natural Pizza
1802 Avenue M
(718) 870-0050

Wendy's Plate
434 Avenue U
(718) 376-3125 (vegetarian)

Yunkee
1424 Elm Avenue
(718) 627-0072 (Chinese American)

Zillis
1928 Coney Island Avenue
(718) 998-8111

The Avenue Plaza Hotel, 4624 Thirteenth Avenue, (718) 552-3200, is a completely kosher, full-service luxury hotel. The New York Marriott Brooklyn, 333 Adams Street, (718) 222-6520, has a kosher kitchen.

New York City: Manhattan

A Baguette Bar Take Out
303 East Fiftieth Street
(212) 317-0600

Abigael's
1407 Broadway
(212) 725-1407 (sushi, pan-Asian)

Abigael's at the Museum of Jewish
  Heritage
36 Battery Place
(212) 437-4231

A-Kosher Delight
1359 Broadway
(212) 563-3366

Alibaba
515 Amsterdam Avenue
(212) 787-6008 (Yemenite, Israeli)

*All American Health and Café Bar
160 Broadway
(212) 732-1426 (dairy)

Ariel's
9 East Thirty-Seventh Street
(212) 725-0130

Azuri Café
465 West Fifty-First Street
(212) 262-2920

Bagel Bites Café
22 West Eighth Street
(212) 979-0888

Bagels and Company
393 Amsterdam Avenue
(212) 496-9400
243 West Thirty-Eighth Street
(212) 997-7558
500 East Seventy-Sixth Street
(212) 717-0505

Bagels Plus
243 West Thirty-Eighth Street
(212) 997-7558

Barouge Bistro Café
228 West Seventy-Second Street
(212) 875-9020

Baruch Kosher Deli and Grill
115 Lexington Avenue
(212) 686-5400

*Ben's Kosher Delicatessen
209 West Thirty-Eighth Street
(212) 398-2367

Bissaleh Classic Dairy Restaurant
1435 Second Avenue
(212) 717-2333 (Middle Eastern)

BJ's Bagels
130 West Seventy-Second Street
(212) 769-3350

Box Tree/Branch Bar and Grill
250 East Forty-Ninth Street
(212) 758-8320

Broadway Café Pizza and Health Bar
160 Broadway
(212) 732-1728

Café 1-2-3
Two Park Avenue
(212) 685-7117

Café at 92nd Street Y
1395 Lexington Avenue
(212) 415-5796

*Café Classico
35 West 57th Street
(212) 355-5411

Café Roma Pizzeria
459 Park Avenue South
(212) 683-3044
175 West Ninetieth Street
(212) 875-8972

Café Viva
2578 Broadway
(212) 663-8482

Café Weissman at the Jewish Museum
1109 Fifth Avenue
(212) 423-3210

Caravan of Dreams
405 East Sixth Street
(212) 254-1613 (organic vegetarian)

Chef's Table Caterers
2 East Sixty-Third Street
(212) 838-0230

Chennai Garden
129 East Twenty-Seventh Street
(212) 689-1999 (South Indian
vegetarian)

Chick Chack Chicken
121 University Place
(212) 724-2222

*China Shalom II
686 Columbus Avenue
(212) 662-9676

Circa.NY
5 Dey Street
(212) 227-2255
22 West Thirty-Third Street
(212) 244-3730 (dairy)

Colbeh Restaurant
43 West Thirty-Ninth Street
(212) 354-8181 (Persian)

Constantine Date Palm Café
15 West Sixteenth Street
(212) 606-8210

Cuisine Catering
(212) 663-0212

Darna Restaurant
600 Columbus Avenue
(212) 721-9123 (Moroccan, Middle
Eastern)

Deli Glatt Stop Sandwiches
150 Fulton Street
(212) 439-9886

Deli Kasbah BBQ and Grill
251 West Eighty-Fifth Street
(212) 496-1500
2553 Amsterdam Avenue
(212) 568-4600

Diamante Pizza/Diamond District Club
8 East Forty-Eighth Street
(212) 832-3434

Diamond Dairy (on the mezzanine of
the Jewelry Exchange)
4 West Forty-Seventh Street
(212) 719-2694

Dimple
11 West Thirtieth Street
(212) 643-9464 (South Indian
vegetarian café and sweet shop)

Domani Ristorante
1590 Fifth Avenue
(212) 717-7575

Dougie's BBQ and Grill
247 West Seventy-Second Street
(212) 724-2222

Dougie's Dairy Restaurant
222 West Seventy-Second Street
(212) 721-7200

Dovid's Kosher Food Stand
27 Williams Street (40 Exchange Place)
(212) 248-9008

East Side Glatt Take Out
500 Grand Street
(212) 254-3335

Eden Wok
127 West Seventy-Second Street
(212) 787-8700

eee's Café and Bakery
105 East Thirty-Fourth Street (7 Park
   Avenue)
(212) 686-3933

Empire Kosher Chicken Restaurant
2014 Broadway
(212) 721-2508

*Essex on Coney Downtown
17 Trinity Place
(212) 809-3000

Essex Place
21 Essex Place
(212) 358-9218

*Esti Hana Oriental Noodle Shop and
   Sushi Bar
221 West Seventy-Ninth Street
(212) 501-0393

Fine and Schapiro Kosher Restaurant
   and Delicatessen
138 West Seventy-Eighth Street
(212) 877-2874

Galil Restaurant
1252 Lexington Avenue
(212) 439-9886 (Israeli, Moroccan)

G & M Glatt Kosher Caterers
41 Essex Street
(212) 677-0090

Gan Asia Take Out
691 Amsterdam Avenue
(212) 280-3800

Gan Eden
74 West Forty-Seventh Street
(212) 869-8946 (Uzbeki, Russian,
   Israeli)

Garden American Health Bar, Deli,
   and Schwarma
49 Ann Street
(212) 587-8101

Ginger Grill
72 Second Avenue
(212) 254-8002 (South Indian vegetarian)

Glatt China
1365 First Avenue
(212) 496-1500

*Glatt Dynasty Chinese Restaurant
1049 Second Avenue
(212) 888-9119

Glatt Gourmet
435 East Eighty-Sixth Street
(212) 288-3093

Grand Deli
399 Grand Street
(212) 536-3366

Great American Health Bar
35 West Fifty-Seventh Street
(212) 355-5177
106 Fulton Street
(212) 587-0262

Green Tea Lounge (upstairs at
   Abigael's)
1407 Broadway
(212) 575-1407 (sushi, pan-Asian)

*Gusto Va Mare
237 East Fifty-Third Street
(212) 583-9300

H & H Bagels
2239 Broadway
(212) 799-6765

Haikara Japanese Grill
1016 Second Avenue
(212) 355-7000

Har Zion Tasty Restaurant
325 Fifth Avenue
(212) 213-1110

House of Pita
32 West Forty-Eighth Street
(212) 391-4242

*Il Patrizio
206 East Sixty-Third Street
(212) 980-4007

Jerusalem Pita
212 East Forty-Fifth Street
(212) 922-0009

Jerusalem II Pizza
1375 Broadway
(212) 383-1475

Joseph's Café
50 West Seventy-Second Street
(212) 595-5004

Josh's Place
2665 Broadway
(212) 222-3320

JT Café
226 West Seventy-Second Street
(212) 724-2424 (café, bookstore, gift
    shop)

Judaica Treasures Café
226 West Seventy-Second Street
(212) 724-3414

Kaffit
104 West Ninety-Sixth Street
(212) 888-5233 (salads, sandwiches,
    coffee, cakes)

Kashbah
251 West Eighty-Fifth Street
(212) 285-8585

Katz's Deli
205 East Houston Street
(212) 254-2246

Kay Caterers
(212) 877-5659

Kitchen
265 West Thirty-Seventh Street
(212) 695-7700

Kosher Creations Caterers
(212) 663-0121
http://www.koshercreations.com

Kosher Dairy Luncheonette
23 West Nineteenth Street
(212) 645-9315

Kosher Delight
1156 Avenue of the Americas
(212) 869-6699
1359 Broadway
(212) 563-3366

Kosher Deli Sub
2554 Amsterdam Avenue
(212) 795-3240

Kosher Deluxe
10 West Forty-Sixth Street
(212) 869-6699

Kosher Heaven
55 Ann Street
(212) 587-1185

Kosher Tea Room
193 Second Avenue
(212) 677-2947

La Bagel
263 First Avenue
(212) 388-9292

La Fontana
309 East Eighty-Third Street
(212) 734-6343

Le Marais Bistro and Steakhouse
150 West Forty-Sixth Street
(212) 869-0900
15 John Street
(212) 255-3601

*Levana Restaurant
141 West Sixty-Ninth Street
(212) 877-8457

Lou G. Siegel's Take Out
240 West Fourteenth Street
(212) 354-1843

Madras Café
79 Second Avenue
(212) 254-8002

Madras Mahal
104 Lexington Avenue
(212) 684-4010 (Indian vegetarian)

Maharani
156 West Twenty-Ninth Street
(212) 868-0707 (Indian vegetarian)

Makor Café
35 West Sixty-Seventh Street
(212) 601-1008

Mendy's East Restaurant and Sports Bar
61 East Thirty-Fourth Street
(212) 576-1010

Mendy's 42nd Street Deli and Take Out
(dining concourse of Grand Central
Station)
Forty-Second Street and Park Avenue
(212) 856-9399

Mendy's Galleria Meat and Take Out
115 East Fifty-Seventh Street
(212) 308-0101

Mendy's Kosher Delicatessen
30 Rockefeller Plaza
(212) 262-9600

Metric Pizza
1435 First Avenue
(212) 452-1100

Mezonot Take Out
692 Columbus Avenue
(212) 665-0953

*Mom's Bagels at Capstone Café
240 West Thirty-Fifth Street
(212) 494-0440

Mr. Bagel of Broadway
5672 Broadway
(212) 549-0408

Mr. Broadway Deli and Caterer/Me Tsu
Yan
1372 Broadway
(212) 921-2152 (Chinese, Japanese)

Murray's Falafel and Grill
261 First Avenue
(212) 533-1956

My Most Favorite Dessert Company
Restaurant and Café
120 West Forty-Fifth Street
(212) 997-5130

New Madras Palace
101 Lexington Avenue
(212) 889-3477 (South Indian vegetarian)

New York University Kosher Cafeteria
511 University Place
(212) 995-3939

Noah's Ark Original Deli
399 Grand Street
(212) 674-2200

Ozu
566 Amsterdam Avenue
(212) 787-8316 (Japanese macrobiotic)

Park East Grill
1564 Second Avenue
(212) 717-8400

Penguin
258 West Fifteenth Street
(212) 255-3601 (Middle Eastern)

*Piece of Cake Café and Bakery
1370 Lexington Avenue
(212) 987-1700

Pita Express
15 Ann Street
(212) 571-2999
261 First Avenue
(212) 533-1956

Pizza Cave
218 West Seventy-Second Street
(212) 874-3700
1376 Lexington Avenue
(212) 987-9130

Pizza Pazza
866 Avenue of the Americas
(212) 686-8319

Pongal
110 Lexington Avenue
(212) 696-9458 (Indian vegetarian)

Prime Grill
60 East Forty-Ninth Street
(212) 697-9292

Provi Provi
228 West Seventy-Second Street
(212) 875-9020

Quintessence
566 Amsterdam Avenue
(212) 501-9700
263 East Tenth Street
(646) 654-1823

Rectangles
159 Second Avenue
(212) 677-8410 (Yemenite, Israeli)

"R" Heaven
1364 Lexington Avenue
(212) 289-5005

Saffron Indian Cuisine
81 Lexington Avenue
(212) 202-8080

Saravana Bhavan
102 Lexington Avenue
(212) 725-7466 (Indian vegetarian)

Second Avenue Deli
156 Second Avenue
(212) 674-2061

Shalom Chai Pizza
359 Grand Street
(212) 598-4178

Siegel's Kosher Delicatessen
1646 Second Avenue
(212) 288-3632

Sweet Roll
48 Beaver Street
(212) 363-7588 (dairy)

Taam Tov
46 West Forty-Seventh Street
(212) 768-8001 (Uzbeki, Russian,
Israeli)

Take a Pita
247 West Thirty-Eighth Street
(212) 730-7482

Talia's Steakhouse and Grill
668 Amsterdam Avenue
(212) 580-3770

Tevere "84" Italian Restaurant
155 East Eighty-Fourth Street
(212) 744-0210

Tiffin Indian Vegetarian
18 Murray Street
(212) 696-5130

Time Out Kosher Pizza
2549 Amsterdam Avenue
(212) 923-1180

Tuscan Grill
228 West Seventy-Second Street
(212) 875-9020

Udipi Palace
103 Lexington Avenue
(212) 889-3477 (Indian vegetarian)

Va Bene Kosher Ristorante Italiano
1589 Second Avenue
(212) 517-4448

*Vegetable Garden
48 East Forty-First Street
(212) 883-7668

Vege Vege
544 Third Avenue
(212) 679-4710

*Village Crown Italian Dairy Cuisine
96 Third Avenue
(212) 777-8816

Village Crown Moroccan
1435 First Avenue
(212) 452-1100 (Moroccan, Middle
   Eastern, vegetarian)

Viva Natural Pizza
64 East Thirty-Fourth Street
(212) 779-4350

Westside Kasbah
251 West Eighty-Fifth Street
(212) 496-1500

Wolf and Lamb Steakhouse
10 East Forty-Eighth Street
(212) 317-1950

Yom Tuv Basket/Club 47
11 West Forty-Seventh Street
(212) 278-0664

Zenith
888 Eighth Avenue
(212) 791-3511

Most major New York City hotels can make arrangements for kosher catering.

New York City: Queens

*Aaron's Gourmet Take Out
63-36 Woodhaven Boulevard
Rego Park
(718) 205-1992

Annie Chan's Restaurant
190-11 Union Turnpike
Fresh Meadows
(718) 740-1773 (Chinese, sushi)

Annie's Kitchen
72-24 Main Street
Kew Gardens Hills
(718) 268-0960

Arzu
101-05 Queens Boulevard
Forest Hills
(718) 830-3335

Bamboo Garden
41-28 Main Street
Flushing
(718) 463-9240 (Chinese vegetarian)

*Ben's Best Kosher Deli and Restaurant
96-40 Queens Boulevard
Rego Park
(718) 897-1700

*Ben's Deli Restaurant
211-37 Twenty-Sixth Avenue
Bayside
(718) 229-2367

Benjy's Pizza and Dairy
72-72 Main Street
Kew Gardens Hills
(718) 268-0791

Berso's (at the U.S. Open Tennis
   Tournament)
Flushing Meadows Corona Park

Berso Take Home Foods and Catering
64-20 108th Street
Forest Hills
(718) 275-9793

Beth Torah Glatt Kosher Caterers
106-06 Queens Boulevard
Forest Hills
(718) 261-4775

*Bombay Kitchen
113-25 Queens Boulevard
Forest Hills
(718) 263-4733

Buddha Bodai
46-96 Main Street
Flushing
(718) 939-1188 (Chinese vegetarian)

*Buddy's Delicatessen Restaurant
215-01 Seventy-Third Avenue
Bayside
(718) 631-2110

*Burger Nosh
69-48 Main Street
Kew Gardens Hills
(718) 520-1933

Café Baba
91-33 Sixty-Third Drive
Rego Park
(718) 520-1933

Cheburechnaya
92-09 Sixty-Third Drive
Rego Park
(718) 897-9080 (Uzbeki, Russian,
   Middle Eastern)

*Cho-Sen Garden
64-43 108th Street
Forest Hills
(718) 275-1300

Cleopatra Restaurant
181-34 Union Turnpike
Fresh Meadows
(718) 591-0136

Club Rafael Restaurant
116-33 Queens Boulevard
Forest Hills
(718) 268-3308 (Middle Eastern, Asian,
   Russian, American)

Colbeh
68-34 Main Street
Kew Gardens Hills
(718) 268-8181 (Middle Eastern)

DaMikelle II
102-39 Queens Boulevard
Forest Hills
(718) 997-6166 (Italian)

Dan Carmel Pizza
98-98 Queens Boulevard
Forest Hills
(718) 544-8530

*Deli Masters
184-02 Horace Harding Expressway
Fresh Meadows
(718) 353-3030

Diner's Delight
188-09 Union Turnpike
Fresh Meadows
(718) 479-5506

Dougie's BBQ and Grill
72-27 Main Street
Kew Gardens Hills
(718) 793-4600

Eilat Restaurant
97-25 Sixty-Fourth Road
Rego Park
(718) 459-1200

Emperor's Garden
251-15 Northern Boulevard
Little Neck
(718) 281-1500 (Chinese vegetarian)

Erwin's Glatt Kosher Restaurant
John F. Kennedy International Airport
Terminal 4 Food Court
East Wing
(718) 428-5000

Europa Restaurant
95-28 Queens Boulevard
Rego Park
(718) 927-6262

Gabriel's
102-03 Queens Boulevard
Forest Hills
(718) 830-0744

Gan-Eden
181-34 Union Turnpike
Fresh Meadows
(718) 591-0136
102-11 Queens Boulevard
Forest Hills
(718) 459-8800 (Bukharian)

Glatt to Go Self-Service
70-17 Austin Street
Forest Hills
(718) 263-6263 (Middle Eastern
   vegetarian)

Glatt Wok Express
190-11 Union Turnpike
Flushing
(718) 263-6263

Habustan Restaurant
188-02 Union Turnpike
Jamaica Estates
(718) 217-6254

Hapisgah Steakhouse
147-25 Union Turnpike
Kew Gardens Hills
(718) 380-4449

Happy Buddha Vegetarian Restaurant
135-37 Thirty-Seventh Street
Flushing
(718) 358-0079

Heavenly Delights
Queensboro Community College
Bayside
kosher food cart

Hillcrest Bagels and Pizza
180-22 Union Turnpike
Fresh Meadows
(718) 591-1188

Jerusalem Café
72-02 Main Street
Kew Gardens Hills
(718) 520-8940

King David
101-10 Queens Boulevard
Forest Hills
(718) 896-7686 (Middle Eastern)

Kings House Ariel Restaurant
92-60 Queens Boulevard
Rego Park
(718) 899-2405

Kingsway Caterers
193-10 Peck Avenue
Fresh Meadows
(718) 357-4585

Knish Knosh
100-30 Queens Boulevard
Forest Hills
(718) 897-5554

*Kosher Corner Dairy Cafe
73-01 Main Street
Kew Gardens Hills
(718) 263-1177

Kosher Haven Caterers
65-30 Kissena Boulevard
Flushing
(718) 261-0149

K-Roasters Restaurant
180-30 Union Turnpike
Fresh Meadows
(718) 591-4220
100-19 Queens Boulevard
Forest Hills
(718) 997-7135

Maadinei Melech
101-15 Queens Boulevard
Forest Hills
(718) 896-7736

*Mauzone Home Kosher Products
61-36 Springfield Boulevard
Bayside
(718) 255-1188
69-60 Main Street
Kew Gardens Hills
(718) 261-7723

*Maven Take Out
188-09 Union Turnpike
Jamaica Estates
(718) 479-5504

*Max's Kosher Delicatessen
71-19 Austin Street
Forest Hills
(718) 268-1262

Mazurs Market Place/Restaurant
254-51 Horace Harding Boulevard
Little Neck
(718) 428-5000

*Meal Mart Take Out
72-10 Main Street
Kew Gardens Hills
(718) 261-3300

Mel's Place
71-35 Kissena Boulevard
Flushing
(718) 380-3400

Moishe's Kosher Pizza
181-30 Union Turnpike
Fresh Meadows
(718) 969-1928

Naomi's Kosher Pizza
68-28 Main Street
Kew Gardens Hills
(718) 520-8754

Or Yehuda Kosher Restaurant
138-44 Eighty-Sixth Street
Jamaica
(718) 291-3406

Panorama Restaurant
167-01 Union Turnpike
Flushing
(718) 969-9800

Pita House
98-102 Queens Boulevard
Forest Hills
(718) 897-4829

Pita Hut
75-43 Main Street
Kew Gardens Hills
(718) 544-6755

Pizza Professor
141-25 Jewel Avenue
Kew Gardens Hills
(718) 261-6666 (specializes in sweet
    pizzas)

Pninat Hamizrach Prime Grill
178-07 Union Turnpike
Fresh Meadows
(718) 591-3367 (Israeli, sushi)

Prime Grill
69-54 Main Street
Kew Gardens Hills
(718) 261-7077

Queen's Kosher Pita
68-38 Main Street
Kew Gardens Hills
(718) 263-8000

Registan
65-37 Ninety-Ninth Street
Rego Park
(718) 459-1638 (Bukharian)

*Ristorante Micelli
97-26 Sixty-Third Road
Rego Park
(718) 275-0988

Ruchel's Kosher Kettle
123-04 Metropolitan Avenue
Kew Gardens
(718) 441-5886

Salut
63-42 108th Street
Forest Hills
(718) 275-6860 (Russian, Middle
    Eastern)

*Sandy's Surf Delicatessen
101-05 Queens Boulevard
Forest Hills
(718) 459-7875

Shimon's Pizza and Falafel
71-24 Main Street
Kew Gardens Hills
(718) 793-1491

Sogdiana Caterers
73-20 Grand Avenue
Maspeth
(718) 507-4171

Strawberry Café
72-28 Main Street
Kew Gardens Hills
(718) 266-7723

*Surry's Kosher Restaurant and Take-
  Out
179-08 Union Turnpike
Fresh Meadows
(718) 969-5643

Sushi Metsuyan
72-08 Main Street
Kew Gardens Hills
(718) 575-8700 (Japanese fusion
  steakhouse and sushi)

Sweet Bites Café
81-48 Lefferts Boulevard
Kew Gardens
(718) 805-1513

Tajikistan
102-03A Queens Boulevard
Forest Hills
(718) 830-0744 (Afghan)

Tandoori
99-04 Sixty-Third Road
Rego Park
(718) 897-1071

Tov Caterers
97-22 Sixty-Third Road
Rego Park
(718) 896-7788

Vege World
20-02 Utopia Parkway
Whitestone
(718) 352-1616

Wok Two
100-19 Queens Boulevard
Forest Hills
(718) 896-0310

New York City: Staten Island

Dairy Palace
2210 Victory Boulevard
(718) 761-5200

Delicious Grill
1980 Victory Boulevard
(718) 556-2828

Good Appetite Dairy Café
1980 Victory Boulevard
(718) 981-5458

Yum Yum Glatt
2234 Victory Boulevard
(718) 982-1111

Rockland County

Glatt Wok
106 Route 59
Monsey
(845) 426-3600

Jerusalem Pizza
190 Route 59
Monsey
(845) 426-1500

Kyo Sushi and Steak
419 Route 59
Monsey
(845) 371-5885

Sullivan County

Delicious Kosher Pizza
Main Street
South Fallsburg
(845) 434-5845

Dougie's Express
Main Street
Woodbourne
(845) 436-4441

Izzy's Knish Nosh
Route 52
Loch Sheldrake
(845) 434-6674

Kikar Tel Aviv North
Vacation Village
Loch Sheldrake
(845) 434-0600

Mazel Wok
Main Street
Woodbourne
(845) 436-7302

*Shwarma King Monticello
279 East Broadway
Monticello
(845) 794-2803

*Sruly's
Main Street
South Fallsburg
(845) 434-9311

Stargelt
Main Street
Loch Sheldrake
(845) 436-6774

Woodbourne Kosher Pizza and Ice Cream
Main Street
Woodbourne
(845) 434-4790

Westchester County

Cherry Blossom
1382 North Avenue
New Rochelle
(914) 654-8052

*Eden Wok
1327 North Avenue
New Rochelle
(914) 637-9363 (Chinese sushi)

Green Symphony Vegetarian Cuisine
427 Boston Post Road
Port Chester
(914) 937-6537

Off the Grill of Westchester
1279 North Avenue
New Rochelle
(914) 235-0496

Prime Time Kosher Café
1315 North Avenue
New Rochelle
(914) 654-1646

*Wykagyl Deli and Restaurant
1305 North Avenue
New Rochelle
(914) 636-4381

The Rye Town Hilton, 699 Westchester Avenue, Rye Brook, (914) 939-6300, and the Renaissance Hotel, White Plains, (914) 694-5400, have kosher catering facilities.

Ohio

Cincinnati

Breadsmith
9708 Kenwood Road
(513) 791-8817

Just Desserts
6964 Plainfield Road
(513) 793-6627

Pilder's Deli
4070 East Galbraith Road
(513) 792-9961

Queen City Kosher/Ares' Grill
4070 East Galbraith Road
(513) 792-9961

Tel Aviv Café
7384 Reading Road
(513) 631-8808

Cleveland

Abba's
13937 Cedar Road
(216) 321-5660

Contempo Cuisine
13898 Cedar Road
(216) 397-3520

Empire Kosher Chicken Restaurant
2234 Warrensville Center Road
University Heights
(216) 691-0006

Issi's Place
14431 Cedar Road
(216) 291-4251

Jacob's Field Stadium
kosher food stand

Kinneret Kosher Pizza
1869 South Taylor Road
Cleveland Heights
(216) 321-1404

Peking Kosher Chinese
1841 South Taylor Road

Ruchama's Singapore
2172 Warrensville Center Road
University Heights
(216) 321-1100

Yacov's Restaurant
13969 Cedar Road
(216) 932-8848

Columbus

Irv's Deli and Grill
3012 East Broad Street
(641) 231-3653

Kosher Buckeye
2944 East Broad Street
(641) 235-8070

Sammy's New York Bagels and Deli
40 North James Road
(614) 246-0426

Pennsylvania

Bucks County

Sindi Udoppi Dosa
Center Plaza
2163 Galloway Road
Bensalem

Dauphin County

Kitchen Maven
201 Esterton Avenue
Harrisburg
(717) 234-5448

Kosher Mart
800 Hershey Park Drive
Hershey
(717) 534-3119
45 North Market Street
Hershey
(717) 392-5111

Lehigh County

Abe's Place Deli Restaurant
1741 Alien Street
Allentown
(610) 435-1735

Catering by Ann
(610) 664-5327

JCC Snack Bar
702 North Twenty-Second Street
Allentown
(610) 432-3571

Philadelphia

ABGY Catering
(215) 483-2837

Bellaleah's Pizza
7540 Haverford Avenue
(215) 284-0627

Cherry Street Chinese Vegetarian
1010 Cherry Street
(215) 922-8957

Dara's Delights Catering
(215) 856-0100

Dragon Inn Chinese Restaurant
7628 Castor Avenue
(215) 742-2575

Holy Land Grill
7628 Castor Avenue
(215) 725-7000

Holy Land Pizza
8010 Castor Avenue
(215) 725-7444

Jonathan's
130 South Eleventh Street
(215) 829-8101

Kingdom of Vegetarians
129 North Eleventh Street
(215) 413-2290

Kosher Kaos Fastfood
9550 Bustleton Avenue (lower level)

Maccabean
128 South Eleventh Street
(215) 922-5922

Mr. J's Restaurant and Bakery
1526 Sansom Street
(215) 568-2448

Rajbhog Restaurant and Sweets
738 Adams Street
(215) 537-1937 (Indian vegetarian)

Samasa Indian Restaurant
1214 Walnut Street
(215) 545-7776

Shalom Pizza
7598 Haverford Avenue
(215) 878-1500

Simi's Place Glatt Kosher Deli
    Restaurant
300 Levering Mill Road
Bala Cynwyd
(610) 949-9420

Singapore Chinese Vegetarian
    Restaurant
1029 Race Street
(215) 922-3288

Tiberias Cafeteria
8010 Castor Avenue
(215) 725-7444

Time Out Falafel Kingdom
9846 Bustleton Avenue
(215) 969-7545

Traditions Restaurant
9550 Bustleton Avenue
(215) 677-2221

Water Wheel
1529 Sansom Street
(215) 563-9601

Zev's Salads and Catering
(610) 649-5611

The Wyndham Philadelphia at Franklin Plaza, Seventeenth and Race Streets, (215) 448-2000, has kosher catering facilities.

Pittsburgh

Golden China
2209 Murray Avenue
(412) 422-1800

Milky Way
2120 Murray Avenue
(412) 421-3121

Platters Restaurant/King David
2020 Murray Avenue
(412) 422-3370

Sari's/Yacov's Vegetarian
2109 Murray Avenue
(412) 421-7208

Rhode Island
> *Providence*

Café De-Lite
758 Hope Street
(401) 454-5652

Tennessee
> *Memphis*

City Café and Bread Co.
575 South Mendenhall Road
(901) 683-7350

Gottlieb's Deli
5062 Park Avenue
(901) 763-3663

Rubinstein's Deli
4965 Summer Avenue
(901) 682-3801

Schnucks
799 Truse Parkway
(901) 682-2989

Texas
> *Dallas*

Café Fino
7522 Campbell Road
(972) 931-9500

Tom Thumb
11920 Preston Road
(972) 392-2501

> *Houston*

Garden Vegetarian Restaurant
9013 Westheimer Road
(713) 783-6622

King David Center
5925 South Braeswood Boulevard
(713) 729-5741

Madras Pavillion
3910 Kirby Drive
(713) 521-2617

Saba's Mediterranean
9704 Fondren Road
(713) 270-7222

Virginia
> *Richmond*

Restaurant at the Farbreng Inn Hotel
212 North Gaskins Road
(804) 740-2000

Washington
> *Seattle*

Bagel Deli
340 Fifteenth Street East
(206) 322-2471

Bagel Oasis
2112 N.E. Sixty-Fifth Street
(206) 526-0525

Bamboo Gardens Vegetarian Cuisine
364 Roy Street
(206) 282-6616

Kosher Delight
1509 First Avenue
(206) 682-8140

Leah's Café and Bakery
2114 N.E. Sixty-Fifth Street
(206) 985-2647

Leah's Catering
(206) 524-4020

Noah's Bagels
2746 N.E. Forty-Fifth Street
(206) 522-1998

*Nosh Away
419 Rainier Avenue North
Renton
(206) 772-5757

*Pabla Indian Cuisine
364 Renton Center Way
Renton
(425) 228-4625 (vegetarian)

Panani Grill
2118 N.E. Sixty-Fifth Street
(206) 522-2730

Teapot Vegetarian House
125 Fifteenth Avenue East
(206) 325-1010 (Chinese, Thai)

Wisconsin
Milwaukee
JCC Snack Bar
1400 North Prospect Avenue
(414) 271-2627

Canada
Calgary, Alberta
Carriage House Inn
9030 Macleod Trail South
(403) 253-1101

*Karen's Café
1607 Ninetieth Avenue
(403) 225-5311

Toby's
Ninetieth Avenue and 124th Street
(403) 238-5300

Montreal, Quebec
A la Marguérite
6630 Côte Saint-Luc Road
(514) 488-4111

Bête-Aron
9292 Meilleur Street
(514) 384-0065

Bistrole
5095 Queen Mary Road
(514) 487-6455

Casa Linga/Bistroglatt Rahamim
5095 Queen Mary Road
(514) 737-2272

El Morocco II
3450 Drummond Street
(514) 844-6888

Ernie and Ellie's Place
6900 De Carie Boulevard
(514) 344-4444

Exodus Restaurant
5395 Queen Mary Road
(514) 483-6610

Famous Pizza
5710 Victoria Avenue
(514) 731-7482

Foxy's Kosher Pizza
5987 Victoria Avenue
(514) 739-8777

Majestik
5415 Royalmont Avenue
(514) 735-7911

Mitchell's Restaurant
5500 Westbury Avenue
(514) 737-8704

Pizza Manne
5834 Westminster Avenue
(514) 369-0550

Tatty's Pizza
654 Darlington Avenue
(514) 734-8289

Yossi's Dizengoff Café
3460 Stanley Street
(514) 845-9171 (Israeli)

Ottawa, Quebec
Viva Pizza
1766 Carling Avenue
(613) 722-6645

Toronto, Ontario
Bais Burger
3011 Bathurst Street
(416) 785-3047

Café Sheli
Clark Avenue
Thornhill

Chicken Nest
3038 Bathurst Street
(416) 787-6378

Chocolate Moose
2839 Bathurst Street
(416) 874-9092

Colonel Wong's
2825 Bathurst Street
(416) 784-9664

Dairy Treats European Café and Bakery
3522 Bathurst Street
(416) 787-0309

Golden Chopsticks
7800 Bathurst Street
Thornhill
(905) 760-2786

Hakerem Restaurant
3030 Bathurst Street
(416) 787-6504

Hakotel Restaurant
1045 Steeles Avenue West
(416) 736-7227

Jerusalem One
3026 Bathurst Street
(416) 256-7115

King David's Pizza
3774 Bathurst Street
(416) 633-5678

King David's Pizza and Burekas
3020 Bathurst Street
(416) 781-1326
221 Wilmington
(416) 636-3456
531 Atkinson Avenue
Thornhill
(905) 771-7077

*King Solomon's Table (in the
    Montecassino Place Suites Hotel)
3705 Chesswood Drive
Downsview
(800) 567-4878

Marky's Delicatessen
280 Wilson Avenue
(416) 638-1001
7330 Yonge Street
(905) 731-4800

Mati's Pizza and Falafel
3430 Bathurst Street
(416) 783-9595

Miami Grill
441 Clark Avenue West
Thornhill
(905) 709-0096

Migdal David
3022 Bathurst Street
(416) 787-6551

Milk 'n Honey
3457 Bathurst Street
(416) 789-7651

Milk Street Café and Bakery
441 Clark Avenue West
(905) 886-7450

Not Just Yogurt
7117 Bathurst Street
Thornhill
(905) 764-2525

Oasis Café
100 King Street
(416) 368-8805

Orli Café
3464 Bathurst Street
(416) 256-9537

Peri's Deli
3013 Bathurst Street
(416) 787-4234

Tov Li Pizza
5972 Bathurst Street
(416) 650-9800

Umami Fusion
288 Eglinton Avenue West
(416) 483-9018

Umami Sushi
3459 Bathurst Street
(416) 782-3375

Yehudale's Falafel and Pizza
7241 Bathurst Street
Thornhill
(905) 889-1400

Vancouver, British Columbia

Chagall's Creative Cuisine
950 West Forty-First Street
(604) 904-1116

Garden City Take Out
9100 Blundell Road
Richmond
(604) 244-7888

Winnipeg, Manitoba

*Desserts Plus
1595 Main Street
(204) 339-1957

Downstairs Deli
1570 Main Street
(204) 338-4911

Schmoozers Café
123 Doncaster Street

Belgium

Antwerp

Blue Lagoon Chinese
Lange Herentalsestraat 70

Gelkop
Van Leriusstraat

Hoffy's
Lange Kievistraat 52

Time Out Vegetarian
Lange Herentalsestraat 58

USA Pizza
Isabelallei 118A

England

London

Amor
8 Russell Parade

Blooms
130 Golders Green Road

Café on the Green
122 Golders Green Road

Croft Court Restaurant
44 Ravenscroft Avenue

Dizengoff
118 Golders Green Road

Erez
239 Golders Green Road

Kaifeng Chinese
51 Church Road
Hendon

Reubin's
79 Baker Street

Solly's
148A Golders Green Road

Tasti Pizza
252 Golders Green Road

France

Paris

Adolphe
14, rue Richer

Azar et Fils
6, rue Geoffroy Marie

Berberche Burger
47, rue Richer

Casa Rina
18, rue de Faubourg Montmartre

Chez David
11, rue de Montyon

Contini
42, rue des Rosiers

La Grillade
42, rue Richer

La Pita
26, rue des Rosiers

Les Ailes
34, rue Richer

Panino Café
31, rue Saint-Georges

Tel Aviv Haktana
9, rue des Rosiers

Yahalom Restaurant
22, rue des Rosiers

Italy
Rome

Da Lisa
Via Joscolo 16

Gan Eden
Via Eleanora Darborea 40

Zi Fenizia
Via Santa Maria del Pianto 64

Mexico
Acapulco

El Isleño Restaurant (in the Hyatt
  Regency Acapulco Hotel)
(800) 233-1234

Mexico City

Pizzas Koshertel
various locations

Netherlands
Amsterdam

Carmel
Amstelveenseweg 224

Mensa
De Lairessestraat 13

Mouwes Deli
Kastelenstraat 261

Museum Café
Jonas Daniel Meijerplein 2–4

Sal Meyer
Scheldestraat 45

Russia
Moscow

Carmel Restaurant
1 Tverskaya Yamskaya

David HaMelech Club
8 Bolshoj Spasoglenishevsky

Odessa Rosemaren
46-A Malaya Arnautskaya

Switzerland
Geneva

Heimische Kitchen Restaurant Familial
1, avenue Miremont

Zurich

Fein und Schein Dairy Restaurant
Schontalstrasse 14

Schalom Restaurant, Lavaterstrasse 33

Thailand

Bangkok

Bossotel Inn Restaurant

Bakeries, Butchers, Candy, Chocolates, and Markets

A number of American supermarket chains and discount shopping clubs carry selections of kosher products, including poultry and baked goods. These include Acme, Albertsons, America's Choice, Costco, C-Town, Fairway, Finast, Food Emporium, Foodtown, Grand Union, Key Food, K-Mart, King Kullen, Pathmark, Price Club, ShopRite, Stop & Shop, Super Fresh, Waldbaum's, Wal-Mart, and Whole Foods Markets.

Arizona

Phoenix

Karsh's Bakery
5539 North Seventh Street
(602) 944-2753

Segal's New Place
4818 North Seventh Street
(602) 285-1515

S n Z Kosher
5132 Camelback Road
Glendale
(602) 939-7309

Tucson

Feig's Kosher Market and Deli
5071 East Fifth Street

Nadine's Pastry Shoppe
4300 East Pima Street
(602) 326-0735

California

Los Alamitos

Los Alamitos Kosher Meat and Poultry
11196 Los Alamitos Boulevard
(310) 594-4609

Los Angeles

Back East Bialy Bakery
8562 West Pico Boulevard
(310) 276-1531

Beverly Hills Patisserie
9100 West Pico Boulevard
(310) 275-6873

BH International Bakery
7304¼ Santa Monica Boulevard
(213) 874-7456

Carmel Kosher Meats
8914 West Pico Boulevard
(310) 278-6347

City Glatt Continental Kosher Bakery
7667 Beverly Boulevard
(213) 933-4040
12419 Burbank Boulevard
(818) 762-5005

Doheny Kosher Meats
9213 West Pico Boulevard
(310) 276-7232

Dove's Bakery
8924 West Pico Boulevard
(310) 276-6150

Eilat Bakery
513 North Fairfax Boulevard
(213) 653-5553
9233 West Pico Boulevard
(310) 205-8700

Elat Market
8730 West Pico Boulevard
(310) 659-7070

Fairfax Fish
515 North Fairfax Avenue
(213) 658-8060

Fairfax Grocery
517 North Fairfax Avenue
(323) 651-5878

Famous Bakery
350 North Fairfax Avenue
(323) 933-5000

House of Bonjour Bakery
12453 Oxnard Street
(818) 506-7145

Kol Tuv Market
8602 West Pico Boulevard
(310) 652-5355

Kosher Klub Butcher and Market
4817 West Pico Boulevard
(323) 933-8283

Kotlar's Pico Market
8622 West Pico Boulevard
(310) 652-5355

La Brea Kosher Market and Bagel
   Company
410 North La Brea Avenue
(213) 931-1221

Le Palais Bakery
8670 West Pico Boulevard
(310) 659-4809

Little Jerusalem Market
8963 West Pico Boulevard
(310) 858-8361

Livonia Glatt Meat Market
8922 West Pico Boulevard
(310) 271-4343

Mom's Kosher Donuts
13850 Burbank Boulevard
(818) 769-8352

New York Kosher Market
16733 Ventura Boulevard
Encino
(818) 788-0007

Pico Glatt Kosher Mart
9427 West Pico Boulevard
(310) 785-0904

Rami Meat Market
505 North Fairfax Avenue
(213) 651-4293

Renaissance Bakery
14550 Friar Street
(818) 778-6230

Royal Fish
8973 West Pico Boulevard
(310) 859-0632

Roz Kosher Meats and Market
12422–24 Burbank Boulevard
(818) 760-7694

Sam's Kosher Bakery
12450 Burbank Boulevard
(818) 769-8352

Santa Monica Glatt Market
11933 Santa Monica Boulevard
(310) 473-4435

Schwartz's Bakery
441 North Fairfax Boulevard
(323) 653-1683
8616 West Pico Boulevard
(310) 854-0592

Star Meats
12136 Santa Monica Boulevard
(310) 447-1612

Super Sal Market
17630 Ventura Boulevard
(818) 906-2815

Unique Pastry
17979 Ventura Boulevard
Encino
(818) 757-3100

Valley Glatt Market
12836½ Victory Boulevard
North Hollywood
(818) 506-5542

Valley Glatt Meats
12450 Burbank Boulevard
North Hollywood
(818) 766-4530

Ventura Market
18357 Ventura Boulevard
(323) 873-1240

Western Kosher Market
444 North Fairfax Avenue
(213) 655-8870

Oakland

Grand Avenue Bakery
3264 Grand Avenue
(510) 465-1110

Holy Land Kosher Food Market
677 Rand Road
(510) 272-0535

Noah's Bagels
2060 Mountain Road
(510) 339-6633

Oakland Kosher Foods
5640 College Avenue
(510) 653-8902
3256 Grand Avenue
(510) 451-3883

Palo Alto

Molly Stones Market/Kosher Meat
  Department
164 South California Avenue
(650) 323-8361

Sacramento

Bob's Butcher Block Grocery and Deli
6436 Fair Oaks Boulevard
(916) 482-6884

Lang's Loaf
6165 East Cajon Boulevard
(916) 287-7306

San Diego and Vicinity

Aaron's Glatt Market
4488 Convoy Street
(858) 636-7979

Western Kosher Butcher Shop
7739 Fay Avenue
La Jolla
(619) 454-6328

San Francisco

Israel Kosher Meat and Market
5621 Geary Boulevard
(415) 752-3064

Noah's Bagels
3519 California Street
(415) 387-3874

Tel Aviv Strictly Kosher Meat Market
2495 Irving Street
(415) 661-7588

San Jose

Willow Glen Kosher Market
1185 Lincoln Avenue
(408) 297-6604

Colorado

Denver

Bagel Store
942 South Monaco Parkway
(303) 388-2648

Eastside Kosher Grocery
499 South Elm Street
(303) 322-9862

King Sooper Stores
1725 Sheridan Boulevard
(303) 237-4988
Leetsdale and Monaco
(303) 333-1535
Yosemite and Bellview
(303) 793-9080

New York Bagel Boys
6449 East Hampden Avenue
(303) 759-2212

Connecticut

Bridgeport

Slate Kosher Market
1147 Madison Avenue
(203) 579-1699

Stop & Shop Supermarket Bakery
2600 Madison Avenue
(203) 372-0668

Hartford

Cousin's Bakery
Bishops Corner
(203) 236-5756

Crown Market Deli and Bakery
2471 Albany Avenue
West Hartford
(860) 236-1965

Shop & Stop Supermarket Bakery
1235 Farmington Avenue
West Hartford (open 24 hours)

New Haven

Edge of the Woods Market
379 Whalley Avenue
(203) 787-1055

Fox's Deli and Bakery
140 Whalley Avenue
(203) 397-0839

Westville Kosher Bakery
1658 Litchfield Turnpike
(203) 387-2214

Westville Kosher Meat Market
1666 Litchfield Turnpike
(203) 389-1166

Stamford

Cerebone's Bakery
605 Newfield Avenue
(203) 348-9029

Delicate-Essen Meat, Poultry, and
    Grocery
111 High Ridge Road
(203) 316-5570

Stop & Shop Supermarket Bakery
2200 Bedford Street
(203) 356-0109

Delaware

Wilmington

Baker's Rack
1705 Concord Pike
(302) 654-3165

Modern Kosher Meats
1708 Namana Road
(302) 475-9300

District of Columbia

Dahan's Provisions Market
800 Twenty-First Street
N.W. (Marvin Center)
(202) 994-2992

Stacks Bakery
1101 Pennsylvania Avenue, N.W.
(202) 628-9700

Florida

Boca Raton

Boca Kosher Meats
9070 Kimberly Boulevard
(561) 488-9808

Dushan's Bakery
6006 S.W. Eighteenth Street
(561) 395-1080

Oriole Kosher Meats
7351 West Atlantic Avenue
(561) 427-8722

Pita Pan Bakery
23269 State Road 7
(561) 451-9477

Ruthy's Pastries
22191 Powerline Road

Deerfield Beach

Star of David Meats
1806 West Hillsboro Boulevard
(954) 427-6400

Fort Myers

Bubee's Kosher Foods
1939 Park Meadows Drive
(941) 278-5674

Miami Beach and Vicinity

Abraham's Bakery
7423 Collins Avenue
(305) 861-0191

Abraham's Kosher Baker II
757 N.E. 167th Street
North Miami Beach
(305) 652-3343

Glatt Town Grocery and Butcher Shop
1123 N.E. 163rd Street
North Miami Beach
(305) 944-7726

Goren's Vienna Bakery
1233 Lincoln Road
(305) 672-3928

Kastner's Pastry Shop
7440 Collins Avenue
(305) 865-8217

Kosher Gourmet Gallery
456 Forty-First Street
North Miami Beach
(305) 535-7444

Kosher World
514 Forty-First Street
(305) 532-2210

Pastry Lane Bakery
1688 N.E. 164th Street
North Miami Beach
(305) 944-5934

Pastry Lane Bakery II
4022 Royal Palm Avenue
(305) 674-9523

Ziggy's Yogurt
744 Arthur Godfrey Road
(305) 531-6111

Miramar

Eli the Baker
6136 Miramar Parkway
(954) 903-5601

Orlando

Amira's Kosher Market
1351 East Altamonte Drive
(407) 767-7577

Kosher Korner
4846 Palm Parkway
(407) 238-9968

Tampa

Tampa Kosher Meats
2305 Morrison Avenue
(813) 253-5993

West Palm Beach

Century Kosher Market
4869 Okeechobee Boulevard
(407) 686-2066

Chiffon Kosher Bakery
1253 Old Okeechobee Road
(407) 833-7404

Palm Beach Kosher Market
5085 Okeechobee Road
(561) 686-2066

Georgia

Atlanta

Arthur's Kosher Meats
2166 Briarcliff Road
(404) 634-6881

Cake Company
2191B Briarcliff Road
(404) 633-3734

Krispy Kreme Donut Shops
all locations

Kroger Dunwoody Club
2090 Dunwoody Club Drive
(770) 391-9036 (fish, meat, and deli)

Kroger Sage Hill
1799 Briarcliff Road
(404) 607-1189 (groceries, meat)

Kroger Sandy Springs
227 Sandy Springs Place
(404) 256-3434 (bakery)

Kroger Toco Hills
2205 Lavista Road N.E.
(404) 633-8694 (fish, meat, and deli)

Publix Supermarket
2969 North Druid Hills Road
(404) 638-6022

Quality Kosher Emporium
2153 Briarcliff Road N.E.
(404) 636-1114

Superior Baking
3015 West Druid Hills Road
(404) 633-1986

Illinois

Chicago and Vicinity

Breadsmith
3327 Dempster Street
Skokie
(847) 673-5001

Brooklyn Market
1016 Weiland Road
Buffalo Grove
(847) 229-1818

Chaim's Kosher Bakery, Deli, and
    Supermarket
4956 West Dempster
Skokie
(847) 675-1005

Dunkin Donuts
3132 West Devon Avenue
(312) 262-4560
3900 West Dempster Street
Skokie

Ebner's Kosher Meat Market
2649 West Devon Avenue
Skokie
(773) 764-1446

Gitel's Bakery
2745 West Devon Avenue
(312) 262-3701

Good Morgan Kosher Fish Market
2948 West Devon Avenue
Skokie
(773) 8115

Highland Park Kosher Market
1813 Saint John Avenue
Highland Park
(708) 432-0748

Hungarian Kosher Foods
4020 Oakton Street
Skokie
(847) 674-8008 (butcher, deli, bakery,
    grocery; the largest kosher
    supermarket in the Midwest)

J and M Kosher Meat Market
4465 West Lawrence Avenue
(773) 794-0303

King David's Kosher Bakery
1731 Howard
Evanston
(312) 475-0270

Kol Touhy
2923 West Touhy Avenue
Skokie
(773) 761-1800

Kol Tuv Kosher Foods
2938-40 West Devon Avenue
Skokie
(773) 764-1800

Kosher City
3353 Dempster Street
Skokie
(847) 679-2850

Kosher Gourmet
3552 West Dempster Street
Skokie
(708) 679-0432

Moshe's New York Kosher
2900 West Devon Avenue
(773) 338-3354

New York Kosher Sausage Company
2900 West Devon Avenue
Skokie
(773) 338-3354

North Shore Kosher Bakery
2919 West Touhy Avenue
(773) 262-0600

Roumanian Kosher Sausage Company
7200 North Clark Street
(773) 761-4141

Shaevitz Kosher Meats and Deli
712 Central Avenue
Highland Park
(847) 432-8334

Shalom Bakery
1165 North Arlington Heights Road
Buffalo Grove
(847) 808-9300
869 Sanders Road
Northbrook
(847) 272-4343

Slovin and Solomon Kosher Meat
  Market
4004 Main Street
Skokie
(847) 673-3737

Tel Aviv Bakery
2944 West Devon Avenue
(312) 764-8877

Tel Aviv Kosher Shopping Plaza
4956 West Dempster Street
Skokie
(708) 675-1005

Kentucky
Louisville
Han's Pastries
3089 Breckinridge Lane
(502) 452-9164

JCC Snack Bar
3600 Dutchman's Lane
(502) 459-0660

Strathmoor Market
2733 Bardston Road
(502) 458-2276

Louisiana
New Orleans Area
Dorignac's Food Center
710 Veteran's Memorial Boulevard
Metairie
(504) 834-8216

Maine
Portland
Penny Wise Supermarket
182 Ocean Avenue
(207) 772-8808

Maryland
Baltimore
Adler's Bakery
1860 Reisterstown Road
(410) 653-1119

Carvel Ice Cream
102 Reistertown Road
(410) 486-2365

Dunkin Donuts
1508 Reisterstown Road
(410) 653-8182
7000 Reisterstown Road
(410) 764-6846

Dunkin Donuts/Baskin Robbins
6125 Montrose Road

Goldman's Kosher Bakery and Pastry
  Shop
6848 Reisterstown Road
(410) 358-9625

Knish Shop
508 Reistertown Road
(410) 484-5850

Kosher Market at Safeway Supermarket
201 Reisterstown Road
(410) 413-1196

Krispy Kreme Donuts
10021 Reisterstown Road
(410) 356-2655

Pariser's Bakery
6711 Reisterstown Road
(410) 764-1700

Schmell's Bakery
104 Reisterstown Road
(410) 484-7343

Seven Mile Market
4000 Seven Mile Lane
(410) 653-2000

Shlomo's Kosher Meat
506 Reisterstown Road
(410) 602-7888

Sion's Bakery
302 Reisterstown Road
(410) 486-4196

Wasserman and Lemberger Kosher
  Meat Market
7006 Reisterstown Road
(410) 486-4191

Rockville

Dunkin Donuts
Vera Mills Road

Katz's Supermarket and Café
4860 Boiling Brook Parkway
(301) 468-0400

Kosher Mart
184 Rollins Avenue
(301) 468-4840

Wheaton

Shalom Kosher Market
2307 University Boulevard
(301) 946-6500

Wooden Shoe Pastry Shop
11301 Georgia Avenue
(301) 942-9330

Massachusetts

Boston and Vicinity

Anthony Bakery
4 Lake Street
Peabody
(508) 535-5335

Boston Cookie
Framingham Mall
Route 30
Framingham
(508) 872-1052

Bread Basket Bakery
151 Cochituate Road
Framingham
(508) 875-9441

Brick Oven Bakery
237 Ferry Street
Malden
(617) 322-3269

Brighton Kosher Meat Market
1620 Commonwealth Avenue
Brighton
(617) 277-0786

Butcherie
428 Harvard Street
Brookline
(617) 731-9888

Cheryl Ann's Bakery
1010 West Roxbury Parkway
Chestnut Hill
(617) 469-9241

Cookies Express
252 Bussey Street
East Dedham
(978) 461-0044

Donut Shak
487 Westford Street
Lowell
(978) 937-0178

Donuts with a Difference
35 Riverside Avenue
Medford
(781) 396-1021

Dough-C-Donuts
1460 Massachusetts Avenue
Arlington
(617) 643-4550

Dunkin Donuts
1316 Beacon Street
Brookline
(617) 232-9252

Fabiano Bakery
7 Somerset Avenue
Winthrop
(617) 846-5946

Green Manor Bakery
31 Tosca Drive
Stoughton
(617) 828-3018

J & E Baking
10 Bedford Park
Bridgewater
(508) 279-0990

Kosher Mart
154 Chestnut Hill Avenue
(617) 254-9529

Kupel's Bakery
421 Harvard Street
Brookline
(617) 566-9528

La Ronga
509 Somerville Avenue
Somerville
(617) 625-8600

Leaven and Earth Bakery
406 Harvard Street
(617) 566-8798

Lederman's Bakery
1223 Centre Street
Newton
(617) 527-7896

Lieberman's Bak-Ree
107 Shirley Avenue
Revere
(617) 289-0041

Newman's Bakery
248 Humphrey Street
Swampscott
(781) 592-1550

Rain's Bakery
55 Nichols Road
Framingham
(508) 877-3927

Rosenfeld Bagel
1280 Centre Street
Newton
(617) 527-8080

Ruth's Bake Shop
987 Central Street
Stoughton
(781) 344-8993

Sara's Kitchen
South Shore Plaza
Braintree
(617) 843-8803

Stop & Shop Bakery
155 Harvard Street
Brookline
(617) 566-4559

Taam Tov Bakery
305A Harvard Street
Brookline
(617) 566-8136

Tabrizi Bakery
56A Mount Auburn Street
Watertown
(617) 926-0880

Titterington Bakery
48 Cummings Park
Woburn
(781) 938-7600

Tuler's Bakery
551 Commonwealth Avenue
Newton
(617) 964-5653

Zeppy's Bakery
937 North Main Street
Randolph
(781) 963-9837

In-store bakeries in Stop & Shop stores in Allston, Brookline, Foxboro, Framingham, Lexington, Natick, Norwood, Stoughton, Swampscott, and Worcester are certified kosher, as are the in-store bakeries in Shaw's Supermarkets and Star Markets in Allston, Brighton, Canton, Sharon, and Sudbury.

New Bedford Area

Super Stop & Shop Bakery
221 Huttleson Avenue
(508) 990-4700

Springfield

Abe's Meats
907 Summer Avenue
(413) 733-3504

Liberty Bakery
801 Liberty Street
(413) 734-2114

Stop & Shop Bakery
470 North Main Street
East Longmeadow
(413) 525-5747

Michigan

Detroit Area

Farmer Jack
6585 Orchard Lake Road
Bloomfield
(810) 851-3850
13115 West 10 Mile Road
Oak Park
(810) 542-1920
29800 Southfield Road
Southfield
(810) 559-8121

Lakewood Market and Food Center
2520 Greenfield Road
Oak Park
(810) 967-2021

Zeeman's New York Bakery
25258 Greenfield Road
Oak Park
(810) 967-3905
30760 Southfield Road
Southfield
(810) 646-7159

Minnesota

Minneapolis

Bakery Express
8793 Anderson Lakes Center
(952) 943-1663

Gelp's Old World Bakery
2445 South Avenue
(612) 377-1870

Wuollet Bakeries
2447 Hennepin Avenue South
(612) 381-9400

Missouri

Kansas City

New York Bakery and Delicatessen
7016 Troost Street
(816) 523-0432

Price Chopper
1030 West 103rd Street
(816) 942-4200

Saint Louis

Diamant's Market
618 North and South Road
(314) 721-9624

Dierberg's Bakery
Craig Road
(314) 432-8823

Kohn's Kosher Market
10405 Old Olive Street Road
(314) 569-0727

Mr. Donut
7758 Olive Street Road
(314) 863-8005

Schnucks Market Bakery
8867 Ladue Crossing
(314) 725-7574
12756 Olive Boulevard
(314) 434-7323

Simon Kohn's Kosher Meat Market and
Grocery
10424 Old Olive Street Road
(314) 569-0727

Sol's Kosher Market
8627 Olive Street Road
(314) 993-9977

Nevada

Las Vegas

Albertsons Supermarket
2550 South Fort Apache Road
(702) 242-1136

Lamar Donuts
9031 West Sahara Avenue
(702) 243-1717

Smith's Supermarket
2211 North Rampart Boulevard
(702) 256-5200

Vegas Kosher Mart
4794 South Eastern Avenue
(702) 243-2533

New Jersey

Atlantic County

Isadore's Kosher Market and Deli
1324 Tilton Road
Northfield
(609) 383-3635

Bergen County

Blue Ribbon Kosher Meats
1363 Inwood Terrace
Fort Lee
(201) 224-3220

Butterflake Bake Shop
448 Cedar Lane
Teaneck
(201) 836-3516

Dovid's Fresh Fish Market
736 Chestnut Avenue
Teaneck
(201) 928-0888

Dunkin Donuts
25 Hackensack Avenue
Hackensack
(201) 488-5219
1406 Teaneck Road
Teaneck
(201) 862-0096

Fair Lawn Kosher Bakery
19-09 Fair Lawn Avenue
Fair Lawn
(201) 796-6565

Fancy Delights
492A Cedar Lane
Teaneck
(201) 487-4035

Food Showcase
24-28 Fair Lawn Avenue
Fair Lawn
(201) 475-0077

Glatt Express Market
1400 Queen Anne Road
Teaneck
(201) 837-8110

Glatt World Market
89 Newbridge Road
Bergenfield
(201) 439-9675

Gruenbaum Bakeries
477B Cedar Lane
Teaneck
(201) 836-3516

Harold's Kosher Meats
67-A East Ridgewood Avenue
Paramus
(201) 262-0030

Hot Bagels
607 Saddle River Road
Fair Lawn
(201) 796-9625
976 Teaneck Road
Teaneck
(201) 833-0410

513 Cedar Lane
Teaneck
(201) 836-9190

Korn's Bakery
1378 Queen Anne Road
Teaneck
(201) 833-0114

Kosher by the Case and Less
255 Van Nostrand Avenue
Englewood
(201) 568-2281

Kosher Express
22-16 Morlot Avenue
Fair Lawn
(201) 791-8818

Kosher House
799 Abbott Avenue
Fort Lee
(201) 224-7777

*Ma'adan
446 Cedar Lane
Teaneck
(201) 692-0192

Marketplace
647 Cedar Lane
Teaneck
(201) 692-1290

*Menagerie
41 East Palisade Avenue
Englewood
(201) 569-2704

Miracle Mart
22-08 Morlot Avenue
Fair Lawn
(201) 791-8810

New Royal Bakery/Breakstix
19-09 Fair Lawn Avenue
Fair Lawn
(201) 796-6565

Perfect Pita
13-22 River Road
Fair Lawn
(201) 794-8700

*Petak's Glatt Kosher Fine Foods
19-03 Fair Lawn Avenue
Fair Lawn
(201) 797-5010

Rita's Italian Ices
1371 Teaneck Road
Teaneck
(201) 862-1522

Royal Bakery Too/Breadstix
172 West Englewood Avenue
Teaneck
(201) 833-0114

Sammy's New York Bagels
1443 Queen Anne Road
Teaneck
(201) 837-0515

Sugarflake Bakery
257 Westwood Avenue
Westwood
(201) 664-1253

World of Goodies
198 West Englewood Avenue
Teaneck
(201) 833-9950

Essex County

Gourmet Galaxy
659 Eagle Roack Avenue
West Orange
(973) 736-0060

Moshavi Speciality Market and
    Restaurant
515 South Livingston Avenue
Livingston
(973) 740-8770

Zayda's
309 Irvington Avenue
South Orange

Hudson County

Progressive Donuts
1250 Kennedy Boulevard
Bayonne
(201) 858-1070

Mercer County

Kosher Experience at ShopRite
319 Route 130 North
East Windsor
(609) 448-1040

Twin Rivers Bagel
Abington Drive
East Windsor
(609) 443-8330

Middlesex County

Dunkin Donuts
65 Raritan Avenue
Highland Park
(732) 828-5485

Kosher Experience at ShopRite
1665 Oak Tree Road
Edison
(732) 494-2440

Lachmaynu Bakery
314 Raritan Avenue
Highland Park
(732) 296-6777

Lox, Stock and Deli
228 Ryders Lane
Milltown
(732) 214-8900

Monmouth County

Kosher Experience at ShopRite
280 U.S. Highway 9
Marlboro
(732) 6170-0404
2200 Highway 66
Neptune
(732) 775-4250

Ocean County

Kosher Experience at ShopRite
1700 Madison Avenue
Lakewood
(732) 363-8270

Passaic County

Kosher Hot Bagels and Bialys
237 Main Avenue
Passaic
(973) 472-1244

Somerset County

Kosher Experience at ShopRite
611 West Union Avenue
Bound Brook
(732) 302-9299

Union County

Dunkin Donuts
186 Elmora Avenue
Elizabeth
(908) 289-9327

New York

Albany

Leo's Bakery
26 Maple Street
(518) 482-7902

Kosher Deli in Price Chopper's
  Supermarket
1892 Central Avenue
(800) 727-5674

Buffalo and Niagara Falls

Bagel Land
Hopkins Road at West Klein
(716) 636-8417

Long Island

Bagel Delight
598 Central Avenue
Cedarhurst
(516) 374-7644

Beach Bakery
112 Main Street
Hampton Beach
(631) 288-6552

Brach's Glatt Market
11 Lawrence Avenue
Lawrence
(516) 239-2703

Central Kosher Fishery
554 Central Avenue
Cedarhurst
(516) 295-7616

Chef Jeff's Gourmet
315 West John
Hicksville
(516) 870-0770

Dunkin Donuts
299 Burnside Avenue
Lawrence
(516) 239-2052
120 East Sunrise Highway
Valley Stream
(516) 561-2779

Emouna Glatt Kosher
713 Middle Neck Road
Great Neck
(516) 829-5454

Gotta Getta Bagel
311 Central Avenue
Lawrence
(516) 374-1131
1033 Broadway
Woodmere
(516) 374-5245

Gourmet Glatt Emporium
137 Spruce Street
Cedarhurst
(516) 569-2662

Grandma Seiden's
1564 Union Turnpike
New Hyde Park
(516) 354-3508

Great Neck Glatt
501 Middle Neck Road
Great Neck
(516) 773-6328

Guss's Pickles
504A Central Avenue
Cedarhurst
(516) 569-0909

JM Glatt Kosher
177 West Hempstead Avenue
West Hempstead
(516) 489-6926

Kosher Cook
882 Lakeside Drive
Windmere
(516) 295-4468

Kosher Delight
437 Railroad Avenue
Westbury
(516) 338-4100

Kosher Emporium of Merrick
1984 Merrick Road
Merrick
(516) 378-6463

Marine Kosher Fish
537 Middle Neck Road
Great Neck
(516) 466-1654

Max's Gourmet Appetizing and Deli
1016 Broadway
Woodmere
(516) 374-0617

Oh Nuts
469 Central Avenue
Cedarhurst
(516) 295-0131

Pearl's Kosher Bake Shop
26 Manetto Hills Road
Plainview
(516) 935-5225

*R & S Kosher
2915 Long Beach Road
Oceanside
(516) 753-5166
http://www.glattmeals.com (meat, fish,
    deli, spa cuisine)

Rabinowitz & Sons Kosher Marketplace
3115 Long Beach Road
Oceanside
(516) 763-4597

Roslyn Kosher Foods
1044 Willis Avenue
Albertson
(516) 621-9615

Shloimy's Heimishe Bakery
536 Central Avenue
Cedarhurst
(516) 374-2525

Shop Glatt Mart
172 East Park Avenue
Long Beach
(516) 897-8657

Simcha Glatt Kosher Meats
1620 Marcus Avenue
New Hyde Park
(516) 681-7766

Superior Glatt Kosher Foods
2915 Long Beach Road
Oceanside
(516) 763-5166

Supersol Kosher Supermarket
330 Central Avenue
Lawrence
(516) 295-3300

Tasty Heimishe Bakery
343 Central Avenue
Cedarhurst
(516) 569-5551

Ultimate Yogurt Shop
602 Central Avenue
Cedarhurst
(516) 569-7821

Woodbury Kosher Meat and Catering
428 South Oyster Bay Road
Hicksville
(516) 681-7766

Zomick's Bakery
444 Central Avenue
Cedarhurst
(516) 569-5520

New York City: Bronx

Glatt Emporium
3711 Riverdale Avenue
(718) 884-1200

Glatt Shop
3450 Johnson Avenue
(718) 548-4855

Gruenebaum's Bakery
3550 Johnson Avenue
(718) 884-5656

Heislers Pastry Shop
3700 Riverdale Avenue
(718) 549-0770

Mr. Bagel of Broadway
5672 Broadway
(718) 549-0408

Nathan's Kosher Meat Market
570 West 235th Street
(718) 548-1723

Rolen Bagels
3601 Riverdale Avenue
(718) 884-9555

Swiss Gourmet
1046 Spofford Avenue
(718) 842-8303

New York City: Brooklyn

Bagel Spot
4305 Fourteenth Avenue
(718) 853-4450

Bell Bagel
1556 Troy Avenue
(718) 951-3555

Chocolate House
1078 Fifty-Third Avenue
(718) 633-8060

Crown Kosher Meat
413 Kingston Avenue
(718) 774-9300

Dave's Kosher Meat Mart
3604 Nostrand Avenue
(718) 648-8500

Flaum Appetizers
40 Lee Avenue
(718) 387-7934

Food Basket
5921 Twentieth Avenue
(718) 331-2220

Glatt Butcher
5704 New Utrecht Avenue
(718) 435-5243

Glatt Mart
1205 Avenue M
(718) 338-4040 (the only kosher
    butcher in the city that prepares
    kosher buffalo meat)

Glatt Pack Kosher Meat
4815 Thirteenth Avenue
(718) 633-6346

Glauber's Appetizing and Catering
161 Division Street
(718) 388-3388

Glick Brothers
448 Avenue P
(718) 645-5254
3719 Nostrand Avenue
(718) 769-7705
520 Neptune Avenue
(718) 372-9394

Golden Star Bakery
2914 Coney Island Avenue
(718) 769-5700

Greens
65 Franklin Avenue
(718) 625-0289

Grodko Kosher Butcher Shop
8402 Twentieth Avenue
(718) 449-2924

HealthyDelites.com
17 Carroll Street
(718) 797-4826

Heimishe Gebeks
1274 Fifty-Sixth Street
(718) 435-4956

Holon Market
517 Kings Highway
(718) 336-7758

I & D Glatt
482 Avenue P
(718) 339-8555

International Glatt Kosher
5600 First Avenue
(718) 491-2756

Israel Glatt
4907 Thirteenth Avenue
(718) 436-2948

Jerusalem Glatt Meats
710 Kings Highway
(718) 376-7443

Jerusalem Kosher Meat Market
4516 Fort Hamilton Parkway
(718) 633-5555

Joey Glatt Kosher
936 Kings Highway
(718) 382-2527

King Glatt Mart
936 Kings Highway
(718) 382-4897

Korn's Kosher Bread Basket
877 Sixty-Third Street
(718) 491-2900

Kosher French Baguette
683 MacDonald Avenue
(718) 633-4994

Kosher Korner
492 Kings Highway
(718) 375-3442 (specializes in Middle
   Eastern foods)

Kosherland
1536 Coney Island Avenue
(718) 338-9346

Kosher Meat Farm
2104 Ralph Avenue
(718) 531-7250

Kosher Plaza Supermarket
1223 Coney Island Avenue
(718) 252-8555

Landau's Glatt Kosher Market
65 Lee Avenue
(718) 782-3700

Landau's Supermarket
4510 Eighteenth Avenue
(718) 633-0633

Le Chocolatier Extraordinaire
1711 Avenue M
(718) 258-5800

Lee Avenue Kosher Bakery
73 Lee Avenue
(718) 387-4736

Lieberman and Rubashkin Glatt Kosher
   Butchers
4308 Fourteenth Avenue
(718) 436-5511

Mansoura's Bakery
515 Kings Highway

Mehadrin Supermarket
5124 Twelfth Avenue
(718) 435-2678

Mendy's Supermarket
2213 Sixty-Fifth Street
(718) 837-0782

Nadler's Kosher Meats
613 Brighton Beach Avenue
(718) 648-6900

Ossi's Fish Market
1314 Fiftieth Street
(718) 436-1151

Netzach Israel Meat
5010 Sixteenth Avenue
(718) 851-0051

Pasternack Kosher Butcher
422 Ditmars Avenue
(718) 438-4411

Pick N Pay
1907 Avenue M
(718) 377-4050

Presser Kosher Bakery
1720 Avenue M
(718) 375-5088

R & W Glatt Kosher Butchers
1501 Coney Island Avenue
(718) 377-7391

Ralph Zaken
3069 West First Street
(845) 434-1078

Raskin's Fish Market
320 Kingston Avenue
(718) 756-9521

Rosner Kosher
719 Avenue U
(718) 645-8486

Royal Food Market
1701 McDonald Avenue
(718) 645-0055 (open 24 hours)

Setton's Foods
509 Kings Highway
(718) 375-2558

Shlomy's Heimishe Bakery
4301 Sixteenth Avenue
(718) 854-1766
5017 New Utrecht Avenue
(718) 633-2209

Sola Bakery
2112 East Eighth Street
(718) 339-5857

Steinbergers Kosher Bakery
1753 Clymer Street
(718) 486-9100

Strauss Bakery
5209 Thirteenth Avenue
(718) 851-7728

Sweet Odyssey Candy
1723 Avenue M
(718) 258-2534

Weiss Kosher Bakery
5011 Thirteenth Avenue
(718) 438-0407

Weiss Kosher Meat Market
5520 Thirteenth Avenue
(718) 871-5448
1214 Avenue M
(718) 376-6116

World of Chantilly Fine Kosher Desserts
4302 Farragut Road
(718) 859-1100

Yerushalayim Famous Bakery
1336 Thirty-Ninth Street
(718) 633-5100

Yossi's Sweet House
5717–19 Eighteenth Avenue
(718) 234-7629; (877) 4-YOSSIS

Zion Market and Bakery
4100 Thirteenth Avenue (the only kosher
    Yemenite market in New York City)

New York City: Manhattan

Bagels Plus
243 West Thirty-Eighth Street
(212) 997-7558

Ben's Cheese Shop
181 East Houston Street
(212) 254-8290

Cold Stone Creamery
253 West Forty-Second Street
(212) 398-1882 (customized ice cream)

David's Kosher Meats
221 East Broadway
(212) 964-1232

East Side Glatt Butchers
510 Grand Street
(212) 254-8335
http://www.kosherburgers.com

Eli's Breads
403 East Ninety-First Street
(212) 831-4800

Feinschmecker Fine Foods
1239 First Avenue
(212) 794-2365

Fischer Brothers and Leslie Kosher
    Meat and Poultry and Take Out
230 West Seventy-Second Street
(212) 787-1715

Gertels Bake Shop
53 Hester Street
(212) 982-3250
1592 Second Avenue
(212) 734-3238

Gisella's Secrets
412 East Ninth Street
(212) 777-0695 (sugar-free, salt-free
    bakery)

Grossinger's Uptown Bakery
570 Columbus Avenue
(212) 874-6996

H&H Bagel
2239 Broadway
(212) 595-8000
639 West Forty-Sixth Street
(212) 765-7200 (open 24 hours)

Kosher Marketplace
2442 Broadway
(212) 580-6378

Kossair's Bialys
367 Grand Street
(212) 473-4810

Leibel's Kosher Specialties
39 Essex Street
(212) 254-0335

Long Island Glatt Kosher Meat and
   Poultry
829 West 181st Street
(212) 795-0248

Miller's Cheese and Appetizing
2192 Broadway
(212) 496-8855

Moishe's Home Made Kosher Bakery
181 East Houston Street
(212) 475-9624
115 Second Avenue
(212) 505-8555

Murray's House of Prime Kosher Meat
507 Grand Street
(212) 254-0180

Orwasher's Bakery
308 East Seventy-Eighth Street
(212) 288-6569

*Park East Kosher Butchers and
   Take Out
1163 Madison Avenue
(212) 737-9800

Royale Kosher Bakery Shop
237 West Seventy-Second Street
(212) 874-5642

Supersol Kosher Supermarket
526 Amsterdam Avenue
212-875-1731

Sweetroll
48 Beaver Street
(212) 363-7588

Zabar's Food Shop
2245 Broadway
(212) 787-2000 (wide selection of
   kosher foods and delicacies; also sells
   nonkosher foods)

New York City: Queens

Aaron's Bake Shop
71-72 Yellowstone Boulevard
Forest Hills
(718) 263-5045

*Aaron's Gourmet Emporium
63-36 Woodhaven Boulevard
Rego Park
(718) 205-1992

Aaron's Kosher Meats
156-15 Aguilar Avenue
Flushing
(718) 380-8209

Abe's Glatt Kosher Meats
98-106 Queens Boulevard
Forest Hills
(718) 459-5820

Akboch Kosher Meat Market
98-54 Sixty-Third Road
Rego Park
(718) 896-7276

Amala Grocery
68-24 Main Street
Kew Gardens Hills
(718) 575-1887

Ararat Bakery
220-16 Horace Harding Expressway
Bayside
(718) 225-3478

Bagels and Company
188-02 Union Turnpike
Flushing
(718) 217-7755

Beautiful Buhkara Bakery
64-47 108th Street
Rego Park
(718) 275-2220

Block and Faulk Meats
112-06 Queens Boulevard
Forest Hills
(718) 261-7463

Brach's Glatt Self-Service Meat and
    Supermarket
72-51 Main Street
Kew Gardens Hills
(718) 544-7448

Burkho Meat Store
65-49 Ninety-Ninth Street
Rego Park
(718) 459-8480

Chai Kosher Meats
64-37 108th Street
Forest Hills
(718) 897-9619

Cinderella Sweets
4909 Rockaway Beach Boulevard
Far Rockaway
(718) 318-2100

D&W Kosher Meats
61-42 Springfield Avenue
Bayside
(718) 225-1550

Edal's Kosher Meat and Poultry
79-09 Main Street
Kew Gardens Hills
(718) 380-1366

Eli's Glatt Cut
189-19 Union Turnpike
Flushing
(718) 217-9299

Finest Kosher Meats and Poultry
63-71 108th Street
Forest Hills
(718) 897-3053

Fried's Fish Market
69-36 Main Street
Kew Gardens Hills
(718) 793-8188

G&I Kosher Bakeries
69-40 Main Street
Kew Gardens Hills
(718) 261-1155
72-22 Main Street
Kew Gardens Hills
(718) 544-8736

G&K Kosher Meat and Poultry
115-06 Rockaway Beach Boulevard
Rockaway Park
(718) 474-6704

Gotta Getta Bagel
107-09 Continental Avenue
Forest Hills
(718) 793-1640

Hatov Vehamativ Meat and Groceries
69-38 Main Street
Kew Gardens Hills
(718) 263-7009

Herman Glick & Sons Glatt Kosher
    Food Emporium
100-15 Queens Boulevard
Forest Hills
(718) 896-7736

Hershkowitz Glatt Kosher
164-08 Sixty-Ninth Avenue
Flushing
(718) 591-0750

Isaac's Meat Market
189-19 Union Turnpike
Fresh Meadows
(718) 217-9299

Jay Dee Kosher Bakery
98-92 Queens Boulevard
Forest Hills
(718) 459-5365

JMJ Baking and Catering
28-11 Twenty-Third Street
Long Island City
(718) 392-6222

King David Bakery
77-51 Vleigh Place
Kew Gardens Hills
(718) 969-6165

Kosher Bagels and Bialys
147-23 Union Turnpike
Fresh Meadows
(718) 591-3356

Kosher Fish Market
72-14 Main Street
Kew Gardens Hills
(718) 520-8744

Kosher Palace
103-27 Queens Boulevard
Forest Hills
(718) 830-9792

Kosher World Supermarket
1913 Cornaga Avenue
Far Rockaway
(718) 471-4475

Lazar's Kosher Meats
100-30 Queens Boulevard
Forest Hills
(718) 897-6635

*Main Street Bagels and Appetizing
72-26 Main Street
Kew Gardens Hills
(718) 793-8200

Max and Mina's Ice Cream
71-26 Main Street
Kew Gardens Hills
(718) 793-8629

Mazal Kosher Food
63-66 108th Street
Forest Hills
(718) 459-5707

Mazur's Market Place
254-51 Horace Harding Boulevard
Little Neck
(718) 428-5000

Mendy's Bakery
72-22 Main Street
Kew Gardens Hills
(718) 544-8736

Natural Spice
69-66 Main Street
Kew Gardens Hills
(718) 261-6767 (spices, coffee)

Piquanty Grocery
68-29 Main Street
Kew Gardens Hills
(718) 575-1587

Queens Pita Bakery
68-38 Main Street
Kew Gardens Hills
(718) 263-8000

Ramat Gan Fresh Fruits and Vegetables
71-30 Main Street
Kew Gardens Hills
(718) 544-2774 (carries a selection of
    dried fruits and Israeli specialties)

Sangdast Kosher Meat
81-63 Lefferts Boulevard
Kew Gardens
(718) 805-7900

Simcha Kosher Meats
138-40 Eighty-Sixth Avenue
Jamaica
(718) 206-4861
77-39 Vleigh Place
Kew Gardens Hills
(718) 969-7954

Super Glatt
189-23 Union Turnpike
Fresh Meadows
(718) 776-7727

Supersol Kosher Supermarket
68-18 Main Street
Kew Gardens Hills
(718) 268-6469

Tikvah Kosher Meat Mart
105-45 Sixty-Fourth Road
Forest Hills
(718) 896-8515

Uncle Louie's Gourmet Ice Cream
68-41 Main Street
Kew Gardens Hills
(718) 544-4656

Union Turnpike Meat Corp.
179-14 Union Turnpike
Fresh Meadows
(718) 969-4322

Uzbekistan Tandoori Bread
120-35 Eighty-Third Avenue
Kew Gardens
(718) 850-3426

Wasserman Supermarket
72-68 Main Street
Kew Gardens Hills
(718) 544-7413

Yakaov and David
138-38 Eighty-Sixth Avenue
Jamaica
(718) 739-5436

New York City: Staten Island

Famous Kosher Bakery
2208 Victory Boulevard
(718) 494-1411

Heartland Bagels and Cakes
2311 Richmond Avenue
(718) 761-4280

Kosher Depot Supermarket
460 Bradley Avenue
(718) 477-1584

Kosher Island Glatt Kosher Take Home
  Foods
2206 Victory Boulevard
(718) 698-5800

Payless Glatt Kosher Meats
77 Richmond Hill Road
(718) 370-1788

Rockland County

A & B Famous Fish
84 Route 59
Monsey
(845) 425-3390

Kessler Brothers Kosher
Green Street
Woodbridge
(845) 434-4500

Monsey Glatt Kosher
190 Route 59
Monsey
(845) 425-6328

Monsey Kosher Plaza
84 Route 59
Monsey
(845) 352-5040

Rockland Kosher Supermarket
34 Main Street
Monsey
(845) 425-2666

Wesley Kosher Supermarket
455 Route 306
Monsey
(845) 364-7217

Westchester County

Carvel Ice Cream Bakery
19 Quaker Ridge Road
New Rochelle
(914) 738-5222

Heisler's Pastry
1321 North Avenue
New Rochelle
(914) 235-8201

Lincoln Park Pastry Shop
634 McLean Avenue
Yonkers
(914) 965-7463

Sammy's Kosher Meat Market
720 Bedford Road
Bedford Hills
(914) 241-4477

Sammy's New York Bagels
134 North Avenue
New Rochelle
(914) 235-7800
1461 Weaver Street
Scarsdale
(914) 472-0500

Supersol Kosher Supermarket
11 Quaker Ridge Road
New Rochelle
(914) 636-4821
1066 Wilmot Road
Scarsdale
(914) 472-2240

Syon Kosher Meats
2558 Central Park Avenue
Yonkers
(914) 779-8100

Ohio

Cincinnati

Dunkin Donuts
9385 Colerain Avenue
(513) 385-0930

Graeter's Ice Cream
41 East Fourth Street
(513) 381-0653

Marx Hot Bagels
477 East Kemper Road
(513) 671-0278

Philder's Kosher Foods
7601 Reading Road
(513) 821-7050

Cleveland and Vicinity

Abba's Market and Grill
13937 Cedar Road
(216) 321-5660

Boris Butcher Shop
14406 Cedar Road
(216) 382-5330

Brooklyn Bagels
190 South Taylor Road
Cleveland Heights
(216) 321-0738

Chocolate Emporium
14439 Cedar Road
(216) 382-0140

Lax and Mandel Bakery and Deli
2070 South Taylor Road
Cleveland Heights
(216) 932-6445
14441 Cedar Road
South Euclid
(216) 381-5730

Shimon's Kosher Poultry and Fish
1923 South Taylor Road
Cleveland Heights
(216) 371-0555

Tibor Kosher Meat Market
2185 South Green Road
Cleveland Heights
(216) 381-7615

Unger's Kosher Bakery and Food Shop
1831 South Taylor Road
Cleveland Heights
(216) 321-7176

Columbus

Bexley Kosher Market
3012 East Broad Street
(614) 231-3653

Blessed Cookie
3 Nationwide Place
(614) 221-4442

Martin's Kosher Foods
3685 East Broad Street
(614) 231-3653

Sammy's N.Y. Bagel and Deli
40 North James Road
(614) 237-2444

Oregon
Portland
Albertsons Deli and Bakery
5414 S.W. Beaverton Hillsdale Highway
(503) 246-1713

Safeway Supermarket
6745 S.W. Beaverton Hillsdale Highway
(503) 292-5111

Strohecker's Market
2855 S.W. Patton Road
(503) 223-7391

Pennsylvania
Harrisburg
Grant Food
4450 Oakhurst Boulevard
(717) 652-7795

Weiss Market
4300 Linglestown Road
(717) 540-6010

Northampton County
Buy the Dozen Bakery
219 Haverford Avenue
Nazareth
(610) 667-9440

Philadelphia
Bestcake Bakery
1594 Haverford Avenue
(215) 878-1127

Best Value Market
8566 Bustleton Avenue
(215) 342-1902

Genuardi's Family Market/
 Glatt Kosher Deli
737 Huntington Pike
(215) 379-6900

Krispy Kreme
2327 Cottman Avenue
(215) 708-8040

Laromme Bakery
10186 Bustletown Avenue
(212) 969-6003

Liss Bakery
6242 Haverford Avenue
(215) 474-8550

Michael's Bakery
6635 Castor Avenue
(215) 745-1423

Milk n Honey Grocery
7618 Castor Avenue
(215) 342-3224

New York Bagel Baker
7555 Haverford Avenue
(215) 878-8090

Simon's Glatt Kosher Meat
6926 Bustleton Avenue
(215) 624-5695

Weiss Bakery
6635 Castor Avenue
(215) 722-4506

Pittsburgh
Kosher Mart
2121 Murray Avenue
(412) 421-4450

Krispy Kreme
461 Clairton Boulevard
(412) 650-9733

Pastries Unlimited/Simple Treat Bakery
2119 Murray Avenue
(412) 521-6323

Prime Kosher/Murray Avenue Kosher
1916 Murray Avenue
(412) 421-1015

Rhode Island
Providence
David Kosher Bakery
721 Hope Street
(401) 331-4239

Kaplan's Bakery
756 Hope Street
(401) 621-8107

Tennessee
Memphis
Carl's Bakery
1690 Jackson Street
(901) 276-2304

Kroger Supermarket
540 South Mendenhall Parkway
(901) 683-8846

Texas
Austin
Randall's Grocery and Bakery
5311 Balcones Street
(512) 302-2500

Dallas
Kosher Link
7517 Campbell Road
(214) 248-3773

Tom Thumb Bakery and Deli
11920 Preston Road
(214) 392-2501

Houston
Ashcraft Bakery
1301 North First Street
Bellaire
(713) 666-2163

Kosher Deli and Bakery at Minyard
Food
714 Preston Road
(214) 691-4539

Kroger Supermarket Bakery
10306 South Post Oak Road
(713) 721-7691

Le Moulin European Bakery
5645 Beechnut Street
(713) 799-1618

New York Bagels
9724 Hillcroft Street
(713) 723-5879

Simon's Gourmet Kosher Foods
5411 South Braeswood Boulevard
(713) 729-5333

Three Brothers Bakery
4036 South Braeswood Boulevard
(713) 666-2551

Virginia
Norfolk
Kosher Place
738 West Twenty-Second Street
(804) 623-1770

Richmond
Kroger Supermarket
1601 Willowlawn Road
(804) 288-2885

Washington
Seattle
Albertsons Food and Drug Store
various locations

Bagel Deli
340 Fifteenth Street East
(206) 322-2471 (bagels, bialys,
   brownies)

Krispy Kreme
12505 Aurora Avenue North
(206) 396-2728

Noah's Grocery
4700 Fiftieth Street
(206) 725-4267

Varon's Kosher Market
3931 Martin Luther King Way South
(206) 723-0240

Wisconsin

Milwaukee
Kramer's Kosher Korner
5101 West Keefe Avenue
(414) 442-2625

Canada

Calgary, Alberta
Baskin Robbins
512-10916 Macleod Trail South
(403) 278-6611

Izzy's Kosher Meats and Deli
2515 Ninetieth Avenue S.W.
(403) 251-2552

Halifax, Nova Scotia
Stone Hearth Bakery
Argyle Street
(902) 425-7752

Toronto, Ontario
Amazing Donuts
3772 Bathurst Street
(416) 398-7546

Ely's Fine Foods
3537 Bathurst Street
(416) 782-3231

Grodzinski Bakery
3456 Bathurst Street
(416) 789-0785

Isaac's Bakery
221 Wilmington Street
(416) 630-1678
3390 Bathurst Street
(416) 789-7587

Kosher and Natural Foods
3413 Bathurst Street
(416) 789-7174

Kosher City Plus
3468 Bathurst Street
(416) 782-6788

Kosher Food Warehouse
75 Doncaster Avenue
(905) 764-7575

Kosher Grocer
3041 Bathurst Street
(416) 785-3001

Vancouver, British Columbia
Omnitsky Meat Market
5866 Cambie Street
(604) 321-1818

Royal Bagel Factory
701 Queensbury Avenue
North Vancouver
(604) 257-5111

Sabra Bakery and Grocery
3844 Oak Street
(604) 733-4912

Winnipeg, Manitoba
Bathurst Market
1570 Main Street
(204) 338-4911

City Bread
238 Dufferin Avenue
(204) 586-8409
232 Jarvis Avenue
(204) 586-8469

Gunn's Bakery
247 Selkirk Avenue
(204) 582-2364

Omnitsky's Kosher Foods
1428 Main Street
(204) 586-8271

Belgium

Antwerp
Kleinblatt Bakery
Provincierstraat at Wippstraat

Brussels
Yarkow Market
avenue des Sept Bonniers 83

Great Britain

London

Carmelli Bakery
128 Golders Green Road

Grodzinski Bakery
223 Golders Green Road

Taboon Bakery
17 Russell Parade

Italy

Rome

Limentani Settino Bakery
Via Portico d'Ottavio 1

Netherlands

Amsterdam

Marcus Ritueel Butcher
Ferd. Bolsstraat 44

Theeboom Bakery
Tweede Sweelinckstraat 5
Maasstraat 16

Switzerland

Zurich

Kosher Bakery
Braverstrasse 110

Kosher Butcher
Lowenstrasse 12

Other Resources for the Kosher Consumer

Kosher Cooking Classes

Cook Euro
(212) 687-9898
incook@earthlink.net
La Cucina Kasher (Tuscany, Italy);
   La Cucina Kasher (Emilia Romagna,
   Italy); La Cuisine Cachère de
   Provence (France): tours that
   combine five days of regional kosher
   cooking classes with sightseeing and
   shopping.

Dawn R. Schuman Institute, Chicago
(847) 509-8282
Course: Barbara Freedman Teaches
   Kosher Cooking

De Gustibus
Macy's Cooking School, New York City
(212) 439-1714
http://www.degustibusinc.com
grtcooks@aol.com
Highlights kosher chefs each season.

Jewish Community Center Cooking
   School, New York City
Julie Negrin, Director of Culinary Arts
Registration: (646) 505-5708

http://www.jccmanhattan.org;
http://www.jcckitchen.org
Also has classes in ethnic cuisines,
   cooking for children, and
   understanding wine.

Levana Kirschenbaum
cookbook author, owner of Levana
   Restaurant
(212) 874-6100
http://www.levankirschenbaum.com

Makor
(212) 601-1000
http://www.makor.org

Ninety-Second Street Y, New York City
(212) 415-5500
http://www.92Y.org

Susie Fishbeen, author of Kosher Palate
   and Kosher by Design
http://www.Kosherbydesign.com

Kosher Gyms

Studio 613, 65 Route 59, Monsey, New
   York, (845) 356-6613 (women only)

Kosher Gym, 1800 Coney Island
Avenue, Brooklyn, New York, (718)
376-3535

Kosher Kitchens

Go Kosher America
(888) 465-6743
http://www.gokoshr.org
A koshering service for consumer,
commercial, and catering situations.

Publications

Kashrus Magazine
P.O. Box 204
Brooklyn, NY 11204
(718) 336-8544
http://www.kashrusmagazine.com
Five issues a year; $18 one year, $33 two
years, $45 three years, $60 four years.

*Kosher Today: The Official Trade
Publication of the Kosher Food Industry*
225 West Thirty-Fourth Street
New York, NY 10122
(212) 643-9164
http://www.koshertodayonline.com
subscription@koshertodayonline.com
$25 a year

Taste NewYork Magazine
P.O. Box 74-7949
Flushing, NY 11374
(718) 302-2093
Kosher food and dining in the New
York City area.

The Jewish Homemaker
420 Lincoln Road, Suite 409
Miami Beach, FL 33139
(800) 237-2304; (305) 673-3530
http://www.homemaker.org
Bimonthly publication that
incorporates *The Kosher Food Guide*
of the OK Laboratories.

Web Sites of Interest to Kosher Consumers

http://www.dmoz.org/Shopping/Food/
Ethnic_and_Regional/Kosher.com

Links to Web sites for kosher food,
vitamins, and recipes.

http://www.haruth.com
Links to kosher sites; information on
kosher cooking and travel; lists of
kosher restaurants worldwide.

http://www.hillel.org
The B'nai B'rith Hillel Foundation's site
has a guide to Jewish life on campus
and descriptions and contact information for college Hillel groups throughout the United States and worldwide,
including information on schools that
have kosher dining arrangements for
their students. Schools or Hillels with
kosher meal plans include Bingham-
ton University, Boston University,
Brandeis University, Brown University, Case Western Reserve University,
Cornell Hillel, CUNY Brooklyn
College, Dartmouth Hillel, Harvard
Radcliffe Hillel, Hillel at Columbia
University and Barnard College, Hillel
at the George Washington University,
Hillel of Towson University, Indiana
University Hillel, Hillel of York Uni-
versity (Toronto), Johns Hopkins Uni-
versity Hillel, Massachusetts Institute
of Technology Hillel, New York
University Hillel/Bronfman Center,
Oberlin College Hillel, Princeton
University Hillel/Center for Jewish
Life, Rutgers University Hillel, SUNY
Stony Brook Hillel, University of
Albany Hillel, University of Arizona
Hillel, University of Chicago Hillel,
University of Maryland, University of
Massachusetts/Amherst Hillel, Uni-
versity of Michigan Hillel, University
of Pennsylvania Hillel, University of
Rochester, University of Southern
California Hillel, Vanderbilt Univer-
sity, Washington University, and Yale
University Hillel.

http://www.jewishfood.com
Links to kosher food sites, kosher
businesses, and recipes.

http://www.jewishcelebrations.com/
restaurants
Information on kosher restaurants
worldwide.

http://www.jewishlink.com
Listing of kosher restaurants in the New
York City area.

http://www.kashrut.com
Information on newly certified products
and kosher product alerts; kosher
travel links

http://www.koshercooking.com
Recipes.

http://www.koshercreations.com
Recipes.

http://kosherdine.com
Information on kosher restaurants
worldwide.

http://kosherfinder.com
Information on kosher restaurants
worldwide.

http://www.kosherline.com
Information on kosher travel, home
catering, wine, and restaurants.

http://www.koshernic.com
Directory of kosher restaurants and food
worldwide.

http://www.kosherquest.org
Recipes, updates, and alerts on kosher
certification.

http://www.kosherzone.com
Kosher restaurants, markets, bakeries
listed by time zone; kosher travel.

http://www.shamash.org
Information on kosher restaurants
worldwide.

http://www.tastekosher.com
Information on kosher restaurants and
kosher travel, discount dining
coupons.

http://www.thejewishweek.com
Sources of Judaica, including kosher gift
baskets.

http://www.totallyjewish.com
Kosher restaurants, markets, bakeries,
butchers worldwide; kosher hotels in
Great Britain.

http://www.zipple.com
Information on kosher cookbooks,
recipes, wine, travel, and kashrut
authorities.

Notes

Chapter One: What Is Kosher?

1. When you purchase kosher canned tuna, you are also assured that it contains no bits of porpoise or dolphin, which are non-kosher, highly intelligent mammals. Porpoises and dolphins are tuna's natural predators and can be caught up in the tuna nets and then processed with the fish.
2. Although bees are not kosher, honey produced by bees is kosher. According to the Torah, the real source of honey is the flowers from which it is made.

Chapter Three: Understanding the Kosher Symbols

1. Arkansas, California, Connecticut, Illinois, Kentucky, Louisiana, Maryland, Massachusetts, Michigan, Minnesota, Missouri, New Jersey, New York, Ohio, Pennsylvania, Rhode Island, Texas, Virginia, Washington, and Wisconsin. Canada has a federal kosher labeling law.

Chapter Four: The Growth of Kosher Certification

1. The *mashgiah* need not be a rabbi (although all Orthodox and Conservative rabbis must master a detailed knowledge of the laws of kashrut before they can be ordained). Any observant Jew trained to look out for kashrut problems can give certification. Kosher inspectors and supervisors must be well versed in

the laws of kashrut as set down in a detailed 576-page text written in Hebrew and Aramaic, as well as in contemporary knowledge about food chemistry and processing.

2. The Food and Drug Administration, which inspects food processing plants (other than meat or poultry plants, which are the province of the U.S. Department of Agriculture), may visit once a year or less. Some plants are visited on average only once every ten years. In addition, the nation's approximately two hundred thousand nonkosher fast-food restaurants are not subjected to any oversight by federal health authorities.

3. Food labeling laws allow for a certain ambiguity regarding ingredients. A "natural flavor" may actually contain more than one hundred different flavor components, including flavor-enhancing animal derivatives from such nonkosher animals as beavers (the extract castoreum) and civet cats. Carmine food coloring is derived from the pulverized shells of a beetlelike insect. Flavorings may also contain biotechnologically produced ingredients processed with such nutrients as blood or animal tissue. Other examples of hidden ingredients are soya flour, which may be treated with an enzyme derived from the stomachs of swine; varieties of vegetable shortening containing emulsifiers—which allow two substances to be mixed together—that may be derived from animals; emulsifiers in baked goods, chocolates, and candies that may be glycerides derived from nonkosher animals rather than of vegetable origin; meat tenderizers containing lactose, a dairy ingredient; and creamers labeled "nondairy" that state and federal regulations allow to contain a small percentage of milk fat.

Chapter Five: Meats and Poultry

1. The United States has recently experienced a nationwide scare about "mad cow disease" (bovine spongiform encephalopathy, or BSE) and the fear that infected beef might find its way into the human food consumption chain. BSE, which destroys an animal's brain and central nervous system, leading to death, is

thought to be caused by prion proteins that incubate in cattle's brain and nerve tissue. The rules of kosher slaughter may help protect consumers from purchasing infected beef, for a number of reasons:

- Any cows or cattle showing signs of injury or disease are automatically rejected for kosher slaughter. So called "downer" cattle—animals that because of injury or illness cannot walk or stand—would never be accepted. In addition, internal abnormalities found after slaughter would render the beef unsuitable for kosher processing. (General use of downer cattle for human consumption and the use of high-risk parts from cows older than thirty months was not banned by the U.S. Department of Agriculture until December 30, 2003. Early in 2004, the Food and Drug Administration took further steps to close loopholes in its livestock feed ban, including prohibitions against feeding cattle mammalian blood or blood products, as well as a ban on using material from downer cows in cosmetics or dietary supplements.)
- Kosher beef comes from animals that have been killed by having their throat slit, rather than by a strike or other trauma to the head, the method generally used to kill cattle for the nonkosher market. This latter method can scatter brain tissue, which may contain prion proteins, through the bloodstream and body of the animal.
- Certain cuts of meat, such as T-bone and Porterhouse steaks, are not allowable for kosher consumption. These cuts, which contain parts of the spinal cord and vertebrae, may contain prion proteins.

Additional information about mad cow disease can be obtained from the Centers for Disease Control and Prevention (CDC) at http://www.cdc.gov, the Food and Drug Administration (FDA) at http://www.fda.gov, and the U.S. Department of Agriculture (USDA) at http://www.usda.gov.

2. USDA regulations permit livestock and poultry to be stunned before slaughter with blows to the head, electric shock, or tranquilizer injections. None of these methods are permitted by kosher ritual. Late in 2003, the Department of Agriculture banned the air injection stunning of cattle before slaughter, but other similar methods are still permitted.

3. Many animals approved by the USDA for human consumption are unacceptable for kosher use. For example, USDA regulations allow nontumorous parts of a chicken to be sold; they also allow a chicken leg to be approved even if it came from a bird that had a tumor on another part of its body. To be kosher, a chicken can have no tumors anywhere. Also, USDA standards do not address questions about the conditions in which the chickens were raised or what they were fed.

4. According to the New York Beef Industry Council, experiments performed by the New York State Department of Agriculture and Markets indicated that the penetration of salt from the koshering process is less than ⅛ inch from the surface. If you are concerned about sodium in your diet, rinsing the beef or poultry in water before cooking will help reduce the salt content.

5. Empire Kosher Chicken maintains a customer hotline to answer cooking questions and to provide information on product availability. The company also offers free literature and recipes. Empire can be contacted at (800) 367-4734, Monday through Thursday, 8 A.M. to 5 P.M., Eastern Time, or Friday, 8 A.M. to 3 P.M.; through its Web site at http://www.empirekosher.com; or by e-mail at empire@acsworld.net. Questions about Wise poultry can be directed via e-mail to info@wisekosher.com.

Chapter Six: Wine and Spirits

1. Jewish immigrants arriving in the United States who needed to make kosher wine for their religious ceremonies found that the only grapes available were a local variety known as Concord.

With a high-acid, low-sugar content, these grapes were unlike the ones they had known in Europe. To compensate for the differences and to balance the natural acidity, the winemakers added sugar during processing. The result was the sweet syrupy drink that many people still associate, erroneously, with all kosher wines.

2. Some kosher wines have the word *Mevushal* on their label; in Hebrew, the word literally means "cooked or boiled wine." Mevushal wines, which have been flash-pasteurized (heated briefly, then brought back to normal temperature) before bottling, can be uncorked and poured by anyone—observant Jew or Gentile—and still be considered kosher. For observant Jews, this "cooked wine" is no longer officially considered wine and therefore, like other kosher foods and products, can be handled by anyone and still keep its kosher status. (This ruling goes back to biblical times, when boiled wine was considered unfit as a sacramental offering.) Flash pasteurization does not affect the taste or quality of the wine.

Chapter Seven: Kosher and Healthy

1. The leanest cut of kosher beef is round; most fish is considered lean; turkey or chicken with the skin removed is considered lean.
2. This includes processed meats such as hot dogs and breaded chicken cutlets. At the time of writing this book, however, the labeling of fresh poultry and meat is voluntary, and information may or may not be displayed at the point of purchase.
3. According to the FDA, a 2,000-calorie-a-day diet is generally recommended for most moderately active women, teenage girls, and sedentary men. Many older adults, children, and sedentary women need only 1,600 calories. A 2,500-calorie-a-day diet may be suitable or appropriate for many men, teenage boys, and active women. In 2003, the USDA issued new recommendations on caloric intake. Recognizing that a majority of Americans

(64 percent) are overweight and sedentary and need to eat less, the agency now calls for most women between the ages of thirty-five and seventy to eat 1,600 to 1,800 calories a day and for most men in that age group to eat 2,000 to 2,200 calories a day.

4. This refers to ingredients that are added or combined to form the product. Exceptions are made for products such as mineral water: the mineral content does not have to be listed since the minerals are considered an inherent part of the product, not added ingredients.

5. In 2003, the FDA loosened its regulations for health claims on food labels, allowing companies to make "qualified health claims" for certain foods. Food makers still have to seek FDA approval first, and the FDA will then respond by grading each potential claim: "A" for scientifically proven claims, "B" where the science is good but not conclusive, "C" where there is limited science to support a claim, and "D" where there is hardly any evidence. B, C, and D claims would be considered "qualified" and could be put on a food label next to a short disclaimer that describes how much proof there is—or isn't.

6. Some "low-fat" or "fat-free" products make claims that they are a certain percentage fat-free. This term will now have to accurately reflect the amount of fat present in 100 grams of food. Thus a food with 3 grams of fat per 100 grams would be "97 percent fat-free." Consumers should also note that fat-free products may contain more sugar or more sodium to improve their taste. Therefore, the calorie count may not be much lower than for comparable products that are not fat-free.

7. In 1996, the 1990 Nutrition Labeling and Education Act was amended to include milk and some dairy products (cottage cheese products and sour half-and-half, a lower-fat sour cream) that had been previously exempted by the FDA. Beginning in 1997, 2 percent milk, which has 5 grams of fat per serving, could now be called "reduced-fat," not "low-fat," as it has long been labeled. One percent milk, which contains 2.5 grams fat per serving, can qualify for "low-fat," and skim milk, which has

no fat at all, can be labeled "fat-free" or "nonfat." The new rules do not apply to yogurt.

Chapter Eight: Kosher for Vegetarians

1. There are over ten million vegetarians in the United States. Many people believe that vegetarians are thinner and healthier and live longer than meat-eaters. Some actuarial statistics seem to bear this out. According to the American Dietary Association, vegetarians appear to be at lower risk for osteoporosis, kidney stones, gallstones, and breast cancer. Some studies show a positive link between vegetarianism and health. In general, says the ADA, heart disease, high blood pressure, adult-onset diabetes, obesity, and some forms of cancer tend to develop less often among vegetarians than nonvegetarians.

2. A vegetarian diet is an ideal also stressed by of several Eastern religions, including Taosim and Hinduism. Many Buddhists are vegetarians because their code, the Eightfold Path, calls for them not to harm living things. The two million Jains of India are strict vegetarians. They will not even eat root vegetables because the whole plant dies when the root is harvested for food. Members of the Seventh-day Adventist church, a now worldwide Protestant denomination formally established in America in 1863, are expected to adhere to the biblical principles of diet and health—in effect, the Jewish dietary laws. They abstain from alcohol and tobacco and are encouraged to follow a vegetarian diet. It is estimated that half of the 7.7 million Seventh-day Adventists are vegetarians.

3. Jewish law commands that not only must you protect animals from pain or harm, but you must also protect the environment and natural resources of the earth. You are admonished not to waste food and not to wantonly pollute. Some contemporary rabbis go even further and say it is not proper to eat plants or animals that are in danger of extinction, even if those plants and animals are kosher, or to ingest known carcinogens or to smoke.

Chapter Nine: Kosher for the Lactose-Intolerant

1. The ability to *tolerate* lactose in adulthood is probably a genetic mutation, since in most cultures (except certain western European societies), our ancestors did not drink milk after early childhood. In 2001, scientists identified the genetic basis for lactose intolerance. A test based on this finding will enable lactose intolerance to be diagnosed from the DNA in a drop of blood.

2. Milk allergy is not the same as lactose intolerance. Milk allergy, which occurs in less than 1 percent of adults, is characterized by typical allergy symptoms that range from asthma and runny nose to diarrhea, abdominal pain, dermatitis, and hives.

3. Dairy products are high in calcium, riboflavin, protein, phosphorus, and magnesium, which help protect against osteoporosis, a debilitating bone disease. Those who cannot eat dairy foods comfortably should increase their intake of nondairy calcium-containing foods such as dates, prunes, legumes, broccoli, leafy green vegetables such as kale and Chinese cabbage, canned salmon and sardines with the bones included, calcium-fortified soy milk, and tofu.

4. Isoflavones may reduce menopausal symptoms, help prevent and fight cancer, reduce the risk of heart disease, aid in the control of diabetes, prevent kidney disease, lower cholesterol, and help fight osteoporosis.

Chapter Ten: Cooking Kosher

1. For many of the recipes in this chapter, my special thanks go to my late mom, Beatrice Garfunkel, and to my aunt, Florence Fialkoff; her daughter and granddaughter, Lynn Kozbial and Maren Kozbial; my sister and brother-in-law, Sandy and Gerry Muroff; Zena and Michael Muroff; Claire and Nat Muroff; Harry and Martha Pollack; Marcia and Artie Tureck; Joyce and Aaron Garvin; Susan Meltzer; and Carol Zuckerman.

Bibliography

Bank, Richard. *The Everything Jewish Book*. Avon, Mass.: Adams Media, 2002.

Boneler, Rabbi Milton. *The Kabbalah of Food*. Boston: Shambhala, 1998.

Dimont, Max. *The Jews in America*. New York: Simon & Schuster, 1978.

Dosick, Rabbi Wayne. *Living Judaism*. San Francisco: HarperSanFrancisco, 1995.

Duyff, Roberta Larson. *The American Dietetic Association's Complete Food and Nutrition Guide*. Minneapolis, Minn.: Chronimed, 1996.

Friedman, Seymour E. *The Book of Kashruth*. New York: Bloch, 1970.

Goldman, Ari L. *Being Jewish: The Spiritual and Cultural Practices of Judaism*. New York: Simon & Schuster, 2000.

Kolatch, Alfred J. *The Jewish Book of Why*. New York: Jonathan David, 1981.

Kolatch, Alfred J. *The Second Jewish Book of Why*. New York: Jonathan David, 2000.

Lipshutz, Rabbi Yacov. *Kashruth*. Brooklyn: Mesorah, 1999.

Maimonides, Moses. *Guide for the Perplexed*. Chicago: University of Chicago Press, 1974.

Nathan, Joan. *Jewish Cooking in America*. New York: Knopf, 1994.

Olitzky, Rabbi Kerry M., and Judson, Rabbi Daniel (eds.). *The Rituals and Practices of a Jewish Life*. Woodstock, N.Y.: Jewish Lights, 2002.

Roden, Claudia. *The Book of Jewish Food*. New York: Knopf, 1997.

The Author

Trudy Garfunkel is the author of *On Wings of Joy: The Story of Ballet from the 16th Century to Today* (Little, Brown, 1994; rev. ed., E-Reads, 2002), *Letter to the World: The Life and Dances of Martha Graham* (Little, Brown, 1995), and *Start Exploring Ballet* (Running Press, 1996). She is also a contributor to *The Oxford Companion to United States History* (Oxford University Press, 2001) and to New York City Ballet's ongoing Repertory Notes project. For a number of years, Ms. Garfunkel was publicity and advertising manager at the Dial Press; she now heads her own public relations and marketing consulting firm in New York City. *Kosher for Everybody* is Trudy Garfunkel's second book on the subject of kashrut, the successor to *The Kosher Companion* (Birch Lane, 1997).